MOTHERHOOD MISCONCEIVED

MOTHERHOOD MISCONCEIVED

*Representing the
Maternal in U.S. Films*

EDITED BY

HEATHER ADDISON

MARY KATE GOODWIN-KELLY

ELAINE ROTH

STATE UNIVERSITY OF NEW YORK PRESS

Published by
STATE UNIVERSITY OF NEW YORK PRESS, ALBANY

For information, contact
State University of New York Press, Albany, NY
www.sunypress.edu

Production, Laurie Searl
Marketing, Anne M. Valentine

Library of Congress Cataloging-in-Publication Data

Motherhood misconceived : representing the maternal in U.S. films / edited by Heather Addison, Mary Kate Goodwin-Kelly, and Elaine Roth.
   p. cm.
Includes bibliographical references and index.
ISBN 978-1-4384-2811-6 (hardcover : alk. paper)
ISBN 978-1-4384-2812-3 (pbk. : alk. paper)
   1. Motherhood—United States.　2. Motherhood in motion pictures.　3. Sex role in motion pictures.　I. Addison, Heather.　II. Goodwin-Kelly, Mary Kate, 1971–　III. Roth, Elaine, 1968–

HQ759.M8745 2009
302.23'4308520973—dc22   2008054157

10 9 8 7 6 5 4 3 2 1

To our significant others and to our children,

but most of all—to our mothers

CONTENTS

III. Horrific Mothers and the Mothers of Horror

IV. Maternal Anxieties of Class, Race, and Gender

ILLUSTRATIONS

x   ILLUSTRATIONS

ACKNOWLEDGMENTS

Motherhood Misconceived has had a long gestation period, and we are grateful to all of our contributors for staying the course and seeing the project through to publication. We also appreciate the friends and colleagues who have given us advice and insight along the way: Grace Tiffany of Western Michigan University; Rebecca Brittenham and Lesley Walker of Indian University South Bend; Astrid Henry and associates of the Center for Women's Intercultural Leadership at Saint Mary's College; Barry Keith Grant of Brock University; Charles Berg of the University of Kansas; and Larin McLaughlin, our editor at SUNY Press. Cynthia Kuhn of Metropolitan State College of Denver and Erin Webster-Garrett of Radford University invited us to share our thoughts on "Hollywood Motherhood" with the Women's Caucus at the Rocky Mountain Modern Language Association conference in October 2004, an occasion that proved an important jumping-off point for this collection.

We thank the online journal *Genders* for letting us reprint a shorter version of Kathleen Rowe Karlyn's essay "Scream, Popular Culture, and Feminism's Third Wave: 'I'm Not My Mother,'" which originally appeared in issue 38 (2003), and the print journal *Weber: The Contemporary West* for allowing us to use Madonne Miner's article "Not Exactly According to the Rules: Pregnancy and Motherhood in *Sugar & Spice*," which was published in volume 24.2 (2008).

Of course, none of this would have been possible without the unwavering support of our families. A special thank you to our parents: Ed and Joanne Kelly, John and Judy Fischer, and Emily Roth. And to Oscar Barrau; Rich, Connor, and Justin Addison; Chris, Nate, Claire, and Will Goodwin-Kelly: thanks for your patience. You mean the world to us!

INTRODUCTION

Heather Addison, Mary Kate Goodwin-Kelly, and Elaine Roth

In the early twenty-first century, motherhood has been marked by extraordinary cultural visibility; indeed, it has become seemingly ubiquitous in public discourse. Naomi Wolf, Susan Douglas, Meredith Michaels, Judith Warner, and other feminist authors have written high-profile books that explore experiences of motherhood in contemporary U.S. culture and criticize what they variously identify as the "misconceptions," "myths," or "madness" of maternal ideology.[1] The release of such books has prompted reviews, discussions, and analyses of maternal issues in the *New York Times* and *Newsweek*, on *Nightline* and National Public Radio, and elsewhere.

The publication of Lisa Belkin's cover article "The Opt-Out Revolution" in the October 23, 2003, issue of the *New York Times Magazine* struck and exposed a national nerve connected to motherhood as it relates to women's employment, child-rearing practices, and public policy. The author's evidence for the "opting out" trend she identifies is primarily limited to a handful of Princeton University–educated mothers who left high-powered jobs to stay at home and raise their children. Despite the limited scope of Belkin's investigation, "The Opt-Out Revolution" generated enormous buzz and garnered an unprecedented number of letters to the editor, while also becoming, at that time, the most emailed *New York Times Magazine* article in that publication's history (Peskowitz 87). The voluminous and varied responses to the article signal a national interest in conversations and social change that could more fully address the needs and desires of contemporary mothers, both those who stay at home and those who are in the workforce.[2] Since the turn of the millennium, motherhood has been central to debates regarding other aspects of U.S. domestic and foreign policy as well, from ongoing arguments about the parenting rights of gays and lesbians to Cindy Sheehan's stance against the war in Iraq.

Simultaneously, the figure of the mother has been put *on display*. Popular magazines such as *People*, *Star*, *Us*, and *In Touch* have repeatedly spotlighted celebrity moms, offering visual and gossipy details of their pregnancies and early motherhood experiences. As these publications expose confirmed pregnancies or speculate about the possible pregnancies of current stars, they invite and encourage consumers to deploy critical, penetrating gazes on the bodies of maternal or "potentially" maternal women. For example, an April 2005 photograph of Britney Spears on the cover of *Star* magazine is accompanied by a caption that queries, "Britney Pregnant? Is She Eating for Two?," blatantly urging readers to survey Spears's body for evidence of her possible expectant status. On this same cover, readers learn that "Pregnant Demi [Moore]" plans a "Secret Summer Wedding" and faces "Her Pregnancy Fears at 42." With a focus on the postpartum phase of maternity, the cover of a September 2004 issue of *People* declares, "Baby Love! Suddenly, show-biz comes second: First-time celeb moms talk about their brand-new lives," and features photographs of Gwyneth Paltrow, Debra Messing, and Brooke Shields with their babies. And in a July 2006 issue, *In Touch* offers readers its "Exclusive Bump Watch!" in which it declares, "Motherhood is now the hottest role in Hollywood."

As these captions reveal, sexual icons increasingly grab headlines through the intersection of sexuality and maternity. Shields, whose fame derives from her skin-baring Calvin Klein ads and films such as *The Blue Lagoon* (1980), and Demi Moore, whose nude pregnant body graced the August 1991 cover of *Vanity Fair* in what now seems a watershed moment in the increased visibility of pregnant bodies in contemporary American culture, stand as examples of this trend. Indeed, as B. Ruby Rich observed in 2004, in "baby-booming Hollywood . . . maternity, no longer an obstacle to sex appeal, has instead become its urgent accessory" (Rich 25). Angelina Jolie, one of the most iconic celebrity figures of the decade, exemplifies this shift. Consistently rated as one of the sexiest, most beautiful women in the world,[3] Jolie is also famous as the mother of six young children, three of whom were adopted internationally. The July 2008 cover of *Vanity Fair* asserts Jolie's sexuality as a pregnant woman, yet excludes the most visible evidence of pregnancy: her belly. A medium close-up of Jolie presents her with a sensual open-mouthed expression and a barely concealed chest. The accompanying story by Rich Cohen, "A Woman in Full," offers readers a glimpse into why Jolie "in her second pregnancy, feels so sexy."

Even as they intersect, however, sexuality and maternity do not suggest increased freedom for mothers, but rather continued and perhaps even greater cultural and ideological scrutiny of their bodies and activities. The summer 2007 cultural obsession with Britney Spears's parental behavior and Angelina Jolie's increasingly slender figure highlights the intense public surveillance that accompanies the celebrity mom.[4] For example, the August 27, 2007, *People* magazine cover announces "Booze, Betrayal and Greed: The Battle for Britney's Boys" and asks "Is She a Danger to her Kids?," while an inside feature in the same issue queries "Is Angelina Dangerously Thin?" below images of Jolie hand-in-hand with one of her children.

Maternal scrutiny has been created (if not fabricated) and showcased on daytime television as well.[5] As Miriam Peskowitz details in her book *The Truth Behind the Mommy Wars*, in November 2003 *Dr. Phil* aired a program titled "Mom vs. Mom," which perpetuated a false binary[6] by pitting "working mothers" against "stay-at-home" mothers and divided its largely female audience into two camps seated on opposite sides of the aisle (33). According to Peskowitz, the show's two experts, Heidi Brennan (a public policy advisor for the Family and Home Network) and Joan K. Peters (author of *When Mothers Work: Loving Our Children Without Sacrificing Ourselves* and *Not Your Mother's Life: Changing the Rules of Work, Love and Family*), reported that the conversation during taping was very "compelling," and extremely "attentive to all the complex issues of parenting" (33). Yet, when the show finally aired, the "relatively careful" conversation the experts had witnessed and participated in was replaced with a "heavily edited show" featuring an audience full of mothers insulting one another. In effect, the *Dr. Phil* show opted to construct a spectacle of combative mothers rather than airing the original conversation which, through the inclusion of many voices, spoke to the need for real change in our social structure regarding mothering and domestic policy.

Another noteworthy if carefully constructed media moment of the early twenty-first century that acknowledged this need for transformation occurred when Congresswoman Nancy Pelosi put motherhood on display on the steps of Congress. On the occasion of her own history-making swearing-in to become Speaker of the House of Representatives in January 2007, Pelosi stood on the House floor of the Capitol surrounded by children and grandchildren, calling for substantive reform and legislation to help parents and families.[7] The enormity of this image in the political landscape was matched during the course of the 2008 election season, when we repeatedly witnessed Hillary Clinton flanked by her daughter and mother as she ran to become the first female Democratic nominee for president of the United States,[8] and Governor Sarah Palin, John McCain's vice-presidential running mate and a mother of five, facing both intense praise and criticism for seeking the second-highest office in the land while raising five children, including a baby with Down syndrome and a pregnant seventeen-year-old daughter.[9] And motherhood became visible on another one of the world's biggest stages when, in the course of its coverage of the 2008 Olympic Games in Beijing, NBC devoted airtime to the stories of athletes who balance the demands of Olympic competition with their responsibilities as mothers, including forty-one-year-old swimmer and five-time Olympian Dara Torres and thirty-three-year-old soccer player and three-time Olympian Kate Markgraf.[10]

It was this type of remarkable maternal visibility—and the scrutiny that is its inevitable companion—that inspired our focused consideration

of motherhood in popular culture. In recent years, it appeared that a critical mass had been reached: mothers and motherhood were being discussed,
admired, criticized, and desired with greater and more spectacular frequency.
A dominant, influential purveyor of this omnipresent maternal visibility is
the American film industry, particularly Hollywood, which we define as the
moving image entertainment industry centered in and around Los Angeles,
California, including all of its products—films, of course, but also all related
extrafilmic materials, such as publicity and advertisements. We sought to chart
the evolution of American commercial cinema's maternal discourse over the
last century, intending to use our investigations to account for the "new"
popularity of motherhood and maternal images in the twenty-first century.
What we discovered, however, was a striking consistency in Hollywood's
constructions of motherhood. Although the recent pervasiveness of maternal
discourse may seem unprecedented, mothers have always been central figures
in mainstream American films and the culture surrounding Hollywood. From
Lillian Gish's iconic mother in *Intolerance* (1916) overseeing the emergence of
different civilizations, to the way that motherhood redeems the protagonist's
otherwise excessive behavior in *Erin Brockovich* (2000), the representation of
motherhood on-screen and in related discourse has served an ideological agenda.
Indeed, Hollywood's fascinating "misconceptions" of motherhood suggest that
hegemony is maintained through the management of maternity. Mothers re-
produce dominant ideology (quite literally), yet also become ready targets if
they fail to uphold prevailing notions of "good" motherhood. Thus, Hollywood
mothers are repeatedly demonized or deified (often through death).[11] This
limited repertoire of maternal portrayals all too often serves misogynistic and
conservative ends. Hollywood has, with relatively few exceptions, foregrounded
a youthful, white, middle-class, heterosexual paradigm of motherhood, to the
exclusion of other possibilities. For almost a century, it has mobilized particular
constructions of maternity in the service of the status quo.

The current exchange between Hollywood and independent cinema
has produced some encouraging interventions in the range of Hollywood's
maternal representations, though the increasing fluidity between these two
modes of production has tended to collapse the differences that have made
them distinct. Four entries in this collection, by Madonne M. Miner, Elaine
Roth, Mary M. Dalton and Janet K. Cutler, suggest the possibilities that
some independent films offer. However, the often close connections between
Hollywood and independent cinema preclude the latter from providing a
ready "solution" to Hollywood's problematic constructions of motherhood: for
a reading of an independent film that ultimately reinforces the ideological
underpinnings of Hollywood's maternal paradigm, see Mary Kate Goodwin-
Kelly's chapter.

Notably, there have been few sustained scholarly inquiries into cinematic representations of motherhood, a conspicuous oversight given the

pervasiveness and cultural significance of this figure. Only two monographs, both of them excellent, have focused on cinematic mothers: *Mother-hood and Representation: The Mother in Popular Culture and Melodrama* by E. Ann Kaplan (1992) and *Cinematernity: Film, Motherhood, Genre* (1996) by Lucy Fischer. A wide range of feminist film critics has pursued the topic in shorter formats, including Mary Ann Doane, Linda Williams, Barbara Creed, and Kaja Silverman. We contribute to this ongoing debate about the representation of motherhood in mainstream cinema by bringing together a broad range of approaches, building on the study of genre (especially melodrama) and psychoanalysis that formed the basis of earlier work. In particular, *Motherhood Misconceived* includes cultural studies approaches that locate the ideology of maternity in specific historical contexts, such as the publication of significant books on the topic of motherhood. For instance, Mike Chopra-Gant's chapter discusses *Generation of Vipers* (1943), a popular book maligning mothers, while Tamar Jeffers McDonald takes up Betty Friedan's *The Feminine Mystique* (1963). Also addressed is the impact of major historical events or trends, as when Mark Harper connects the relationship of the cold war to maternal space, or Heather Addison charts the rise of consumer culture.

Despite the volume's emphasis on historical context in the analysis of specific manifestations of screen motherhood, we are asserting the ubiquitous and ideological nature of mainstream cinematic constructions of the maternal—and arguing that Hollywood has remained remarkably static in this regard. Therefore, we privilege a thematic rather than a chronological organization. Our collection first considers the spectacle of pregnancy; then analyzes the mother-daughter relationship, especially as it intersects with female sexuality; registers the vilification of mothers as predators, narcissists, or absent victims; and finally surveys instances in which cultural anxieties have been displaced onto marginalized maternal figures.

Part I considers how a cinematic focus on the pregnant body works both to contain, but occasionally also to liberate, female characters. Examining *Fargo* (1996), Mary Kate Goodwin-Kelly highlights the film's visual fixation on the pregnancy of its police chief and considers the ways this conspicuous, if unspoken, obsession with the chief's impending maternity affects and in fact undermines the film's representation of her authority. In the second chapter, Tamar Jeffers McDonald uses historical analysis to contextualize *The Thrill of It All* (1963) in relation to the publication of Betty Friedan's *The Feminine Mystique*, and illustrates how then-current anxieties about the role of stay-at-home wives, the pros and cons of employment for mothers outside the home, and contraception and birth control played out in a script involving a female protagonist's shift from television spokeswoman to pregnant stay-at-home wife. In the final chapter of this section, Madonne Miner situates *Sugar & Spice* (2001) as a kind of hybrid heist film/teen picture, arguing that while conventional male heist films consistently work to exclude and eliminate team members, *Sugar & Spice*'s strategic performance of pregnancy functions to disrupt generic conventions and, albeit to a limited degree, encourage principles of expansion and inclusion. Ultimately, each of these chapters deals with films in which pregnancy or the pregnant body is a central narrative or visual concern.

In Part II, Heather Addison, Gaylyn Studlar, and Elaine Roth consider the mother-daughter relationship, especially as it has been articulated between adult children and their mothers and deployed to regulate female sexuality. Focusing on motion picture fan magazines as evidence, Addison argues that early Hollywood embraced the rhetoric of the consumer age, urging "modern mothers" to remain as youthful and attractive as their daughters. Studlar contends that the multifaceted discourse created around two early Hollywood stars, Mary Pickford and Joan Crawford, and their mothers, functioned to contain these stars' sexuality by deflecting public perceptions of gross immorality. Finally, Roth examines the complicated dynamics between a single mother and her two teenaged girls in *Gas, Food, Lodging* (1992), an independent film that derides neither mother nor daughters for their sexual desires.

The remaining sections chronicle the all-too-frequent presentation of mothers as the source of horror or as scapegoats for wider cultural anxieties. They complement the focus on the pregnancy stage highlighted in Part I by offering a series of close readings of films featuring mothers who have moved onto the project of raising children—with potentially disastrous consequences, according to the logic of the films. In Part III, Mike Chopra-Gant uncovers a tellingly negative history of the now-ubiquitous term "mom" and examines the figure of the vitriolic and self-serving "mom" in post–World War II Hollywood films. In his analysis of Alfred Hitchcock's *Psycho* (1960), Mun-Hou Lo argues that the figure of Mrs. Bates, more than simply functioning as one of the most famous "bad moms" of all, encourages the film's spectators to repudiate homosexuality through violence against the maternal body. In the third chapter of Part III, Mark Harper examines the apparatuses of paranoid surveillance that surround the "cold" mother figure in *Ordinary People* (1980) and finally eliminate her from the nuclear family. Kathleen Rowe Karlyn maps out the connections between Second and Third Wave feminism, Hollywood, and constructions of motherhood as she investigates the role of the mother as a source of history and knowledge in the horror *Scream* cycle (1996–2000).

The ideal of good motherhood (white, middle-class, devoted, selfless, and so on) becomes the yardstick by which women are judged; deviation from this pattern is justification for disparagement—or at least suspicion. Mothers can be denigrated for any number of choices or behaviors that are identified as inadequacies or excesses, such as pursuing careers or otherwise being inattentive to the needs of their children.[12] Indeed, what Linda Williams has said regarding films of the 1930s and 1940s films might be said of Hollywood cinema more generally: "The device of devaluing and debasing the figure of the mother while sanctifying the institution of motherhood is typical of 'the woman's film' in general and the sub-genre of the maternal melodrama in particular" (Williams 300).

In Part IV, Aimee Berger, Janet K. Cutler and Mary M. Dalton remind us that devaluation and debasement are often a function of identity markers such as class, race, and gender. Berger's investigation of the cinematic representations of Southern white working poor mothers and her identification of the frequency with which these representations link the poor white Southern mother with maternal neglect lead her to conclude that this displacement of anxiety about maternity locates white poverty as a regional rather than a national problem. In her chapter, Janet K. Cutler examines cinematic representations of black maternity, comparing the John Stahl and Douglas Sirk versions of *Imitation of Life*, 1934 and 1959, respectively, to the autobiographical documentaries *Suzanne, Suzanne* (1982) and *Finding Christa* (1991) made by Camille Billops and her husband James Hatch. Cutler demonstrates how Billops and Hatch's personal, nonfiction works present a view of motherhood and mother-child relationships that contradicts the image of a self-sacrificing black maternal figure embodied by the "Mammy" figure of 1930s–1950s commercial cinema. Finally, Mary M. Dalton undertakes an analysis of *Transamerica* (2005) and its unusual journey of discovery, in which a preoperative transsexual woman learns that she is the father of a teenaged boy and slowly builds a maternal relationship with him. Both the film and Dalton's chapter raise the possibility of moving beyond portrayals that demean or criticize mothers, suggesting new ways to consider motherhood in popular culture.

It is our hope that further scholarly writing on maternity in cinema will continue this trajectory, spotlighting and examining alternatives to Hollywood's persistent "misconceptions" of motherhood such as the nontraditional maternal figures who can be found in some independent cinema. We also wish to note that this volume owes a substantial debt to the large body of feminist film theory that grounds a number of our chapters. Such theory is one of the dominant and invaluable discourses of the film studies discipline, and our volume draws upon it repeatedly, regardless of the extent to which its use is explicitly foregrounded. Finally, though a major goal of our collection is to critique the maternal ideology of mainstream Hollywood films, we also want to acknowledge the pleasure that such films afford and that the institution of motherhood yields. As film fans, mothers, and daughters, we seek not to lessen the joys of maternity or of film viewing, but rather to improve our understanding of Hollywood's role in constructing and reinforcing specific ideologies about motherhood.

NOTES

1. See *Misconceptions: Truth, Lies, and the Unexpected on the Journey to Motherhood* by Naomi Wolf, *The Mommy Myth: The Idealization of Motherhood and How It Has Undermined All Women* by Susan Douglas and Meredith Michaels, *Perfect Madness: Motherhood in the Age of Anxiety* by Judith Warner, *The Truth Behind the Mommy Wars: Who Decides What Makes a Good Mother?* by Miriam Peskowitz, and *Motherhood Manifesto: What America's Moms Want—and What to Do About It* by Joan Blades and Kristin Rowe-Finkbeiner.

2. Meg Wolitzer's *The Ten Year Nap* (2008) is a novel exploring the interconnected lives of a handful of women from the so-called opt-out generation. The book, to some degree a product of the culture of Belkin's essay, has garnered a fair amount of media attention itself.

3. In November 2004, Jolie was *Esquire* magazine's "Sexiest Woman Alive"; she was featured on the cover of *People Weekly's* annual "100 Most Beautiful" issue in 2006; and in 2007, a British television show, "The Greatest Sex Symbols," named her as the greatest sex symbol of all time.

4. At the time of this writing, morning shows, twenty-four-hour news channels, and online blogs were discussing the subject of "pregorexia." Much of the discourse on pregorexia, a term used to describe women's "excessive" efforts to control their weight during pregnancy, often through diet and exercise, attributed an apparent increase in this phenomenon to thin celebrities and the media attention they garner during their pregnancies. In an article titled, "Pregorexia: Does this bump look big on me?," which appeared on the *TimesOnline* website, Catherine Bruton wrote, "According to some experts, images of svelte celebrity mums-to-be such as Nicole Kidman and [Nicole] Richie with their "barely-there" bumps are inspiring expectant mothers to diet and exercise to excess to stay slim during pregnancy and speed the departure of those post-baby pounds." An article pursuing the same topic and titled " 'Pregorexia' Inspired by Thin Celebs?" appeared on CBSNews.com.

5. A recent example is the case of Nadya Suleman, a single, unemployed mother of six who gave birth to octuplets in early 2009. Suleman has been an object of intense fascination—and criticism—as daytime news programs have questioned her decision (and even her right) to use *in vitro* fertilization to produce her large family. See especially the Ann Curry interview with Suleman, broadcast on February 9, 2009 on the *Today* show.

6. Peskowitz astutely observes, "Currently there is no room in our cultural vocabulary to talk about mothering and work in any but the most oppositional and mutually exclusive terms, and as a result, all this work that women do remains invisible" (74).

7. Meanwhile, websites such as MomsRising.org and the zine *Hip Mama* speak to the needs and struggles of contemporary mothers, including working and lower-class mothers who are all too often overlooked or made invisible by dominant media coverage.

8. In the concession speech that she delivered on June 7, 2008, after losing an incredibly close primary race to Senator Barack Obama, Senator Clinton told supporters and the nation as a whole, "I ran as a daughter who benefited from opportunities my mother never dreamed of. I ran as a mother who worries about my

daughter's future and a mother who wants to lead all children to brighter tomorrows. To build that future I see, we must make sure that women and men alike understand the struggles of their grandmothers and mothers, and that women enjoy equal opportunities, equal pay, and equal respect."

9. The *New York Times* described Palin's candidacy as "the Mommy Wars: Special Campaign Edition. But this time the battle lines are drawn inside out, with the social conservatives, usually staunch advocates for stay-at-home motherhood, mostly defending her, while some others, including plenty of working mothers, worry that she is taking on too much" (Kantor and Swarns).

10. *Sports Illustrated* also ran a feature story by Michael Farber, titled "Mother Load," about U.S. athletes/mothers competing in the 2008 Olympics in Beijing, China. In this article, Melanie Roach, Olympic weightlighting competitor and mother of a seven-year-old boy, recalls meeting other athletes/mothers, including Dara Torres, in the Olympic Village. In a quote about that meeting that speaks to the conflicted feelings and the social scrutiny that many mothers experience, Roach said, "[When I came back] I struggled with the idea that I was encouraging moms to leave their children to pursue their dreams, but then I realized the opportunity I had to inspire other athletes not to put off having children . . . I think we've shown women can come back stronger, physically and sometimes mentally."

11. The year 2007 saw the emergence of a number of films dealing with the inadvertently pregnant woman or teen. *Waitress, Knocked Up,* and *Juno* each explore the trials facing protagonists dealing, in their various ways, with unplanned pregnancies. Perhaps because the narratives of these films did not overtly demonize these maternal figures, at least some of the films themselves have been criticized for their glamorization of unexpected pregnancies, particularly teen pregnancies. In particular, *Juno* was singled out as making teen pregnancy appealing. On CNN's AC360, Anderson Cooper, investigating an apparent "Pregnancy Pact in Glouchester, MA" involving seventeen teenaged girls at a single high school who reportedly agreed to get pregnant, interviewed a psychologist who blamed Hollywood for essentially advocating teen pregnancies. The guest psychologist identified the most "insidious" cause of the teen pregnancy trend as "celebrity baby bliss" or the ubiquity of media representations of celebrities with babies. The supposed "pact," first reported in *Time* magazine, was covered on MSNBC, the *Today Show,* CNN's *Inside Edition,* and NPR's *All Things Considered,* among others. Like AC360's coverage, much of the report considered the role that Hollywood played, through films such as *Juno* and *Knocked Up* and the glamorization of the teen celebrity Jamie Lynn Spears (whose pregnancy and early motherhood were the object of much attention), in making teen pregnancy seem attractive to teens.

12. Absent or working mothers have paid the price in notable films such as *Imitation of Life* (1934; 1959), *Mildred Pierce* (1947), *The Hand That Rocks the Cradle* (1992), or *American Beauty* (1999).

BIBLIOGRAPHY

American Beauty. Dir. Sam Mendes. Dreamworks SKG, 1999.
Belkin, Lisa. "The Opt-Out Revolution." *New York Times Magazine* (23 October 2003): 42+.

Blades, Joan, and Kristin Rowe-Finkbeiner. *Motherhood Manifesto: What America's Moms Want—and What to Do About It*. New York: Nations Books, 2006.

Bruton, Catherine. "Pregorexia: Does this bump look big on me?" *New York Times Online*. (18 August 2008).

Cohen, Rich. "A Woman in Full." *Vanity Fair* (July 2008): 68+.

Douglas, Susan, and Meredith Michaels. *The Mommy Myth: The Idealization of Motherhood and How It Has Undermined All Women*. New York: Free Press, 2004.

Erin Brockovich. Dir. Steven Soderbergh. Jersey Films, 2000.

Farber, Michael. "Mother Load." *Sports Illustrated* (18 August 2008): 60+.

Fargo. Dir. Joel Coen. Gramercy Pictures, 1996.

Finding Christa. Dir. Camille Billops and James Hatch. Third World Newsreel, 1991.

Fischer, Lucy. *Cinematernity: Film, Motherhood, Genre*. Princeton: Princeton University Press, 1996.

Friedan, Betty. *The Feminine Mystique*. 1963. London: Penguin Books, 1992.

Gas, Food, Lodging. Dir. Alison Anders. Cineville, 1992.

The Hand That Rocks the Cradle. Dir. Curtis Hanson. Hollywood Pictures, 1992.

In Touch (July 2006): front cover.

Imitation of Life. Dir. Douglas Sirk. Universal Pictures, 1959.

Imitation of Life. Dir. John M. Stahl. Universal Pictures, 1934.

Intolerance. Dir. D. W. Griffith. Triangle Film Corp., 1916.

Juno. Dir. Jason Rietman. Fox Searchlight Pictures, 2007.

Kantor, Jodi, and Rachel L. Swarns. "A New Twist in the Debate on Mothers." *New York Times Online* (1 September 2008). 2 September 2008 <http://www.nytimes.com/2008/09/02/us/politics/02mother.html?pagewanted=1&ref=politics>

Kaplan, E. Ann. *Motherhood and Representation: The Mother in Popular Culture and Melodrama*. London and New York: Routledge, 1992.

Knocked Up. Dir. Judd Apatow. Universal Pictures, 2007.

Mildred Pierce. Dir. Michael Curtiz. Warner Bros. Pictures, 1945.

100 Greatest Sex Symbols. Channel 4, United Kingdom, 2007.

"100 Most Beautiful." *People Weekly* (8 May 2006): front cover.

Ordinary People. Dir. Robert Redford. Paramount Pictures, 1980.

People Weekly (13 September 2004): front cover.

People Weekly (27 August 2007): front cover.

Peskowitz, Miriam. *The Truth Behind the Mommy Wars: Who Decides What Makes a Good Mother?* Emeryville: Seal Press, 2005.

" 'Pregorexia' Inspired by Thin Celebs?" *CBS News Online* (11 August 2008). 15 August 2008 <http://www.cbsnews.com/stories/2008/08/11/earlyshow/health/main4337521.shtml>

Pyscho. Dir. Alfred Hitchcock. Shamley Productions, 1960.

Rich, B. Ruby. "Day of the Woman." *Sight and Sound* (June 2004): 24–27.

"Sexiest Woman Alive, The." *Esquire* (November 2004): front cover.

Star Magazine (4 April 2005): front cover.

Sugar & Spice. Dir. Francine McDougall. New Line Cinema, 2001.

Suzanne, Suzanne. Dir. Camille Billops and James Hatch. Third World Newsreel, 1982.

The Thrill of It All. Dir. Norman Jewison. Universal Pictures, 1963.

Transamerica. Dir. Duncan Tucker. Belladonna Productions, 2005.

Waitress. Dir. Adrienne Shelly. Night and Day Pictures, 2007.

Warner, Judith. *Perfect Madness: Motherhood in the Age of Anxiety*. New York: Riverhead Books, 2005.

Williams, Linda. " 'Something Else Besides a Mother': *Stella Dallas* and the Maternal Melodrama." *Home Is Where the Heart Is: Studies in Meldorama and the Woman's Film*. Ed. Christine Gledhill. London: BFI Books, 1987. 299–325.

Wolf, Naomi. *Misconceptions: Truth, Lies, and the Unexpected on the Journey to Motherhood*. New York: Random House, 2003.

Wolitzer, Meg. *The Ten Year Nap*. New York: Riverhead Books, 2008.

Wylie, Philip. *Generation of Vipers*. New York and Toronto: Farrar and Rhinehart, 1943.

I

THE CELLULOID STORK

Picturing Pregnancy

ONE

PREGNANT BODY AND/AS SMOKING GUN

Reviewing the Evidence of *Fargo*

MARY KATE GOODWIN-KELLY

In the Coen brothers' independently produced film *Fargo* (1996), a suburban car dealer, Jerry Lundegaard (William H. Macy), arranges to have
his wife kidnapped—"a no-rough-stuff-type deal" he insists—in order to
collect the ransom money from his rich father-in-law and get himself out
of some unspecified trouble. The arrangement goes awry, however. Instead
of one kidnapper, Jerry acquires two; the nonverbal Gaear Grimsrud (Peter
Stormare), originally enlisted to carry out the kidnapping, is accompanied
by the excessively talkative Carl Showalter (Steve Buscemi). The agreed
on "simple" plan for an abduction and an exchange of money results in
a series of homicides and the need for a police investigation. The investigation is headed up by the visibly pregnant Chief Marge Gunderson
(Frances McDormand).

In an interview produced by Polygram Filmed Entertainment that ran
prior to a cable television airing of *Fargo*, director Joel Coen described the
film and its central characters: "The movie's sort of an ensemble piece. It
deals with the character [played by] Bill Macy who's a car salesman. And
it deals with the policeman: the character that Fran plays is the chief of
police of Brainerd, Minnesota, who *happens* to be pregnant at the time
the story is happening" (emphasis mine). My interest in this brief quotation lies in the way it spotlights a particular feature of *Fargo*, namely, the
film's textual (and extratextual) representations of Chief Gunderson. The

15

quotation underscores the impression that the film, at least on the level of dialogue, effectively works to advance: that the pregnant status of the chief of police played by McDormand, Joel Coen's wife, is an incidental and rather insignificant aspect of the film's narrative. That is, although Coen extratextually acknowledges the pregnancy of the film's female protagonist, the understated nature of his reference to Marge's pregnancy—the pregnancy as a matter of happenstance—works in conjunction with the film characters' inattention to that pregnancy (no character, other than Marge, ever acknowledges her pregnancy verbally) to downplay its textual and social importance.[1]

Yet if the film and filmmakers work to downplay the significance of the chief's pregnancy in these specific ways, a close analysis of *Fargo* reveals the specific textual functions that her (exceedingly visible) sexual difference and pregnancy perform. In this chapter, I demonstrate that in fact much of the film's humor hinges on the representation of its unconventional "dick" and her specific social difference: her status as a pregnant woman. I illustrate that while on the one hand we are encouraged to share the film's pleasure in this atypical figure who transcends the boundaries of societal and generic expectations, and we can take some pleasure in the agency she is afforded, her agency and transgressive potential are arguably undercut by the film's obsessive (if dialogically unspoken) preoccupation with her physical and physiological conditions.

We are first introduced to Marge in a scene that conveys the film's acute visual attention to her body and its relation to her professional involvement. This scene, which follows immediately after we witness the plot-central triple homicide committed by Jerry Lundegaard's hirelings, is staged in the home of Marge and her husband Norm. We initially find the couple sleeping. At slightly above bed level, on Marge's side of the bed, the camera shoots the slumbering couple and then the disruption of their sleep as Marge receives a seemingly routine middle-of-the-night phone call. The call prompts Marge to sit up and rise out of bed, and, as she does so, the camera holds at bed level (rather than adjusting its angle or position to capture the image of Marge's entire head and upper body), literally catching Marge's enlarged belly as it appears to move into the camera's lens. This compositional technique distorts the physicality of Marge's pregnant body, making it appear larger than it really is. A cut then shifts the location of the scene from the bedroom to the kitchen where Marge and Norm are momentarily shown, through a medium-long shot, at the breakfast table. Marge is now clad in a police uniform—the maternity version—with her visible police star serving as our first sign of her professional occupation. The editing contributes to the overall visual impact of this scene, ordering the shots and the film's logic such that immediately prior to the moment that we learn of Marge's professional status as an agent of the law (and begin to understand the reason for the late night phone call) she is visually overde-

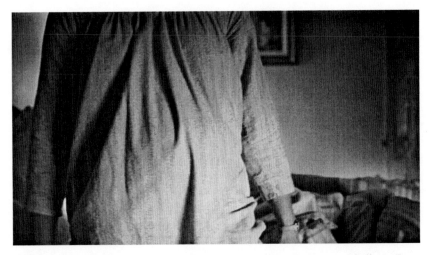

Figure 1. The camera emphasizes Chief Marge Gunderson's pregnant belly in *Fargo* (1996).

termined as a pregnant woman. Representational tactics such as these are employed throughout the film, framing Marge as the excessive embodiment of sexual difference within a "masculine" professional landscape.

This point is further illustrated in a subsequent scene at the site of the triple homicide. At this site, Marge has occasion to demonstrate her investigative proficiency, and the film handles the occasion by representing her skills of detection while simultaneously making her the source of humor. Surveying the crime scene and the evidence it provides, Marge accurately explicates the crimes for Lou, the other cop on the scene: "Okay, so we got a trooper [who] pulls someone over . . . We got a shooting . . . These folks drive by . . . There's a high-speed pursuit . . . Ends here and then this execution type deal. I'd be very surprised if our suspect was from Brainerd . . . And I tell you what, from his footprint he looks like a big fella." Marge's assessment of the evidence serves as proof of her professional abilities at the moment that she offers it, precisely because the audience has already witnessed the actual criminal events and we are able to corroborate her story in our own minds. But immediately after accurately deducing the specifics of the homicidal events based on what she sees, Marge grimaces and bends over in a gesture that seems to echo her reaction to the site of some of the homicide victims. Lou responds with naïve curiosity:

LOU: You see something, Chief?

MARGE: No, I . . . just . . . think I'm gonna barf.

LOU: Chief. You okay, Margie?

> MARGE: Yeah, I'm fine. It's just morning sickness. Well, that
>   passed. Now I'm hungry again.

Marge's status as a pregnant chief fuels the offbeat humor driving this scene. The informal vernacular of Marge's response and the ironic source of her nausea at the crime scene—not the sight of the victims' mutilated bodies but the physiological state of her own body—are clearly written and executed for comic effect. Consequently, the professional acumen and perceptiveness that Marge demonstrates are immediately undercut by personal features that are humorously represented—her dis-ease linked to pregnancy and the language with which she describes it. The scenario functions both to parody the expected intensity and seriousness of typical crime film narratives and to exaggerate the atypical presence of a pregnant woman in this setting. The diegetic function of Marge's morning sickness deserves particular attention in relation to this strategic exaggeration given the fact that, as we later learn, Marge is already seven months pregnant. Morning sickness is a condition that, except in rare cases, tends to affect women in the early months of their pregnancies. Thus, it is rather late in the pregnancy for her to be experiencing or showing these symptoms.[2] Here, then, the illness (we do not actually see her vomit but we see her bend over, an action she then explains by mention of her morning sickness), as well as her reference to it, represent the excessive efforts of the film to register Marge's pregnancy, in this case while she is literally on the job. Indeed, the decision to have the seven-month pregnant investigator get sick after demonstrating her professional aptitude seems to register, through a kind of transference, the filmmakers' anxiety regarding this woman's place in society. And these deliberate details reduplicate the effect of the camera work in the previous bedroom scene, which made Marge's belly, and thus her pregnancy, exceedingly visible.

While Marge does her job well, she never does so on an empty stomach; the film represents her perpetually eating (or else talking about food) throughout her ongoing investigation of this case. One occasion in which the film highlights Marge's simultaneous intake of food and case details takes place when she returns to the Brainerd police headquarters carrying a bag of night crawlers that she has purchased for Norm on her way back from the investigation. She opens her office door to find Norm unexpectedly seated at a desk in her office, having brought lunch for the two of them. This scene is cinematically constructed such that the actual exchange of food for worms takes place within a frame that captures the bag of night crawlers, the spread of food from Arby's, Norm's head and torso, and Marge's enlarged abdomen (but crops Marge's head out of the visible image—a compositional device that now establishes itself as a motif in *Fargo*). As the scene unfolds, the dialogue is fairly banal: Norm thanks her for the night crawlers and she thanks him for lunch. But as she is inspecting the lunch that Norm has brought for her, we hear her say, "Oh, yeah, looks pretty good," while what we *see* is a close-up of the large worms, through what is actually Norm's point of view. On a technical level, what we are witnessing is a kind of spectatorial manipulation involving a disruption of the conventional eyeline match and a subsequent disconnect of sound and image. The effect of this manipulation, though, is the coding of Marge's eating as culturally gross and excessive. Through this disjunction of sound and image, the film asks us to read the always-hungry Marge as eager to consume even the most grotesque fare. In so doing, it works in conjunction with this scene's framing strategies and furthers the effects of previous scenes I have described that represent Marge's pregnant status in exaggerated ways. The framing of Marge's body in this scene, shot in a space marked as her professional domain, at least momentarily divests Marge herself of professional agency as it invests instead in her extended belly. While the physical and physiological phenomena and behaviors *Fargo* seizes upon in its portrayal of Marge—enlarged belly and increased appetite—are standard realities experienced by pregnant women, the manipulation of formal features wielded in creating this portrayal results in a mockery of her. The film visually overdetermines Marge's identity as a pregnant woman and foregrounds her expectant condition within a male-dominated professional space in the interest of humor. This scene ends when Marge's professional partner enters her office to give an update on case leads. Notably, Marge consumes the case information while also consuming her Arby's sandwich and fries, offering responses to the evidence in between every bite.

A subsequent scene underscores the film's fascination with Marge's eating by aligning the camera with Marge's point of view as she visually and then literally takes in all of the options at an all-you-can-eat lunch buffet. The scene opens with a close-up of one of the many offerings on the buffet. A high-angled tracking shot shows an unidentified hand making selections—piling on the biscuits, chicken, meatballs, casseroles, and fricassee. A cut reveals that it is in fact Marge going through the buffet line. We see her head, torso, and part of her tray in the frame as she tops off the last of her three plates. As she turns from the buffet line toward the camera, its angle lowers to capture just her belly and the full tray, again cropping her head from the frame. She sits down to feast with Norm, who has also gone through the line behind her. Once again, one of Marge's officers interrupts her meal to inform her about some developments in the triple homicide case. And once again, details about the case are discussed along with details about the food. As before, Marge's eating habits are represented as excessive if not grotesque, this time due to the quantities of food she apparently consumes in one sitting.

Lynne Joyrich has argued (in relation to television sitcoms) that the fact that texts employ "the form of comedy, constructing role reversals as the source of 'harmless' humor and 'mere' entertainment, should not exempt them from critical scrutiny. If anything, the pleasure that they provide helps mask the more sinister fantasies to which they give voice" (Joyrich 106–107). Rather than dismissing *Fargo*'s representation of Chief Gunderson as harmless humor, I submit, following Joyrich's critical claim, that the film's representation of her taps into a site of social conflict having to do with women's power, agency, social mobility, and relation to danger.

As Kirsten Marthe Lentz writes in her article, "The Popular Pleasures of Female Revenge (Or Rage Bursting in a Blaze of Gunfire)":

> Films problematize representations of armed women through the ambivalent way they position women *vis-à-vis* danger. A woman's use of guns does distance her (albeit only slightly most of the time) from her overdetermined position of victimhood, but often this distance is tenuous or obviously temporary. It is this tension between *being in danger* and *being dangerous* which supplies both the pleasure of her deadly power and the problem of her defeat. (376)

This ambivalence that Lentz describes exists in a number of films of the 1990s such as *Thelma and Louise* (1991), *Blue Steel* (1990), and *The Silence of the Lambs* (1991). But in *Fargo*, the tension between a woman's "being in danger" and "being dangerous" is represented through a female body that is pregnant and therefore further coded, conventionally, as vulnerable and in need of protection. If, as Lentz asserts, women tend to be figured in an overdetermined position of victimhood in Hollywood cinema—a positioning potentially disrupted or at least complicated by their wielding of guns—*Fargo*'s depiction of the armed and pregnant policewoman potentially increases this tension between dangerous and endangered even further.

In fact, there are a number of implications of the film's representation of the armed Marge. On the textual level (in terms of its significance exclusively within this text), with this image, the lethal potential that is initially conferred on the character of Marge by her police uniform is finally confirmed by her wielding of a gun by the film's end. On a larger scale, through its representation of the pregnant woman as dangerous agent, this particular rendition of Marge seems to respond to a long history of filmic representations of pregnant women's "fragile" or "vulnerable" bodies.[3] The sight of the pregnant Marge with gun in hand signals not only her lethal potential but also a degree of agency and social mobility rarely granted to female protagonists, particularly mothers or expectant women, in Hollywood films. At the same time, the image also taps into debates about reproductive rights, women's choice, and tensions between family and career. Indeed, it is the potential controversy that this figure embodies (along with her anomalous existence in a relatively mainstream if eccentric crime film) that *Fargo* seizes upon and exploits for its own promotion. Remarkably, we only

Figure 2. Pregnant Chief Marge Gunderson (Frances McDormand) wields a gun at the end of *Fargo* (1996).

actually see Marge holding a gun on one occasion in *Fargo*, in a scene that takes place in the film's final ten minutes. It is particularly striking, then, that at least three noticeably different photo stills of her aiming her gun in this scene have circulated alongside the film.[4] By reproducing and circulating these photographs of Marge as a part of the promotion and publicity for the film, the filmmakers and distributors apparently both anticipated and tried to capitalize on the cultural resonance of the "armed and loaded" pregnant female body and, simultaneously, reinforced its power and resonance, effectively encouraging us to read the film through that anomalous image.

In terms of *how* precisely we are to read this image, though, the film and filmmakers are somewhat more ambivalent. In the scene from which the image is taken, Marge is in the process of driving through the woods in search of the suspects in the triple homicide case when she spots a stolen vehicle to which they have been linked. When she gets out of her car, Marge is immediately drawn (along with the film viewers) to the curious sound of what she (and we) eventually learn is a woodchipper, which Gaear is in the process of using to mutilate his co-criminal, Carl. When Gaear realizes Marge has caught him in this act, he throws a log at her and then tries to flee. With two shots, Marge shoots and hits but does not kill Gaear, allowing her to take him into custody alive. On the one hand, the image of Marge with gun in hand seems to offer a progressive challenge to the "fragile" pregnant woman stereotype that is well established within film history. And to some extent the potential challenge posed by this image is memorialized for viewers by all of the circulating photo stills of it. Yet one particularly fascinating aspect of the scene from which this image derives is that, unlike climactic scenes of other films of the 1990s that feature women as agents of the law whose visible sexual difference figures centrally, it does not present a drawn-out chase or confrontation between the heroine and her antagonist in which suspense derives specifically from the question of whether or not the heroine will survive. Instead, the suspense of this scene stems primarily from the mysterious noise that we and Marge hear as she seeks out the criminal in the woods. All of the sound and visual cues of the scene heighten the viewer's curiosity about this noise, and make the source of the noise as much the object of pursuit as the criminal himself. Indeed, the non-diegetic music that adds to the suspense of the scene peaks not at the moment that Marge ultimately shoots and wounds her sought-after criminal but rather prior to that—at the moment that we and Marge finally discover that the noise is that of a woodchipper as it is being used by Gaear to obliterate his former partner in crime. The suspense, then, is punctuated by dark humor as the mystery of the sound is answered by the sight of the absurdly unimaginable. As a result of the film's staging of this scene and its visual and auditory emphasis, what we remember from it after the film is not so much Marge's handling of her gun (specifically) and of the situation (more generally), but rather the woodchipper and the grotesque death that apparently befell Carl at the hands of Gaear and his weapon of choice. Ultimately, while prior to this point the film has repeatedly undermined Marge's agency and authority with its obsessive attention to the physical and physiological effects of her pregnancy, here Marge's deft professional and physical abilities are overshadowed by Gaear's absurd efforts to destroy the evidence of his own crimes. That is, at this concluding moment when Marge's professional prowess might be showcased most prominently, the film's steadfast preoccupation with Marge's body is momentarily replaced by its attention to the mutilation of someone else's.

Interestingly, the backside of the *Fargo* DVD case is dominated by a photo of Marge with her gun drawn and an inset photo of Gaear operating the woodchipper. By simultaneously highlighting these two aspects of this scene as standout features of the entire film, the filmmakers and the film's promoters invite a comparison between these two characters (and their behaviors) that the scene itself suggests. The film asks us to find humor in the grotesque things that the male criminals do to the bodies of others,[5] while the source of humor associated with Marge derives from her own embodiment.

The visibility of the law enforcement agent is often emphasized, if not thematized, in filmic scenarios in which the agent is coded as sexually different—that is, when the agent is female.[6] And, as I have argued, *Fargo* registers its own reaction to Marge's visible social identity and state of maternity in specific ways that belie its various textual and extratextual efforts to understate their significance. But in *Fargo*, the acknowledgment of that visibility registers almost entirely through camera work that is not subjectivized; that is, the camera draws attention to Marge's visibly pregnant (and therefore specifically sexed) body and it codes that body as significant, but it does not rely on point of view or reaction shots to do so. Thus, we do not ascribe this vision or portrayal of Marge to a particular fictional character; rather, we attribute it to the film itself. And therefore, the film's obsessive preoccupation with Marge's physical and physiological condition manifested in its representation of her enlarged body and her excessive (or at least excessively visible) eating and vomiting, read not as "harmless humor" or "mere entertainment"—nor as strictly generically (dis) functional—but rather as the film's (or filmmakers') own anxious response to the cultural phenomenon that this character, simultaneously dangerous and in danger, represents.

As I have emphasized, no character in *Fargo* (other than Marge) speaks of her condition and, for the most part, the film represses any subjective reaction to the visibly pregnant police chief. This ongoing inattention to the culturally anomalous status of Marge as pregnant police officer makes one occasion when her pregnancy does register through the reaction of another character all the more noteworthy. Roughly midway through the film, aware that some problems have arisen in the "real sound" abduction of his wife, Jerry Lundegaard enters his dealership's service garage looking for Shep, the mechanic who has been the intermediary between Jerry and the thugs he has hired. Jerry walks into the camera's frame as he approaches another mechanic and asks, "Where's Shep?" The mechanic responds, "talking to a cop," as his eyes direct Jerry toward Shep. "A cop?" Jerry responds with a clear sense of surprise and alarm as he looks over his shoulder in the direction the mechanic has just signaled. "*She said she was a cop!*" the mechanic emphatically insists before landing his eyes again on the scene Jerry has apparently just witnessed—that of Marge and Shep talking in a glassed-in office that allows them to be seen but not heard. The miscommunication that marks this exchange is revealing. Jerry's response to the mechanic—"a cop?"—is not one of disbelief at the sight of Marge and the claim that she is a cop. Rather, it is one of surprise and alarm at the very mention of a cop—any cop—given the criminal activity he's been engaged in with Shep. The mechanic's response, however, suggests his own surprise at the sight of the pregnant female cop and his assumption that Jerry's reaction is one of disbelief based on visible evidence rather than alarm at the mere mention of Shep's speaking with a law enforcement agent. Through this brief exchange marked by miscommunication and false assumptions, the film very subtly reveals what is otherwise repressed: a subjective reaction to this specific incarnation of law enforcement.

In a chapter on television and reproductive politics in *Re-Viewing Reception*, Lynne Joyrich describes "the general shock and discomfort the

gestational body seems to elicit within our historical and social formation."
Drawing on the writing of Faye Ginsburg, she highlights the liminal position that pregnant women are put in, "temporarily located between two
structural states and thus unassimilable to any one role." She continues, "the
legality of abortion allows for the uncertainty of the final outcome: the state
into which the woman may move (motherhood or nonmotherhood) is no
longer predetermined (or punitively enforced as such), and thus, the social
and contingent (versus 'natural' and necessary) order of reproduction is exposed" (Joyrich 112). If pregnant women occupy a "liminal" status between
motherhood and nonmotherhood, Marge's liminal status is complicated by
the fact that she is coded as both one enlisted to "serve and protect" and
one in need of protection. Even if Marge has chosen motherhood within a
personal realm—a choice registered through the visibility of her pregnant
body—her professional choice necessarily situates her "in harm's way," fur-
thering the uncertainty (of the final outcome of her pregnancy) that the
legality of abortion makes possible. Thus, if the visibility of pregnant bodies
in general creates social discomfort or unease, as Joyrich has argued, the
image of the pregnant and uniformed Marge Gunderson with gun in hand
poses a specific threat linked to choice—for family *and* career (specifically,
a male-identified and potentially dangerous career). *Fargo* responds to the
threat posed by Marge through its obsessive attention to the physical and
physiological effects of her body, which effectively undermines the agency
and authority it otherwise affords her.

    The ambivalence that I read in *Fargo*'s depiction of Marge was echoed
extratextually in a *Fresh Air* interview with the film's co-writer and producer,
Ethan Coen, that originally aired in October 1998. Terry Gross, the host
of *Fresh Air*, remarked:

> One of the things I really like about [*Fargo*] is that although the
> criminals are all actually pretty dumb, Marge, the police chief who
> *looks* like she might be mocked in the movie, is actually a very
> good cop with a very big heart and very likeable. I just really love
> the way that you handle this character in the movie. So, tell me
> about creating Marge.

Ethan Coen responded by saying:

> Well, you know, it's funny you say that—a lot of people liked her
> and I'm sure that's why the movie did well. I always thought she
> was the bad guy. [He laughs] I don't know, I just related to Steve
> Buscemi's character [Carl] more—he seemed like a classic sane
> person in an insane land. Marge definitely, Fran's character, sort of
> embodying the insane land. You know I kind of found her a little bit

alarming, as did Fran [McDormand]. We were all sort of surprised, actually, that people liked her quite as much as they did.

When Gross asked Coen what he found alarming about Marge, he responded, "Well, she's . . . she is, she is definitely, I mean there are admirable things about her but she is also definitely, ah, sure of herself to an alarming degree. I mean not, certainly not given to introspection." Strikingly, Coen's on-air description of Marge underscores the film and filmmakers' preoccupation with this character's "embodiment" that I have argued comes across on screen. If Marge embodies the "insane land," it is the "insanity" of this land that offers the possibility (and cinematic anomaly) of this character's simultaneous professional and social occupations as police chief, wife, and expectant mother—all roles carried out by a self-assured woman.[7] The filmmakers' unease with this social scenario is literally and finally sounded in the film's closing moments. Marge, having just solved the triple homicide case, is pictured embracing Norm while talking with him in their bed. The diegetic sound records their contented refrain "just two more months," while the non-diegetic sound underscores the film's anxious focus on Marge's state of maternity, playing the film's mournful theme song that has been transformed into a haunting lullaby.

The film's obsessive preoccupation with Marge's physical and physiological condition, manifested in its representation of her enlarged body and her excessive eating and vomiting, read not as "harmless humor" or "mere entertainment" but rather as the film's (or filmmakers') own anxious response to the cultural phenomenon that this character, simultaneously dangerous and in danger, represents. *Fargo* registers its own anxieties about sexual difference through its literal *reshaping* of the criminal investigator at the same time that it seems to want to convince us that Marge's pregnancy is a non-issue. That is, while the film characters do not speak of Marge's pregnancy, the film "speaks" of it almost obsessively and anxiously through various cinematic maneuvers. Indeed, the overblown ways in which Marge's bodily transformations are visually registered in *Fargo* seem a kind of symptomatic reaction to the social mobility and agency she represents. Her body becomes the smoking gun, if you will, of the Coens' own discomfort with what she represents.

NOTES

1. In *Cinema Without Walls*, Timothy Corrigan argues that "auteurs have become increasingly situated along an extra-textual path in which their commercial status as auteurs is their chief function as auteurs: the auteur-star is meaningful primarily as a promotion or recovery of a movie or group of movies, frequently regardless of the filmic text itself . . . promotional technology and production feats become the new 'camera-style,' serving a new auteurism in which the making of a movie . . . or its

unmaking . . . foreground an agency that forecloses the text itself" (Corrigan 105–106). Corrigan goes on to say that today's auteurs, placed "before, after and outside a film text," can effectively usurp the work of that text and its reception (106). I include this quotation because I think it highlights the way that commentary by filmmakers such as the Coen brothers, who have achieved this status as contemporary auteurs, can function to "set" meanings in the minds of viewers that might otherwise (based on just a viewing of the film) remain ambiguous or less determined. My point here is that Joel Coen's contention that the police chief "happens" to be pregnant potentially works to "fix" the significance of the police chief's pregnant status.

2. I want to thank Sharon Willis for calling this fact to my attention.

3. Filmic representations of pregnant women's "fragile" bodies have a long history. Indeed this fragility was registered on film during the era of the Production Code when we were unlikely to *see* pregnancies in classical Hollywood films (due to the climate of extreme limitations related to representations of sex, crime, childbirth, miscegenation, etc.), even when the narratives of those films dealt with pregnant women. In *Stagecoach* (1939), for example, the body of the pregnant Lucy Mallory is never emphasized in such a way as to make her pregnancy apparent (she covers herself with a shawl throughout much of the film and the camera never highlights her pregnant state) and no one ever mentions the words "pregnant" or "pregnancy." Yet her pregnancy is signaled by the concern about her condition expressed by those around her and finally by her fainting spell. I want to thank Donald Larsson and Sandy Camargo for responding to a query I posted on SCREEN-L and reminding me of the pregnancy of Lucy Mallory in *Stagecoach*.

4. I have encountered these stills on the film's DVD case, accompanying reviews in the popular press, and in an academic anthology, among other places.

5. In a scene prior to this one, Carl, looking bloody-faced and mutilated, returns to the house where Gaear has been hiding out with Jerry's kidnapped wife. When Gaear greets him with a look of disgust and disbelief, Carl responds, "You should see the other guy."

6. *Blue Steel* (1990) and *The Silence of the Lambs* (1991) provide cases in point. In *Blue Steel*, Jamie Lee Curtis plays a rookie New York cop, Megan Turner, whose visibility as a police officer makes her the object of curiosity, suspicion, and repeated interrogation. In *The Silence of the Lambs*, FBI trainee Clarice Starling, played by Jodie Foster, struggles to establish her authority in relation to the men whom she encounters. Despite Starling's excellence in all areas of her professional development, it is her sexual identity that makes her more suited than her male colleagues for an assignment that involves interviewing psychiatrist/killer/cannibal Hannibal Lecter. As she carries out her assignment, Starling is repeatedly figured as the object of her male counterparts' gaze. Both Turner and Starling are subject to interrogations (executed both visually and verbally) about their career aspirations due to their gender and sexual identities. Both of these films involve a textual negotiation of woman as victim and woman as independent heroine and, in each case, the female protagonist's sexuality is employed as a device to gain access or information.

7. Interestingly, Gross offered her praise of Coen's "handling" of the Marge character immediately after playing an audio clip of the scene in which Marge has a bout with "morning sickness" at the site of the triple homicide—a scene that I think showcases the film's ambivalence particularly well because it presents Marge

accurately deducing the specifics of the homicidal events (signaling her agency and professional aptitude) and then vomiting immediately afterward (registering, through a kind of transference, the film's anxiety and dis-ease regarding this working woman). Gross's reading of *Fargo* attests to the fact that, on the one hand, Marge is figured as a perceptive and able cop within professional and generic realms conventionally controlled by men. As so many feminist scholars have pointed out, a female character's mastery of a "masculine" practice and domain affords one familiar possibility for women's viewing pleasure. Gross foregrounds the issue of visibility and representation, saying that Marge "*looks* like she might be mocked" (an apparent though indirect response to Marge's pregnant condition and the extremely unconventional image of a visibly pregnant cop), but the pleasure she derives from Marge's representation is apparently unaffected by the visual "mocking" that I have highlighted.

BIBLIOGRAPHY

Blue Steel. Dir. Kathryn Bigelow. Twentieth Century Fox, 1990.

Coen, Ethan. Interview by Terry Gross. *Fresh Air* (21 October 1998). National Public Radio. WXXI, Rochester. 21 Oct. 1998.

Coen, Joel. Interview. Polygram Film Productions, R.V. Polygram Filmed Entertainment, 1996.

Corrigan, Timothy. *Cinema Without Walls: Movies and Culture after Vietnam*. New Brunswick: Rutgers University Press, 1991.

Fargo. Dir. Joel Coen. Gramercy, 1996.

Joyrich, Lynne. *Re-Viewing Reception: Television, Gender, and Postmodern Culture*. Bloomington: Indiana University Press, 1996.

Lentz, Kirsten Marthe. "The Popular Pleasures of Female Revenge (Or Rage Bursting in a Blaze of Gunfire)." *Cultural Studies* 7.3 (1993): 374–405.

Silence of the Lambs. Dir. Jonathan Demme. Orion Pictures, 1991.

Stagecoach. Dir. John Ford. United Artists, 1939.

Thelma and Louise. Dir. Ridley Scott. MGM, 1991.

TWO

MOTHER'S DAY

Taking the Mother Out of Motherhood
in *The Thrill of It All*

TAMAR JEFFERS MCDONALD

The Thrill of It All (1963) is not a much-seen film now, although I will be arguing that it remains of value—but not for being one of the series of Doris Day "sex comedies,"[1] or as a witty parody of early television advertising,[2] as it is occasionally called. Neither of these accounts is strictly accurate: Beverly Boyer, the character played by Day, is married in this film and therefore not subject to being chased by urbane wolves as in her similar comedies, *Pillow Talk* (1959), *Lover, Come Back* (1961), and *That Touch of Mink* (1962). Further, the advertising parody is not at the story's heart; the spoof of live television advertisements has as much to do with Day's then-contemporary star persona as the realities of sponsored television. What fascinates about *Thrill* is how nakedly and ambivalently it presents a range of problems perceived as urgent in 1963: the role of stay-at-home wives; the pros and cons of employment for mothers outside the home; contraception and birth control. In its portrayal of a housewife whose coping with home chores, children, and being a wife is not enough to occupy her mind, *Thrill* uncannily anticipates the findings of Betty Friedan's *The Feminine Mystique*, published the same year. Due to the lead-in times of production and distribution, *Thrill* must have been under way before Friedan's book hit the stores on February 19, 1963, and the review columns of newspapers and magazines a month later. Yet this film, the first feature written by comedian Carl Reiner, undeniably portrays the hollowness at the heart of the supposedly "happy housewife heroine,"[3] which was Friedan's subject, and represents, in its determined returning of Beverly to the home at the end of the film, a counterattack on Friedan's feminist cry for freedom. The excessive plot exigencies needed to get her back in the home illustrate just how shaky the arguments in support of the feminine mystique were. In its portrayal of a marriage in which the wife fights for equality but the husband battles for supremacy, *Thrill* accurately depicts the very disparities it hopes to discount. Building intricate metaphors around polarities of dirt/cleanliness, public/private, amateur/professional, male/female, the film seems now not so much a light comedy as a depressing snapshot of "ordinary" American life in the white suburbs of the early 1960s, exposing the frustration felt by many women before the rise of the feminist movement later in the decade.

Interestingly, the few filmographies that mention *Thrill* often portray it as a breezy comedy.[4] The synopses they present are significant in omitting many narrative elements that contribute to the film's misogynistic stance. Just as women's lives and women's history have often been untold, left in the interstices of events considered important, Beverly's story languishes unremarked in the interstices of accounts of the film. While offering a similarly brief plot outline here, I will also give prominence to events that seem to symbolize Beverly's oppression in her own home.

Dr. Gerald Boyer (James Garner) is an obstetrician; his wife, Beverly, looks after their two small children, Andy and Maggie, and the family home, with the aid of a live-in maid. Gerald and his wife are invited to dinner by the late-middle-aged Fraleighs in gratitude for helping them conceive. There they meet the elder Mr. Fraleigh, a wealthy, eccentric businessman whose product, Happy Soap, sponsors a live weekly television commercial. Beverly exclaims that her children love Happy Soap, and Mr. Fraleigh is so charmed that he demands she repeat this on television. She declines until she is told her one-time salary: $332. The resultant commercial seems a disaster because of Beverly's amateurishness, but the public recognizes that she is genuine, call the studio in support, and buy the product. As a result, Beverly is offered $80,000 a year to be the Happy Soap spokeswoman. Her home life, however, suffers, since her new busy schedule always clashes with her husband's. He insists she give up the job, but she refuses. He decides to get her pregnant, but the couple are never alone long enough for him to try. Finally he resorts to subterfuge, pretending to have an affair, murmuring "Gloria" while pretending to be drunk. Beverly's resultant misery causes her to forget the product's name on air. At a studio party after this debacle, Mrs. Fraleigh goes into labor and Beverly heads to the hospital with her. They get stuck in traffic; with the help of her husband's advice by phone, Beverly manages to prepare for the birth until he can arrive. Beverly helps

Gerald deliver the child, then bursts into tears. Without recrimination about the affair, Beverly tells her husband she wants to "go back to just being a doctor's wife." They go home and find their children excited to hear how they spent their evening: they want Mommy to have a baby too. Beverly and Gerald agree euphemistically to "discuss" the matter.

This brief account hints at the distasteful lengths the film will go to in order to get its heroine back in the nursery. What I study here in detail are three specific incidents that fully illuminate the parameters of the dispute between Beverly and her husband, making *Thrill* a fascinatingly overt document of the sex wars of the early 1960s. Before turning to these incidents, a short account of the contemporary context of the film is necessary, in order to highlight some of the significances of the terrain the Boyers are fighting over.

SEX AND THE SINGLE (AND MARRIED) GIRL[5]

While woman's sexuality and agency can hardly be said to be easy or unvexed issues at any time, the years from 1953 to 1963 provoked huge successive waves of anxiety in the popular media around the figure of the sexualized woman. The period I am considering here begins with the publication of Alfred Kinsey's *Sexual Behavior in the Human Female* and ends with the release date of *Thrill*, as well as Betty Friedan's best seller, *The Feminine Mystique*. During this time frame, popular attention became fixated on the potential transgressions of the single, desirous girl who might be prepared to flout the double standard, before shifting to the even-more-troubling potential rebellion of the married woman, a figure previously held to be safe and secure because of her constrained and familiar place within a domestic context.

Kinsey published his report[6] to enormous media attention in August 1953; its main revelation was that fifty percent of Kinsey's sample of unmarried females were not virgins. If his group were representative of the American populace in general, this would then mean that half the nation's single women had become "experienced." The popular media began obsessing over this perceived "new" woman and her troublesome sexuality, prompting a wave of articles and investigations. By 1959, Nora Johnson, writing an article on "Sex and the College Girl" for the highbrow magazine *Atlantic Monthly*, noted, "The modern American woman is one of the most discussed, written-about, sore subjects to come along in ages. She has been said to be domineering, frigid, neurotic, repressed, and unfeminine. She tries to do everything at once and doesn't succeed in doing anything very well" (57). Around this time, Hollywood films also caught on to this figure, with the new woman provoking a mixture of anxiety, desire, and prurience by being prepared to flout the double standard, and such texts as *The Best of Everything*, *A Summer Place* (both 1959), *Where the Boys Are* (1960), *State Fair* (1962),

Sunday in New York, and *Under the Yum Yum Tree* (both 1963) brought the troubling, actively sexual, single young woman to the nation's screens. Yet perhaps the challenge presented to the status quo by the rebellious married young woman was even more potentially troubling.

By September 1962, when *Esquire* published Gloria Steinem's first piece of writing, "The Moral Disarmament of Betty Co-Ed," the author felt she could claim that sexual matters were now being handled far more maturely than in previous years because of advances in birth control. Steinem's article contradicts the traditional view of the decade under investigation here (1953–1963) as a time of female sexual timidity, asserting that the spirit of boldness with regards to sexual experimentation is not new. She writes, "Constant fear was hardly the condition prior to the pill in this country, but removing the last remnants of fear of social consequences seems sure to speed American women, especially single women, toward the view that their sex practices are none of society's business" (155). Though stressing a continuum of active female sexuality, Steinem here celebrates the recent advances in birth control. Specifically praising the increased responsibility for her own sexuality given a woman by the pill, Steinem also mentions the diaphragm as a viable birth control method. Significantly, both forms of contraception place the mechanisms of pregnancy prevention in the control of the woman, unlike the male condom. The idea of the woman safely indulging her passion is a very potent one as it negates the threat of inevitable punishment for sex that society had previously wielded at its female members. Without a child, the physical evidence of sexual relations, the woman's sexual status remains invisible, unreadable—and thus threatening.

Contemporary questionings and accounts of the new desirous female thus appeared during this period in texts as diverse as scientific reports, mainstream films, and popular periodicals both low- and highbrow. These various sources bring to the surface many of the contemporary anxieties and assumptions about normative sexual relations, including, fundamentally, that sex is something men want and women grant or withhold. Significantly, both issues are also central to *The Thrill of It All*, which intriguingly incorporates this traditional viewpoint within its narrative, but also subscribes to the contrary new idea that women want sex too.

The film thus adopts both the traditional view of the sexes' contrasting attitudes to sex, in showing Gerald Boyer trying to initiate intimacy with his wife while she evades his attentions, alongside the newer notion that women were as libidinous as men: on other occasions, Beverly is interested in sex as well. This clash between traditional assumptions and current assertions is crystallized on the film's promotional poster. In the photograph of the couple, the Boyers are seen reclining, facing each other as they prepare to kiss.[7] Both have one hand in full view, showing the first two fingers crossed, in the traditional sign of making a wish. The tagline over their heads reads:

> She's hoping He's ready . . .
> He's wishing She's willing . . .

While Gerald's wish is the traditional one of a man for an acquiescent woman, her hope is portrayed in harmony with the contemporary figure of the desirous woman, seeking a partner prepared for action. This suggests the potential for his sexual failure as much as her sexual refusal: he hopes she *will* do it, she hopes he *can*. While the film does not pursue the possibility of sexual impotence in Gerald, at which the poster might seem to be hinting, it does devote time to tracing his feelings of emotional inadequacy once his wife begins not only to work outside the home, but to earn more than he does. Returning to the three incidents that reveal the terms of the Boyers' marriage, I now explore these feelings of inadequacy that prompt the actions Gerald takes in order to return to his accustomed state of mastery. Notably, these feelings revolve around, and set up parallels between, concerns over money, food, babies, and dirt.

THRILL'S IMAGERY SYSTEMS

The first of the incidents illuminating the dialectics of the relationship between Beverly and her husband occurs toward the beginning of the film, on the day when, having been told she is at last pregnant, Mrs. Fraleigh invites Gerald and his wife to dinner in gratitude. Gerald telephones to tell Beverly not to prepare dinner, but Andy, their son, does not deliver the message, and thus when Gerald arrives home to change into evening dress, he finds her in houseclothes rather than evening wear, putting the finishing touches on a large roast. Gerald nevertheless announces that they will go to the Fraleighs. Though Beverly protests, not wanting to waste "a six dollar and thirty-four cent standing rib roast," her husband insists. Beverly again mentions money as a reason not to go: she has given their live-in maid the evening off, and "paying a sitter a dollar an hour when we already have a housekeeper just seems a sin!" Gerald's response to this is significant: leaning seductively close to his wife, he tells her: "Bev, even the best of us sin every once in a while. Tonight's your night." The camera fastens on Beverly's facial expression: she absorbs this rejoinder, showing she has got the underlying message by winking. Simultaneously, the musical score underlines with a flourish the salacious nature of Gerald's line. He has offered a trade: if she gives up her annoyance at the wasted food, her nagging about money, he will give her sex. That Beverly is seen happily agreeing to this deal demonstrates the film's displaying the new awareness of female sexual desires.

This connection between finance and autonomy recurs several times. For example, it is made very obvious that Beverly accepts the Happy Soap jobs so as to earn her own money and contribute to the family's finances. As the couple argue over her job, Gerald offers his definition of "our money": "*Our money* is what I earn by being a doctor. What you earn is yours." Beverly is not allowed to contribute to the family welfare with her earnings, but only with her labor within the household.[8] Cooking and childcare are made her career: a career that, in complete contrast to the advertising contract, has no salary attached to it. Beverly is thus meant to labor for her own keep. Although the film does not investigate her motives in wanting the money from the Happy Soap job, we can perhaps posit that it is not merely increasing the family's wealth that drives Beverly. As her husband notes, "It's not as if we needed the money." Beverly needs the money herself ("she" versus "we"), in order to feel that she has some control over her own life. When Gerald makes the decision to abandon the dinner Beverly has cooked, he assumes he has the right to do so because that "six dollar and thirty-four cent standing rib roast" has been purchased with *his* six dollars and thirty-four cents. Beverly has labored to turn the meat into a roast dinner, but she did not earn the money that paid for it. Her desire for a salary then seems not so much predicated on increasing the household coffers as giving herself the right to make decisions over what is eaten and what is left untasted.

This idea carries through into the second major incident that lays bare the relationship between Beverly and her husband. Again, themes of money, children, marriage, career, food, and dirt are intricately woven into a scene that at first appears merely to further the narrative and provide slapstick humor, but on closer examination reveals the very terms and terrain of the marriage being fought over by the Boyers.

In this scene, Beverly is visited by Mike, the Happy Soap executive, who has come to offer her a year's promotional contract. He finds Beverly in the cellar surrounded by baskets of tomatoes: she is bottling her own ketchup. Like the beef that she cooked and Gerald decided would go uneaten, the ketchup points up Beverly's position of inferiority in the marriage. This labor is decidedly unnecessary, since ketchup is an inexpensive product and could easily be bought ready-made. Furthermore, the shots of the Boyers' garden reveal no tomato plants; Beverly has therefore presumably had to purchase the tomatoes. Unlike the thrifty housewife of earlier times who bottled and preserved all possible crops to eke out the family's rations, to whom making ketchup was therefore just another instance of "waste not, want not," affluent Beverly is engaged in this task for mere "busy work." It is an invented task designed to fill the empty hours. This point is further highlighted when Gerald calls the ketchup-making one of Beverly's "hobbies." Not only does Beverly have no job outside the home that contributes a salary to the family, she also has no significant labor within the home that necessitates her presence there. Her time should therefore be free for hobbies, but Beverly has only the PTA and ketchup. In this she very much resembles the resentful and confused women that Betty Friedan wrote about, and for, in *The Feminine Mystique*, women whom it was assumed belonged in the home, even if it was supplied with so many labor-saving devices and assistants that they had nothing to do there:

> I've tried everything women are supposed to do—hobbies, gardening, pickling, canning, being very social with my neighbours, joining committees, running PTA teas. I can do it all, and I like it, but it doesn't leave you anything to think about—any feeling of who you are. . . . There's no problem you can even put a name to. But I'm desperate . . . I begin to feel I have no personality. (qtd. in Friedan 19)

The film rather overstates the case for the frustrated housewife by giving her nothing to occupy herself with but ketchup and the PTA. Faced with a choice of staying home to look after these matters, or going out to a job that puts her on television, on billboards, and in magazines, why would Beverly hesitate? Yet the film's conclusion returns her to the sterility of the former situation and can only suggest more sex and babies as a solution to her emptiness.

The film's ambivalence about Beverly's position in the marriage, whether she has the right to expect more, or whether Gerald rightly manipulates her back into her "proper" place in the home, is marked through the recurrence of symbolism around notions of dirtiness and cleanliness. To a certain intriguing extent, this imagery system might be contingent with Doris Day's star persona, as her being soaked—in water or mud—is a recurrent motif in her films.[9] As a *Life* magazine article published at the time of the film's release partly appreciated: "The formula: drench her in pools, tubs or suds" ("Tomato on Top" 106). This tendency becomes complicated by *Thrill's* other imagery systems, however, when dirtiness is linked with money. It is significant that the tomatoes all over the Boyers' cellar may seem, from the scene's beginning, to be rife with possibilities for slapstick and messy humor, but Beverly only succumbs to the inevitable pratfall into a basketful at the moment when Mike mentions the huge salary Happy Soap would pay her. The implication seems clear: money makes Mommy dirty. The film continues this theme by showing Beverly increasingly unfit for her motherhood responsibilities through contact with commerce: as she gets better at delivering the live television spots, she gets worse at being at home during crises, which concomitantly multiply because of her absence.

If money makes Mommy dirty, then science makes Daddy clean, even though he delivers babies for a living and thus must be covered in afterbirth and blood on a daily basis. While *Thrill* is ambivalent about the constrictions of Beverly's life and whether or not she has any rights, it ultimately weights the case against these rights—to work, to make decisions, to an active sexuality—by making her husband not merely a professional, versus her amateur status, but in making his specialty obstetrics. She works to sell; he works to give life. Gerald Boyer's role as a baby doctor is vital to the film's paradoxical project of valorizing pregnancy and childbirth, while simultaneously downgrading motherhood. In *Thrill* it is male Dr. Boyer, not his wife, who produces babies. Woman's biological input has been demoted. Not only does the man deliver the babies, but he also seems to be in charge of when they come. From the first scene in which the couple argue over the uneaten beef, where Gerald boasts to Beverly how he "helped a woman become pregnant today," to the final moment when they have made up their quarrel because Beverly has resigned, it is Dr. Boyer who controls female reproduction in the film. Indeed, as another look at the beef scene confirms, Gerald seems to have the power not only to make other women pregnant through his professional advice, but also to keep Beverly from becoming so if he chooses. When he cajoles her to forget her annoyance over the wasted food, he promises her sex: "Tonight's your night." There is no implication here that a baby will result from this act, however. Gerald is not seeking to reward or punish Beverly to that extent at this point. However, in a later scene, when Gerald finds himself contrasting Mrs. Fraleigh's reverential attitude to children—"There's nothing more fulfilling in life than having a baby"—to his wife's careerist desires, he decides to put Beverly in the position of appreciating this. He gets his assistant to send Beverly flowers and make dinner reservations, in order to set up an evening of seduction. When the assistant queries, "Is it Mrs. Boyer's birthday?" the scheming doctor replies, "No, but it may be *somebody's*." Gerald can clearly be seen plotting to get his wife pregnant in order to return her to the home. He must therefore be able to control his own fertility, by which we can assume he would generally use a condom for contraceptive purposes. Remembering that *Thrill* appeared at a time when discussions about the increased availability of the pill and diaphragm were rife throughout the media, the film's insistence on Beverly's reproductive system being subject to Gerald's control appears as an act of almost hysterical nostalgia.

The Thrill of It All can thus be seen to emphasize the importance of male control both of motherhood (Gerald determines how many children his wife will have, and when) and of female sexual agency, using Gerald's status as an obstetrician to disguise the fact that it is his gender, not his professionalism, that gives him the right to decide when Beverly will conceive and, as another incident when he turns down her advances shows, even have sex. Beverly can be reactive but not proactive sexually, as evinced in a scene in which, one rare evening when she is at home without commitments, she propositions Gerald: "What are you doing this evening? I'm baking you something special—with r-r-rum in it." Day's voice as she performs this line gives a sexy growl to the beginning of the word "rum," with Beverly offering to prepare a special meal to get her husband in the mood for sex. Here the film steps away again from traditional assumptions in the direction of then-new assertions about women's desires for sex, but the outcome of the scene suggests it does not endorse the woman openly suggesting intimacy: though Beverly suggests sex, Gerald rejects her, saying he is too busy. While within the narrative this rejection is depicted as part of Gerald's plan to imply he is having an affair, the scene still demonstrates the woman asking for, and the man denying her, sex, reversing the traditional trajectory of such conversations.

The final moment of key significance comes at the end of the film, when the Boyers return home after delivering Mrs. Fraleigh's baby together. Previously Gerald had told his children he could only keep babies when, as in their cases, Mommy had helped him bring them. His choice of wording—when Mommy *helps*—again underlines Gerald's perception of his own instrumental, and the woman's incidental, status to the birth. When Beverly and Gerald arrive home after their *rapprochement*, they find their own children waiting up, ready to insist they should have brought the child home: "When Mommy helps we get to keep the baby." At this point the film has Beverly embrace her own fate: although she was not present at the scene in which Andy, Maggie, and their father discussed keeping a new baby the next time their mother helped, she now joins in with the children's demands: "Yes, dear, a promise is a promise." Packing the children off to bed, she assures them that she and Daddy will discuss the matter, "tonight, if Daddy's not too tired." Beverly here signals to her husband her acceptance of male dominance within the sex act: her possible fatigue, having delivered a commercial and helped with the baby, is not of importance, since he will be doing all the hard work in their coupling while she remains passive below him. Furthermore, she is complicit in her husband's control of her sexuality and fertility when she asks for sex in a coded manner she can deem approved, since it will result in children rather than mere pleasure.

This rather distasteful ending, the children unwittingly cheering as their mother asks to be impregnated again, is augmented by the fact that the adultery plot has not been exploded. In previous Doris Day comedies, such as *Pillow Talk* and *Lover, Come Back*, much of the humor is derived from the male lead's plots against the dignity or chastity of the Day character, and from Day's reaction when she realizes she has been fooled. Her vengeance and his realization that he needs her then make up the final reel of the films. In *Thrill*, however, though the invention of "Gloria" seems to follow

Figure 3. The happy ending of *The Thrill of It All* (1963) mandates that Beverly (Doris Day) become pregnant again.

the same pattern—a subterfuge to which the audience is party while the Day character is not—there is a lack of resolution. "Gloria" is never mentioned again: Beverly does not recriminate the supposed affair, and Gerald does not confess she was merely a pretense to get her to resign. The stakes for which the couple are playing are too high to have an easy resolution; if Gerald were to explain that "Gloria" was a ruse to get Beverly back home long enough to impregnate her and thus ensure her television career was over, his wife would be so furious that there could be no simple closure for the film. Instead, a sacrifice has to be made, and it is Beverly who is making it even while she believes she is saving her marriage. The film ends as it began, with multicolored cartoon rockets exploding over the characters as the couple go upstairs to bed. At the beginning of the film, these rockets burst over Mr. and Mrs. Fraleigh as she announces her pregnancy, signifying joyful celebrations over the announcement of the baby; at the end, however, they underline again the importance of masculinist intervention in the home. Appearing this time before the pregnancy has been accomplished, the phallic rockets seem to evoke the ejaculation of sperm, thus stressing again the significance only of the male's contribution to conception.

CONCLUSION: BEING DADDY, DOING MOMMY

Thrill presents a tangled yet fascinating account of then-current views on a range of topics including the battle of the sexes, career wives versus careerist wives, female sexual agency and control, and backlash desires for male mastery.

While the film seems to close down Beverly's options, returning her to the home in the final scenes, it cannot erase, especially with this ending, the sense of emptiness and sterility in Beverly's life that it has evoked for most of its running time. *Thrill* thus can be seen endorsing Friedan's notions of the "problem that has no name"[10] at the same time as it attempts to deliver a comedy undermining the dissatisfaction of the housewives who suffered it.

The film weights the case against Beverly's career ambitions, even as it shows she only wants the money in order to have control of her own life, by making that career as inane and meretricious as advertising. Beverly's contact with the cleaning product makes her dirty, because she takes money for it, while her husband's career as a baby doctor is sanitized, the taint of dirtiness involved in dwelling in a world of blood and afterbirth erased because he brings new life into the world. As a doctor, Gerald is more than a man, he is a god, bringing life; Beverly's job, by contrast, involves her merely being what she is at home: a woman, subject to, and useful as an example of, her gender. The film becomes confused, however, when it tries condemning Beverly for being a mommy on television instead of at home, implying she is wrong to be talking about, instead of being at home doing, the housework. Scenes in the home have already shown there is little for her to do there: apart from cooking the roast and shampooing Maggie's hair, all of Beverly's chores are accomplished by the housekeeper, leaving her plenty of empty time to make ketchup. The film tries to combat this incoherent stance by insisting that there is a difference between the roles of each parent, that while the male's depends on ontology—*being* Daddy—the female's depends on praxis—*doing* the Mommy chores. This is made clear in several of the exchanges between the Boyers over her career, when he repeatedly demands she give up the job and "go back to being" the dutiful homebody. At one point the argument runs thus:

> GERALD: Will you give up this asinine career and go back to being a wife?
>
> BEVERLY: Go *back* to being a wife?

Her intonation implies that she has never left off being a wife; but wifehood, like motherhood, is seemingly more than ontology for the woman, it is a state of doing more than a state of being, so that if she is not there to cook, wash, shampoo kids, and be available for sex, she is no longer a mother and wife. At the conclusion of one of their endless job arguments, Beverly avers, "I won't let anything interfere with my wifely duties, I promise." Yet the film implies this is exactly what occurs; her presence in the studio removes her from the home where it is her wifely duty to linger, even if idle, in case someone in the family needs her.

Beverly is seen breaking this promise on the occasions when Gerald comes home amorous and cannot have sex with her because she is too busy, too surrounded by other people, or absent. Delivering the Fraleighs' baby supposedly helps Beverly appreciate her errors, and acknowledge that giving up her job is right: "I want to be a doctor's wife again." Yet what the film has shown us in the delivery scene is a woman who enjoys assisting at a birth: surely instead of "closeness" to her husband, a realization that she needs to rely on him for money, control, and decisions, Beverly could simply be happier with a career as a midwife. By setting up Beverly as a television seller of soap, the film intends to contrast her with her husband, pitting dirty commerce against sanctified new life, but the very excessiveness of this career ends up undercutting the intended impact of the polarization. Of course Beverly would become disenchanted with television advertising: her popularity rests on the fickle public and remains out of her control. A real career that she had trained for, instead of merely repeating on screen a role she performs off it, would give her much more satisfaction. As a television spokeswoman for Happy Soap—paradoxically a job that increasingly makes her unhappy—Beverly is enacting on-screen the roles she is supposed to perform in the home: being well-dressed, sunny, and looking after the family's clean clothes and bodies. That this is not sufficient employment for an adult woman is indicated at several key points in the film, even as it attempts to recruit audience support for returning Beverly to this employment. At one moment, Andy and Maggie come upon their mother in her bedroom, saying over and over, "Hello, I'm Beverly Boyer, and I'm a housewife." Her children quiz her, asking if she really needs to practice her name. This hints at the emptiness in the housewife role that erodes a woman's sense of identity.

Further, when the couple argue over whether making ketchup is a sufficient hobby, a small detail of stage business hints at the film's awareness of the contemporary hoopla about the unhappy, dissatisfied housewife. Countering Beverly's pro-job arguments, Gerald asserts, "Our bank balance is healthy. There's no reason for you to work." This evokes a sarcastic response from Beverly, who picks up a magazine triumphantly: "Dr. Boyer, you are a fraud!" Day then seems to ad lib as she turns the pages of the magazine until she finds the section she wants. "Oohh! I've got you now, dear! I've got you now—right here. And I quote: 'In some cases, household duties—important as they are—are not sufficient to gratify a woman's desire for expression. Mrs. America might do well to start early in her marriage a planned cultivation of outside interests and hobbies.' " Before *The Feminine Mystique*'s full publication, Betty Friedan had pre-published two sections as magazine articles, in *Mademoiselle* and *Ladies' Home Journal*. Here the film shows its awareness of this contemporary media milieu by having Gerald write a similar piece. It seems both ironic that he should be declaring in favor of the "planned cultivation of outside interests" that the film shows him trying to prevent, and somewhat unlikely that a magazine would ask an obstetrician to comment on the then-perceived Woman Problem. Perhaps the film, in making Gerald the author of the article, is attempting to confirm again his status as a professional, a medical man whose opinion is significant, even while his specialty lies elsewhere than psychology and his real reason for being granted supremacy is his gender. By acknowledging the contemporary debate about unfulfilled housewives, but then, finally, suggesting that fulfillment could only come by being fully filled with babies, *Thrill* both contributes to and contests then-current debates over female reproductive and sexual autonomy.

NOTES

1. "In [this], as usual, Doris is a slightly nutty, refreshing-to-look-at girl, stunningly turned out and relentlessly pursued by wolf packs of panting males through decidedly risqué dialogue and situations" ("The Tomato on Top" 104).

2. *Thrill* "was at its merriest when it was spoofing television" ("*Move Over, Darling*").

3. "Happy housewife heroine" refers to the title and subject of Friedan's second chapter.

4. For example: "The major part of the film . . . is an exhilarating and hilarious gallop" (Clark and Simmons 68).

5. This subtitle alludes to Helen Gurley Brown's 1962 best-selling book, *Sex and the Single Girl*, which celebrated the unmarried woman. The book did not criticize wives (seeing, in fact, marriage as the ultimate goal of the single girl), but instructed the unmarried on how both to have a good time and become irresistible, while waiting for "Him" to come along.

6. This detailed the sexual attitudes and practices of his sample, which was made up of 5,431 unmarried white thirty-year-old females.

7. A spatial arrangement implies that they are on a double bed, although neither this bed nor the scene actually features in the film itself.

8. I find an interesting parallel with this notion in Kathleen McHugh's *American Domesticity*, where she discusses several maternal melodramas; in films such as *Imitation of Life* (1934) and *Mildred Pierce* (1945), "housework becomes 'not work' in relation to the 'work' that earns a living." This seems to be the case even if the work that earns a living is the performance of housework, or the talking about it, on television (132).

9. For example, Day falls full-length in mud in *Calamity Jane* (1953) and *Jumbo* (1962) and appears in water in *Pillow Talk*, and *Move Over, Darling* (1963) as well as *Thrill*.

10. This refers to the title of the first chapter in *The Feminine Mystique* (see Friedan 13).

BIBLIOGRAPHY

Clark, Jane, and Diane Simmons. *Move Over Misconceptions: Doris Day Reappraised.* BFI Dossier No. 4. London: British Film Institute, 1980.

Friedan, Betty. *The Feminine Mystique.* 1963. London: Penguin Books, 1992.

Gurley Brown, Helen. *Sex and the Single Girl.* New York: Bernard Geis, 1962.

Johnson, Nora. "Sex and the College Girl." *Atlantic Monthly* (November 1959): 56–60.

Kinsey, Alfred C., et al. *Sexual Behavior in the Human Female.* Philadelphia and London: W. B. Saunders, 1953.

McHugh, Kathleen Anne. *American Domesticity: From How-to Manual to Melodrama.* New York and Oxford: Oxford University Press, 1996.

Meyerowitz, Joanne, ed. *Not June Cleaver: Women and Gender in Post-War America, 1945–1960.* Philadelphia: Temple University Press, 1994.

Morris, George. *Doris Day.* Pyramid Illustrated History of the Movies. New York: Pyramid, 1976.

"Move Over, Darling." *Motion Picture Herald* (25 December 1963): 953.

Steinem, Gloria. "The Moral Disarmament of Betty Co-Ed." *Esquire* (September 1962): 97, 153–157.

The Thrill of It All. Dir. Norman Jewison. Universal, 1963.

The Thrill of It All Press Book. Consulted in the British Film Institute Library, London, UK.

The Thrill of It All Script. Consulted in the British Film Institute Library, London, UK.

"The Tomato on Top Is Doris." *Life* (27 September 1963): 104–106.

THREE

NOT EXACTLY ACCORDING TO THE RULES

―――――――――――――――――――

Pregnancy and Motherhood in *Sugar & Spice*

MADONNE M. MINER

> These are the best days of your life—so far.
>
> —Diane, *Sugar & Spice*

For many white, middle-class, teenage girls, marriage and motherhood constitute major components in dreams for the future. Diane Weston (Marley
Shelton), heroine of Francine McDougall's 2001 film, *Sugar & Spice*, captain
of the A-squad cheerleaders and "a poster child for high school" (as described
by the character Lisa), agrees, but gets the components out of order; not
long into the film we learn that Diane intends to marry her boyfriend Jack
Bartlett (James Marsden), quarterback for the Lincoln High football team
and homecoming king, but not until after she bears their baby. Interestingly, it is the "taking" or heist of Diane's body by pregnancy (Diane cannot control her morning sickness, mood swings, expanding waistline, and
gas outbursts) that prompts a more conventional heist narrative in *Sugar
& Spice*. Recognizing that love alone is not going to provide a future for
her family, Diane determines that to realize her version of the American
Dream she needs far more money than she can make working part-time at
a branch bank located in the local supermarket. Taking a cue from *Point
Break* (1991), a heist film in which Bodhi (Patrick Swayze) and his surfing

friends rob banks while wearing masks of ex-presidents, Diane proposes that the A-squad cheerleaders engage in a heist; they can rob the bank where she works. Disguised as pregnant Betty Dolls, the girls perpetrate a heist that revises genre conventions. Most dramatically, this female heist/teen pregnancy film operates on principles of expansion and inclusion; the squad grows, taking in new members, accepting addition as positive. In contrast, conventional male heist films almost always work to exclude, getting rid of team members, disrupting or destroying family bonds, attempting to enact control over uncontrollable situations through elimination of characters. Produced by New Line, an independent studio that "hopes to counterprogram its way to success, zigging when other studios zag" (Brodesser A6), *Sugar & Spice* appears decidedly revolutionary when compared to male heist films; unlike films coming out of major Hollywood studios, *Sugar & Spice* asks viewers to consider the gendered dynamics of conventional heist films *and* offers viewers positive representations of female teamwork. I will briefly review characteristics of conventional male heist films, then argue that McDougall's film appropriates and revises those conventions to make them applicable to a narrative about adolescent female bodies, female communities, and motherhood.

> In school they tell us dreams can come true, but they don't tell us how.
>
> —Diane, *Sugar & Spice*

Film critic Chris Vognar describes the heist film as follows: "A heist film focuses on the elaborate planning and execution of a robbery, and often on the assembly of a team that collaborates on said planning and execution" (G6). Scholar Nicole Rafter, who prefers the term "caper" to describe this genre, elaborates:

> The *caper* follows a criminal or group of criminals as they plan a long con: the complicated, audacious heist that will set them up for life. The first part of a caper movie is usually consumed by planning; the leader rounds up the gang and targets the bank, racetrack, rich Texan, or train that is to be robbed, after which everyone practices with stopwatches and getaway cars. The remainder is devoted to the execution of the crime and, in most cases, the last-minute failure of the criminals. (143)

The appeal of the caper or heist film may lie in an audience's identification with gang members against the bank, racetrack, rich Texan, and so on, but then, also, in the audience's later identification with forces of the law. Critic George Grella, for example, argues that the heist works on its audience because "we live in the modern age, and we like to see a mechanism at work. Heist movies are about a mechanism. They're about people forming a mechanism and foiling machinery" (qtd. in Vognar G6). Generally, the people who form such "mechanisms" (teams/plans) come from positions of powerlessness relative to the far more powerful "machinery" (banks/corporations/insurance companies) they attempt to foil. And, although Rafter, Vognar, and Grella do not call attention to the fact, traditional heist films feature characters we are accustomed to seeing on center stage: men. While we might go as far back as 1903, to Edwin S. Porter's *The Great Train Robbery*, for an early example of the male heist at work, it is after World War II and a relaxation in the Motion Picture Production Code's prohibition against the presentation of "methods of crime" that the male heist flourishes.[1] To outwit security forces in charge of banks, casinos, racetracks, and jewelry stores, mechanisms of men function together in films from the 1950s and 1960s such as *Criss Cross* (1949), *The Asphalt Jungle* (1950), *Rififi* (1955), *The Killing* (1956), and *Ocean's Eleven* (1960). Recently, we have experienced a resurgence of representations of the male team and its attendant tensions in such films as *Heat* (1995), *The Usual Suspects* (1995), *Reindeer Games* (2000), *Heist* (2001), *Ocean's Eleven* (2001), *The Score* (2001), *Three Thousand Miles to Graceland* (2001), *The Italian Job* (2003), *The Ladykillers* (2004), *Ocean's Twelve* (2004), *Inside Man* (2006), and *Ocean's Thirteen* (2007). These films complicate dynamics among team members by diversifying elements of race, class, or ethnicity, but, like their forebears, do little with female characters. When women are present, they tend to disrupt or disturb the all-male team. But women need not be present for the male mechanism to fail. In almost all of these films, the team finds that after it escapes from the casino or bank with bags of loot, members cannot sustain bonds of brotherhood; they squabble over who will get larger shares, who is in charge, or what their next job will be. Bullets fly. Corpses abound. The dream goes sour.

What happens when the team is composed of women—or, more accurately, of white, middle-class, high school girls? And when these girls determine to engage in a heist not because each dreams in dollar signs, but rather because one of them is pregnant, soon to be the mother of twins? Addressing these questions, McDougall's *Sugar & Spice* refers parodically to male heist films that precede it[2] and contrasts teams of male and female characters. The references and contrasts encourage viewers first to recognize precisely how different the female dynamics of *Sugar & Spice* are from those of its male predecessors and second to consider how processes associated with control of the female body during pregnancy and childbirth present curious parallels to processes associated with the planning and execution of a heist.

Look you guys, I just want to provide a future for my baby.

—Diane, *Sugar & Spice*

Sugar & Spice opens in a police station. A police officer and a group of spectators watch as suspects, unseen by us, line up single-file behind a one-way mirror. Only when the officer directs the suspects to prepare for a camera shot do we get to see these objects of attention: six teenage girls in blue cheerleading uniforms, posed as if for a publicity still, the girl to the far left obviously pregnant. After titles introducing each cheerleader, we move to an interrogation area where we meet the narrator of *Sugar & Spice*, Lisa (Marla Sokoloff). A member of the B-squad team who desperately wants to move up to A-squad, Lisa's story to Detective Sibowitz shapes everything that we see in *Sugar & Spice*. A narrator who addresses a police investigator as a result of her desire to be "one of the gang," Lisa reprises the role of Verbal Kindt (Kevin Spacey) in Mark Singer's *The Usual Suspects*, a male heist film released in 1995.[3] After an opening scene on the wharf, *Suspects* moves to Detective Dave Kuhan's (Chaz Palmintieri's) office, where Verbal tells the story of robberies committed by a team of five thieves. Like Verbal, Lisa introduces each of the suspected cheerleaders, imagines how each is drawn into the heist, conjures up their planning and practice sessions, and conveys her own desire to be part of this team. Unlike Verbal's representation of team-building in *The Usual Suspects*, however, where five previously unrelated thieves come together to take vengeance on the New York Police Department,[4] Lisa claims the initial A-squad is tighter than "Carolina cousins" and images on-screen appear to support her claim. During Lisa's description of each "suspect" to Detective Sibowitz, our eyes follow a box of tampons passed from one girl to the next under the stall walls of a high school lavatory. So closely bound, so physically in synch with one another, these girls get their periods at the same time. Although opening shots and dialogue of *Sugar & Spice* make reference to *The Usual Suspects*, the reference also alerts us to ways McDougall's heist film will differ from Singer's. She attends to bonds already established among her characters and represents those bonds in the female body.

The importance of female bodies to McDougall's film and to the possibility of forming a successful heist team is highlighted again when, a few shots later, we return to the pink-tiled lavatory; it is homecoming night and once more the tampon box is handed from one stall to the next, but this time Diane, occupant of the fifth stall, pushes the box away. Exiting their individual stalls, team members gather around their captain. Before Diane can offer an explanation, each girl reacts:

LUCY: Holy shit. You just became a statistic.

KANSAS: Oh my god. I'm not the first.

HANNAH: But you're not married.

CLEO: Wait: did you say you are pregnant or were pregnant?
          You had it, threw it out, and now you're going to go
          out and dance all night?

Lucy, "the brain," speaks from the position of a disapproving adult culture, aware of generally unhappy data associated with teenage pregnancy; Kansas, "the rebel," is amazed she has avoided the dubious distinction of being the first of their group to become pregnant; Hannah, described by Lisa as "an uber-Christian," cannot comprehend pregnancy before marriage; and Cleo, a Conan O'Brian groupee, wants clarification on how, exactly, the team should read Diane's rejection of the tampon box.

While this initial round of responses certainly does not appear particularly supportive, it indicates more concern for Diane and her future than we see exhibited in the boys' lavatory on that same night. We cut to a scene of blue-tiled walls and five boys in a row at urinals. Jack, team captain and father of Diane's baby, offers his comments:

JACK: Hey guys: I got Diane Weston pregnant.

TEAMMATE: What? Well, all right!

TEAMMATE: You nailed Diane Weston? I'd never wash my johnson
            again.

The image of these five individual males, facing away from us and from each other, giving each other high-fives, supports claims by sociologists and psychologists about differing relational dynamics between boys and girls. The former tend to operate more autonomously; the latter, more affiliatively. In its representation of boy and girl teams, Sugar & Spice portrays males as generally independent of one another, connected only loosely when required by rules of the game, whereas females form a much tighter relational network.[5] The relative autonomy of the males on the football team parallels the autonomy we see so often in male heist films, where individual thieves come together as team members reluctantly and temporarily. They are willing to work together to accomplish a goal, but once that goal is achieved, the team dissolves.

When we cut back to the girls' bathroom, the visuals are far different from those we have just left. The four members of the A-squad, facing the camera and Diane, form a unit of support, and, after Diane declares that she is keeping her baby, they embrace in a five-person hug. Diane explains that she has always planned on getting married and having kids ("I just got a little out of order"), and then compares her situation to that of "another young lady who found herself with child, unmarried, on a long, long road with no place to sleep." While some of us initially may assume Diane refers to the Virgin Mary, her teammates know that she's quoting from a somewhat more contemporary Madonna, whose song, "Papa Don't Preach" tells the story of a girl, "in trouble deep," who makes up her mind to continue her pregnancy. This communal understanding of Diane's reference underlines what the film shows us repeatedly: these girls are a team, caring for one another, thinking along the same lines as one another. Hugging their pregnant captain, the team declares, "We're here for you, Diane," and Diane responds, "I love you guys."

Interestingly, Diane's decision to follow the model articulated in Madonna's song ("I'm gonna keep my baby") goes against prevailing patterns for her class, race, and socioeconomic status. In *Dubious Conceptions: The Politics of Teenage Pregnancy*, Kristin Luker notes: "The more successful a young woman is—and, more important, expects to be—the more likely she is to obtain an abortion. Women from affluent, white, and two-parent homes are far more likely to end their pregnancies than are women from poor, minority, and single-parent homes" (154).[6] Decidedly successful (she's not only head of the A-squad cheerleaders, but also homecoming queen), Diane anticipates further success: she envisions herself at Jack's side as he becomes a senator, or perhaps, president. We know too that Diane comes from a middle-class, two-parent family, as does Jack. One might expect Diane to elect abortion, but she does not. Aside from the practical reason that the film needs Diane's pregnancy as a motive for its heist, the continuation of the pregnancy makes sense in at least three ways: first, the film's representation of Diane's choice serves as an example (a paradoxical one) of an adolescent girl's fantasized control over her body in the face of her parents' desire that she be "not pregnant"; second, the pregnancy allows Diane's surrogate family, her cheerleading team, to come together and provide her with the affection adults withhold; and third, the pregnancy aligns itself with the film's overall orientation toward inclusion and incorporation in contrast to exclusion.

Luker suggests that "the short answer to why teenagers get pregnant and especially to why they continue those pregnancies is that a fairly substantial number of them just don't believe what adults tell them, be it about sex, contraception, marriage, or babies" (11). Diane falls into this camp. No matter what adults may say, she determines she will make her own decision about this pregnancy; she will be in control.[7] Were she alive in an earlier era, or of a different class or race, Diane might assert herself against adult expectations by electing to have an abortion. But in this 2001 film, Diane surprises her parents with her decision to carry her baby to term and only then get married. Paradoxically, deciding to continue the pregnancy means surrendering control of her body to fluctuations wrought upon it by pregnancy.

This paradox dovetails with the decision structure that appears in most heist films: characters elect to engage in heists so as to control their futures, but once they make their first move, they lose control—the heist itself takes over. At the heart of any heist—as at the heart of any pregnancy—is the unpredictable. Past prescriptions against the public presence of pregnant women, even married pregnant women (pregnancy, of course, being a sign of sexual activity), indicate the culture's general unease with the power and potential rebelliousness of this body.[8]

After telling their parents about the pregnancy, Jack and Diane are banished from their middle-class homes. Expressing disapproval of the pregnant, unmarried, adolescent female, adults in the film play into genre conventions for teen and romance films; that is, adults/parents become obstructions to be dismissed, derided, or overcome. Interestingly, part of the fantasy of *Sugar & Spice* arises from the film's reassurance to viewers that even without the support of adults, pregnant teens will fare well.[9] Jack and Diane find an apartment, part-time jobs, and seem to be ecstatic about upcoming parenthood. Diane lets out the waist on her cheerleading skirt (we see a green "V" of material added to accommodate extra inches), indulges in her taste for Ben & Jerry's ice cream, and apparently attracts no censure from high school peers. Her cheerleading squad lines up in her support: Lucy passes along information from a book she reads about what to expect during pregnancy ("Diane, it says here you're going to have mood swings, uncontrollable gas . . . and sex dreams where you actually have an orgasm"); other squad members pull Diane away from an ice-cream vendor at the football game and rescue her from on-the-job orgasmic dreams of Wayne Gretsky. Even Lisa, decidedly not one of Diane's fans, tells Detective Sibowitz, "To the kids at school, Jack and Diane had it all. I mean, come on, their own apartment, staying up late, eating whatever they wanted, plus Jack was getting a discount on R-rated movies at the video store." At least in early sections of *Sugar & Spice*, the consequences of teenage pregnancy appear generally positive, especially with respect to teenage peers. And with respect to adults? They barely seem to matter. After the annunciation scene, we do not see Jack's or Diane's parents again; for that matter, parents are notably absent in this film, decidedly marginalized. With the exception of Kansas's mother, imprisoned for murder, and Fern's father, a "bug-zapper" and trader in illegal guns, *Sugar & Spice* offers few talking roles to adults. This movie uses adult absence to affirm, on the one hand, that teens can make it on their own and, on the other, that, even when present, adults have little to offer.[10]

This teen fantasy receives a slight check as Diane's pregnancy starts taking more of a toll. Accustomed to being in control of her life/her body, this unmarried soon-to-be-mother finds it difficult to orchestrate school, cheerleading practice, Lamaze class, and her part-time job at the bank.

Although her squad supports her, they also fall prey to Diane's unpredictable gas attacks and mood swings. When Hannah, for example, offers to help clean Jack and Diane's dumpy apartment, Diane barks: "Don't Martha-freaking-Stewart me. You don't like it, you try being a pregnant teen" and then lets out a decidedly audible fart. In tiny bits, *Sugar & Spice* suggests that being a pregnant teen is not so easy—especially when you are paying rent, grocery bills, doctor bills, and anticipate more of the same. Bright, responsible, hard-working, and well-organized Diane tells her team she has learned the Beatles had it wrong: love isn't all you need. But quickly, so as not to spoil the fantasy, *Sugar & Spice* offers an out to Diane with another fantasy: to provide for her family, Diane takes a cue from Kathryn Bigelow's 1991 heist film, *Point Break*, suggesting that she—and the squad—rob the grocery-store bank branch where she works part-time.

Sugar & Spice's gesture toward *Point Break* is significant for a variety of reasons. First and foremost is the fact that this genre-breaking heist/surfer/buddy/cops and robbers film is directed by a woman. Surveying over fifty American heist films released between 1941 and 2001, I could find only two directed by women: *Point Break* and *Sugar & Spice*. Interestingly, both films push generic conventions, *Point Break* by conflating conventions of numerous genres, *Sugar & Spice* by introducing female characters into a plotline traditionally reserved for men. While the question of differences between male and female directors is too vexed to pursue here, I will say that Bigelow and McDougall direct films that can be read as "testing the properties" of the heist tradition. In " 'I Wanted to Shoot People': Genre, Gender and Action in the Films of Kathryn Bigelow," Needeya Islam suggests that Bigelow's films "acknowledge the seductive qualities of various popular genres, but question them internally" (96). Further, according to Islam, Bigelow's films "can be considered not so much genre films as films concerned with the way in which genres function" (121). The same can be said of McDougall's *Sugar & Spice*, which, from beginning to end, both makes reference to and asks questions of earlier male-directed and male-driven heist films. Further, in its positive representation of the friendship shared by girls on the A-squad, *Sugar & Spice* goes far toward recuperating a vision of possibilities of true understanding and care among women.[11]

In any case, Bigelow's film provides inspiration for McDougall's character Diane, who feels certain the squad can succeed in pulling off a heist of their own. Lucy responds by hypothesizing that Diane's pregnancy has affected her mind: "Oh my god, I've read about this. It's called pregnancy insanity." But Diane insists she's perfectly sane and proves as much by arguing that although school tells them to follow their dreams, school doesn't tell them how; they have to look to movies for a method: "Thanks to Keanu, I've figured it out. Money makes your dreams come true." Diane's newfound knowledge solidifies her motive. From this point on in the film, planning for the birth of Diane's baby and planning for the heist occur absolutely in tandem; the two activities parallel each other as the girls move from scenes in which they practice Lamaze to scenes in which they practice robbing the lunch lady.

Traditional male heist films generally employ opening shots to introduce gang members and offer some sense of each member's motivation for engaging in communal thievery.[12] *Sugar & Spice* acknowledges this convention, but simultaneously subverts it. Instead of representing each character's desire as an individual desire, *Sugar & Spice* privileges Diane's needs. Although Diane takes note of the ways each girl might spend her share of the loot (Kansas can appeal her mother's prison conviction; Lucy can afford to go to Harvard; Hannah can support a starving child advertised by Sally Struthers; and Cleo can furnish an apartment in leather to attract Conan O'Brian), these individual desires take a backseat to the girls' overarching desire to provide a future for Diane's growing family. As a matter of fact, as the squad considers whether to join Diane in her plan, they refer to themselves as a family. When Kansas declares that she is "in," she adds: "This is the closest thing to a goddamn family I've ever had. If one of us needs something, we all do." Cleo too elects to join: "We're like sisters. We're closer than sisters and you don't turn your back on your family." Although male gangs sometimes work on the idea of brotherhood (*Point Break* is a good example) or on father/son models (*The Score, Three Thousand Miles to Graceland*), it is a very rare male heist film in which the sustenance of family serves as a motive for crime.[13] Instead, male heist films repeatedly declare that families must give way in order for male teams to realize their larger monetary motives.[14] Families repeatedly cause problems in male heist films; they complicate and endanger all-male bonds. But, in *Sugar & Spice*, conservation of Diane's family motivates a crime, the execution of which, interestingly, makes these female criminals more aware of how much they value the familial ties they have established with one another.

It is not just the sororial squad ties the girls have established with one another: as they consider how they might rob the grocery-store branch bank, they also come to appreciate mother-daughter ties. Initially, the girls look to the movies for instructions on how to pull off this caper:

DIANE: People do it in the movies all the time.

LUCY: And they get caught.

DIANE: That's right. So all we have to do is watch a bunch of movies and learn from their mistakes.

Cleo watches *Reservoir Dogs* (1992); Kansas watches *Dog Day Afternoon* (1975); Luz reports on *Heat*; Hannah on *The Apple Dumpling Gang* (1975).

Kansas, dumbfounded that Hannah would have elected to watch Disney's *Apple Dumpling Gang*, berates her, but Hannah retorts that her parents let her watch only G-rated movies: "Those of us who have parents know they have rules because they care." The insult to Kansas provokes a hair-pulling fight in the waiting room of Diane's ob/gyn office as Kansas and Hannah go at it. Significant about this fight is: (1) it assumes that possession of parents (and a family) is a good thing; (2) it occurs in an ob/gyn waiting room where other clients are accompanied by husbands or male partners, but where Diane is surrounded by her surrogate, sororial family; (3) it threatens, but then strengthens, the familial bonds among the girls. Diane, in tears over "the fighting, the backstabbing, the open hostility," calls off the heist and declares "it was silly to think we could learn how to rob a bank from movies." Willing to abandon her plan, Diane follows a pattern Carol Gilligan sees frequently among girls, who value the maintenance of relationships over the continuation of a game or play.[15] But at the moment Diane expresses her willingness to throw in the towel, Cleo moves a sonogram over Diane's extended belly and the "movie screen" at Diane's side shows not one fetus but two. Armed with this new information, Kansas asserts: "OK: we ain't done with this. Those babies are going to have a good start in life. . . . We're going to learn how to rob a bank from people who really know how to do it: criminals. I'm going to visit my mom."

For the most part, this meeting between mother and daughter proceeds happily. Having expected rejection from the daughter she has not seen since birth, Kansas's mother is delighted when Kansas says she has come because she needs her mother's help. Kansas explains that she wants to get some money for a pregnant friend by robbing a bank:

MOTHER: Shitfire, Kansas. That's the sweetest thing I ever heard.

KANSAS: But we can't quite figure out, you know, how to do it.

MOTHER: So you need my help? Oh my god, this is like you asking me for help with your homework.

Kansas's request provides her mother with the role/position of mother. Like a good mother, this inmate readily acquiesces to her daughter's request, calling upon "Mink," along with other women in her ward, to answer her daughter's questions. As mentioned earlier, *Sugar & Spice* operates according to a principle of inclusion. The "taking in" of Kansas's criminal mother and her friends is the first prominent example of this principle. In a subsequent scene, all five cheerleaders meet with prison inmates, learning about the appropriate time for a heist and how to procure guns. While the film contrasts older female inmates dressed in workshirts and pants to fresh-faced teenage girls in their cheerleading outfits, it also brings these two groups of women together as they conspire on behalf of Diane.

Following the inmates' advice, the girls approach a local bug exterminator to request guns. Here too they are confronted with a question of inclusion/exclusion. The Terminator will provide them with rifles taken from South American rebels if they agree to make his daughter Fern a cheerleader: "I got a daughter. She's always dreamt of being a cheerleader. . . . If you put her on your squad—and I mean put her on the squad; don't make her haul around your pom-poms—you give her something to do, then I'll give you the guns." When Fern appears on screen, we see the challenge she poses to the squad; stoop-shouldered, greasy-haired, and smelling of cyanide, Fern is this film's nightmarish representation of white trash. Rather than embrace Fern, the squad stages a robbery of the lunch ladies at school, hoping thereby not only to "practice" heist techniques, but also to procure sufficient funds to pay for guns. The practice robbery proceeds in ballet-like fashion, with each girl performing her assigned role perfectly, but the squad nets only $200. They return to the Terminator, accepting both his guns and his daughter. Interestingly, when the squad opens the wooden box supposedly filled with rifles, they find bits and pieces, analogous to the "broken part" that is Fern. Squad members express dismay, but Diane turns the situation around: "Excuse me, do you guys know what I don't see here? I don't see a problem. I see a great big craft project sitting right in front of me." With glue, tape, and a nail file, the team puts together reasonable semblances of rifles; and with a few practice sessions, they turn Fern into an acceptable member of the squad.

Having rehearsed a robbery and practiced Lamaze, having watched heist films and fetal images, having consulted "experts" in banks and in babies, the girls are ready for the heist and the birth. Or almost ready. A Christmas present from Kansas's mother brings them Betty Doll masks but also leads to Lucy's confession that she has received a scholarship to Harvard and so is going to pull out of the heist. Her rejection of the team raises, once again, questions about families and allegiances. Diane protests that the team went "hands in" on this deal and that if Lucy pulls out, she breaks the National High School Cheerleaders' Association Pledge of Allegiance and Conformity. Lucy responds by saying she'll turn in her pom-poms after Christmas. Then, like Hannah, who earlier harassed Kansas by taunting her about her lack of family, Lucy insults Kansas's mother and fellow inmates: "You guys are insane if you don't think those criminals wouldn't gladly turn you in for a pack of Lucky's." Fiercely, loyally, Kansas insists that inmates don't rat on the children of other inmates: "You don't mess with another inmate and you don't mess with their kid." My point, again, is that in male heist films, characters fight over the division of the spoils or over whether and when to pull the next job; they do not fight over family allegiances.[16]

Lucy exits; Fern steps in as a substitute (becoming "white trash Betty") and the heist is on. Scenes devoted to the actual robbery pay parodic homage to numerous earlier heist films. From the getaway car (Fern's father's Terminator van, complete with enormous bug on the roof) that resembles an escape vehicle stolen by Kevin Costner in *Three Thousand Miles to Graceland*, to the pliable plastic masks that mimic masks in *Point Break*, the long white flower boxes for holding rifles that come from *Dog Day Afternoon*, and the western music and "the walk" from *The Wild Bunch* (1969), *Sugar & Spice* engages with past heist films in order to send them up, to challenge us to see them in a new way: through the lens of female perpetrators, and pregnant female perpetrators at that. When Diane, Kansas, Hannah, Cleo, and Fern step out of the Terminator van, they wear Betty Doll masks *and* the swollen bellies of pregnancy. Rather than expose Diane by allowing her to be the only pregnant perpetrator, all the girls appear to be pregnant. They also all wear red-white-and-blue tops over black slacks; just as their cheerleading uniforms emphasize similarity and unity, so too their American Dream bank-robbery outfits. After affirming their readiness ("We're ready, we're prepared, and this is going to be the best bank robbery ever"), the Bettys move toward the front entrance of the grocery store, but are interrupted by the arrival of Richard Nixon—or, rather, of Lucy in a Richard Nixon mask. This prodigal sister proclaims "I'm part of this squad," and, after a short lecture from Hannah about sisterhood, the freshly reinforced squad walks, in profile, across the screen toward the store's entrance. This walk appears in countless westerns and heist films, from the end of the original *Ocean's Eleven*, to the famous walk into M'pache's fort in *The Wild Bunch*, to the beginning of *Reservoir Dogs*. But no film that I know of has ever cast pregnant girls in "the walk."

Figure 4. Pregnant bandits perform "the walk" of heist films in *Sugar & Spice* (2001).

Once inside the store, the squad has to deal with a few unexpected problems, but, on the whole, the heist proceeds as planned. Unfortunately, leaving the store, Diane passes a display of fresh fish, the smell of which causes her to vomit into one of the money-filled grocery bags. Further, Lisa happens to be at the bank during the robbery; she notices the "illegal dismount" used by Diane and finds an A-squad pom-pom tie. Immediately after the robbery, however, all seems to have gone well. The girls gather in Kansas's grandparents' basement to celebrate and to "launder" the money in Diane's vomit bag. Instead of taking their stolen loot to a fence for laundering (which often poses a major challenge for male heist perpetrators[17]), Diane literally washes the bills and hangs them to dry. Kansas enters, announcing that she has incinerated their costumes and presents Diane with a double-wide cradle from her teammates. The team may be surrounded by bills, but the presence of the baby cradle ensures that they do not forget why they pulled this job. It also serves as a pledge of the girls' future support of their friend.

In conventional male heist movies, the moment of celebration following a successful heist all too often turns into a moment of competition. As teammates touch the dollars they have stolen, they get greedy. *The Killers* (1946), *Criss Cross*, *The Asphalt Jungle*, *Taking of Pelham One, Two, Three* (1974), *Blue Collar* (1978), *City of Industry* (1997), *The Underneath* (1998), *A Simple Plan* (1999), *Reindeer Games*, *Heist*, *The Score*, *Three Thousand Miles to Graceland*, and *The Ladykillers* all portray males selling out, shooting, or otherwise betraying a partner after the heist has been completed. *Sugar & Spice* gestures toward this plot component after police follow up on clues Lisa has given them; news reporters conjecture that the robbery was committed by five high school girls. Diane takes calls from Kansas, who believes Lucy has "ratted us out," and then from Lucy, who cannot understand why Kansas thinks she may have talked to the police. Allegiances among the team appear somewhat frayed, but they do not break. For that matter, we see how strongly the girls support each other as all six of them, in cheerleading uniforms, enter Lincoln High School. Once again, they engage in "the walk," facing front, never looking to the side or behind. Following the lead of their captain, the team enters the school cafeteria, and is confronted with accusations—first from Lisa, who has reported the team to the National High School Cheerleaders Association for using "cradle dismounts from double-based partner stunts that are over shoulder-stance level without using three catchers" and then by a swarm of armed police. The next scene locates all six members of the A-squad in a jail cell.

At this point, we return to the opening "lineup shot" of *Sugar & Spice*, reminding us that we have been watching Lisa's narrative of the heist. After seeing the lineup once more, we shift to Lisa with Detective Sibowitz. She notes: "Even the kids on the short list can see that all the evidence points to Diane and the A-squad." Sibowitz comments that Lisa's testimony will be invaluable in putting the squad behind bars. Lisa responds: "Unfortunately it wasn't them. They were all waiting in my Suburban that day when I ran into the supermarket for some cash. . . . We were on our way to practice." Diane, enacting a strategy that reflects the overall orientation of *Sugar & Spice*, has used her one phone call from jail not to contact Jack, but instead to invite Lisa onto the A-squad in exchange for an alibi. As she says to her team members: "A failure to plan is a plan for failure. We needed an alibi." So Lisa, portrayed throughout the film as arrogant, conceited, self-absorbed, and not particularly talented as a cheerleader, makes the team. As with Kansas's mother and Fern, the team shows itself willing to expand, to take in others instead of eliminating or excluding them. Granted, every inclusion works to the benefit of the team, and yet the team could have made other choices. They don't. They operate by adapting themselves to situations and taking in characters represented as "other."

As noted earlier, Lisa's opening dialogue with Lieutenant Sibowitz resembles that of Verbal Kindt and Inspector Kuhan in *The Usual Suspects*. Both Lisa and Verbal confront a police officer who elicits a story from them, a story about a heist. Both characters tell their stories and, in doing so, position themselves as outsiders who desperately want to change their classification; both desire membership in the "top squad," an embrace from a successful "family" (of cheerleaders, of thieves). At their conclusions, both *Sugar & Spice* and *The Usual Suspects* return to this scene of dialogue between the narrating character and a police investigator. Both films suggest that their narrators have realized their desire: Lisa drives off with members of the A-squad in her Suburban; Verbal's story shows us that the suspects have taken him in as one of their own. But at the end of the male heist, Verbal is the only suspect alive. He walks out of Kuhan's office alone, and, as he walks out, transforms himself into Keyser Soze, mastermind of a heist that has taken the lives of all of his partners and a man who, according to reputation, has killed his own family to establish his invulnerability. In other words, Verbal/Keyser Soze never forms ties of affiliation with the other suspects; he uses the suspects to further his own agenda and, when finished with them, throws them away. In contrast, at the end of the pregnant female heist depicted in *Sugar & Spice*, all team members are alive, well, and bouncing away from jail in Lisa's Suburban. The team has increased in size as it has embraced the twin fetuses in Diane's womb, Kansas's imprisoned mother, and new members Fern and Lisa. This female family successfully pulls off a heist and, instead of eliminating characters, adopts new members.

Well, Lisa was wrong about Bruce.

—*Sugar & Spice*

There's an epilogue to *Sugar & Spice* in which we, through intertitles and inset photographs, learn the fate of the film's major characters. None of their futures is particularly surprising, except that of Lisa. Her photo shows her in wedding gown, next to a character who looks vaguely familiar. The intertitle states: "Well, Lisa was wrong about Bruce." But who is Bruce? Addressed only once by name in the film, Bruce haunts the sidelines of *Sugar & Spice*. He appears momentarily at the A-squad cheerleading tryouts early in the film, dressed in a Tommy Hilfiger outfit and "hoping fourth year's the charm." Diane tells him he looks cute, but he is shouldered aside by Lisa: "Out of my way, fag." Having failed to make the squad, he takes on the role of Lincoln High mascot, most often seen parading around under a huge Lincoln head. He wears his mascot costume in a scene a few moments later, when Diane cartwheels into Jack, knocking the new quarterback unconscious. Bruce, apparently as attracted to Jack as Diane is, rushes to Jack's aid, throwing Jack over his shoulders and carrying him out of the gym. Finally, Bruce receives mention from Lisa as she accounts to Sibowitz for her poor skating performance during the Winter Sports Pep Rally: "I just want to say that normally I'm an excellent skater. Some jealous fag who will remain nameless obviously sabotaged my skates." Why does *Sugar & Spice* marry off Bruce, its most obvious gay character, to Lisa? Despite my claims about the ways this teen pregnancy/heist film operates to include "others" within the family unit developed by the team, it seems perplexed about how to respond to gay or lesbian characters as well as to characters of color. Every reference to homosexuality in *Sugar & Spice* is negative; further, the film engages in what we might call malign neglect of races and ethnicities outside the majority. With respect to homosexuality: when Kansas visits her mother for the first time in prison, her mother offers to introduce Kansas to Mink, "someone special." Kansas assumes that her mother and Mink are lovers: "Jesus Christ, mom. As if my life isn't a great big pile of shit 'cuz you're in here and now I have got to add p.s.: my mom's a dyke too." Kansas's mother tells her daughter to sit down and chill out: "Mink ain't my bitch, if that's what you think. She's a specialist . . . in banks." While Kansas talks to Mink and her mother, other members of the squad sit in a waiting room where a black female inmate mops the floor, gazing lewdly, lasciviously, at the girls' legs. Licking her lips, the inmate comments: "Them's some sweet skirts you got there." Cheerily, Diane replies: "Actually, they're uniforms. We're cheerleaders." We do not see this black inmate again, nor do we see anything beyond a glimpse of students of color at Lincoln High. We are introduced briefly to a Chinese character, "Dim Sum Charlie," when he becomes a suspect in the bank robbery because the grocery clerk feels sure that only Chinese acrobats could have jumped up so quickly to paint the security camera. While *Sugar & Spice* distinguishes itself from male heist films by its apparent willingness to open the heist team to new members, the movie is not open to all; when it comes to homosexual characters and characters of color, when it comes to the epilogue's representation of "happily-ever-after," *Sugar & Spice* declares its allegiance to the values of mainstream teen movies: white, middle-class, and decidedly heterosexual.

NOTES

This chapter appeared in the journal *Weber: The Contemporary West*, Vol. 24.2, Winter 2008. Reprinted with permission.

1. See John McCarty's *Hollywood Gangland: The Movies' Love Affair with the Mob* for a detailed history of changes in the Code during the early 1950s.

2. F. Gary Gray's 1996 *Set It Off* is the only other all-female heist film I have been able to locate. Gray's film sympathetically represents a group of black women who come together to rob a bank once other options have been denied them. It merits extensive analysis. Since this chapter was written, *Mad Money* (2008) has also been released.

3. In "Dis-embodying the Female Voice," Kaja Silverman notes that "the rule of [speech] synchronization is imposed much more strictly on the female than on the male voice within dominant cinema" (133). That is, female voices rarely are heard extradiegetically as voice-over narrators. Lisa breaks this convention; her voice-over aligns her with at least some of the qualities usually ascribed to male voice-over narrators: "transcendence, authoritative knowledge, potency and the law" (134).

4. We learn later that four of the five actually are manipulated onto the team by the fifth, a master-criminal, Keyser Soze.

5. See, for example, the work of Chodorow, Gilligan, and Tannen.

6. Luker continues: "Among well-to-do teens who get pregnant accidentally, about three-fourths seek an abortion; among poor teens, the proportion is less than one-half. Likewise, about 60 percent of white teens terminate their pregnancies, whereas the figure for blacks and Hispanics is about 50 percent" (154).

7. Luker sees contemporary discussions of teenage pregnancy as fraught with tension because teen pregnancy highlights "competing views of family and marketplace, of men and women, of rationality and morality, of rights and obligations. . . . Teenage mothers and their babies reflect and illuminate these cultural and social wars because they pose so pointedly the contradictions inherent in our ways of thinking about them" (11).

8. "Until the 1970s visibly pregnant married women, whether students or teachers, were formally banned from school grounds, lest their swelling bellies cross that invisible boundary separating the real world (where sex and pregnancy existed) from schools (where they did not). The idea that a pregnant unmarried woman would show herself not only in public but in school, where the minds of innocent children could be corrupted, was more unthinkable still" (Luker 2).

9. An important intertextual reference in *Sugar & Spice* is John Mellencamp's 1982 song, "Jack and Diane," about "Two American kids growin' up in the heartland." In Mellencamp's song, the two teens run off "behind a shady tree" and Jack asks that Diane let him do "what I please." By 2001, Francine McDougall was able to represent the sexual attraction between these teens as emanating from both of them.

10. Few adults appear in *Sugar & Spice*. The majority of those who do, how-ever, are fools or buffoons. Investigating officers appear incompetent; the principal of Lincoln High, delivering comments to students at the beginning of the year, is shadowed by the Lincoln mascot, who caricatures what the principal says; Diane's mother introduces herself to Jack's parents by calling attention to her double–D bra size; Fern's father, covered in grease and smelling of cyanide, threatens to kill the girls if they report him for selling guns; and Kansas's mother is in jail for murder. Among this limited adult cast, it is only Kansas's mother who has a major part, and she functions in at least two ways: first, she shows what might happen when female bodies move outside the boundaries of the law (they are incarcerated); and second, she represents a mother who hopes to connect with her daughter, to provide her daughter with something of use (even if that something is instructions for robbing a bank).

11. Contrast *Sugar & Spice*, for example, to films analyzed by Lucy Fischer in her chapter, "Girl Groups: Female Friendship," in *Shot/Countershot*.

12. *The Killing* might serve as an example. Kubrick's camera follows each member of the team to his home or place of work, showing us what each lacks and thereby what he hopes to achieve by joining with others in robbing the vault at a racetrack.

13. In *Dog Day Afternoon* (1975), director Sidney Lumet, working from an actual story, represents Dustin Hoffman robbing a bank for funds to provide his lover with a sex change operation. In Paul Schrader's 1978 *Blue Collar*, Harvey Keitel and Richard Pryor rob their union's safe in order to provide better lives for their wives and children (Keitel's daughter needs braces for her teeth; Pryor's family owes back taxes). And in Joel Coen's 2000 *O Brother, Where Art Thou?* (a fun variation on the heist formula), George Clooney convinces his prison buddies to accompany him on a treasure hunt, the real motive of which is to reunite him with his wife and family. But these truly are exceptions. Generally, male heist films represent the goal of the heist as simple acquisition of greater resources. The films rarely specify how these resources will be used; having them is what is important. See, for example, *The Asphalt Jungle*, *The Great St. Louis Bank Robbery* (1959), *Odds Against Tomorrow* (1959), *The Killers*, *The War Wagon* (1967), *The Good, the Bad, and the Ugly* (1968), *Kelly's Heroes* (1970), *The Taking of Pelham One, Two, Three*, *The Brink's Job* (1978), *Going in Style* (1979), *Crackers* (1983).

14. See *Heat*, for example, in which the leader of the heist team, played by Robert DeNiro, lives by the mantra, "Don't let yourself get attached to anything that you can't leave in thirty seconds flat" or *Thief* (1981), in which James Caan banishes his wife and child, blows up his house, and sets fire to cars on his used-car lot.

15. See Gilligan: "Rather than elaborating a system of rules for resolving disputes, girls subordinated the continuation of the game to the continuation of relationships" (10).

16. See, for example, *The Score*, in which Robert DeNiro and Ed Norton come to blows over who will keep a valuable scepter; or *Heist*, in which Gene Hackman and Danny DeVito battle over gold bars; or *Three Thousand Miles to Graceland*, in which Kevin Costner takes on Kurt Russell for the loot associated with a casino heist.

17. See, for example, *The Asphalt Jungle*, or, more recently, *Three Thousand Miles to Graceland*.

BIBLIOGRAPHY

The Apple Dumpling Gang. Dir. Norman Tokar. Disney, 1975.

Blue Collar. Dir. Paul Schrader. Universal, 1978.

Brodesser, Claude. "The Indies: Surviving Another Year, But Barely." *Variety* (12–18 January 2004): A6.

Chodorow, Nancy. *The Reproduction of Motherhood: Psychoanalysis and the Sociology of Gender.* Berkeley: University of California Press, 1999.

Dog Day Afternoon. Dir. Sidney Lumet. Warner Bros., 1975

Enos, Sandra. *Mothering from the Inside: Parenting in a Women's Prison.* Albany: SUNY Press, 2001.

Fischer, Lucy. *Shot/Countershot: Film Tradition and Women's Cinema.* Princeton: Princeton University Press, 1989.

Gilligan, Carol. *In a Different Voice: Psychological Theory and Women's Development.* Cambridge: Harvard University Press, 1982.

The Good, the Bad, and the Ugly. Dir. Sergio Leone. MGM, 1968.

Heat. Dir. Michael Mann. Warner Bros., 1995.

Heist. Dir. David Mamet. Warner Bros., 2001.

Islam, Needeya. " 'I Wanted to Shoot People': Genre, Gender and Action in the Films of Kathryn Bigelow." In *Kiss Me Deadly: Feminism & Cinema for the Moment.* Ed. Laleen Jayamanne. Sydney: Power Institute of Fine Arts, 1995.

The Killers. Dir. Robert Siodmak. Universal, 1946.

The Killing. Dir. Stanley Kubrick. MGM, 1956.

Luker, Kristin. *Dubious Conceptions: The Politics of Teenage Pregnancy.* Cambridge: Harvard University Press, 1996.

Madonna. "Papa Don't Preach," in *Immaculate Conception.* Warner Bros., 1990.

McCarty, John. *Hollywood Gangland: The Movies' Love Affair with the Mob.* New York: St. Martin's, 1993.

Mellencamp, John. "Jack and Diane," in *American Fool.* Riva Records, 1982.

O Brother, Where Are Thou? Dir. Joel Coen. Touchstone, 2000.

Point Break. Dir. Kathryn Bigelow. Twentieth Century Fox, 1991.

Rafter, Nicole. *Shots in the Mirror: Crime Films and Society.* Oxford: Oxford University Press, 2000.

Reservoir Dogs. Dir. Quentin Tarantino. Live Entertainment, 1992.

The Score. Dir. Frank Oz. Paramount, 2001.

Set It Off. Dir. F. Gary Gray. New Line, 1996.

Silverman, Kaja. "Dis-embodying the Female Voice." In *Re-Vision: Essays in Feminist Film Criticism.* Eds. Mary Ann Doane, Patricia Mellencamp, and Linda Williams. Los Angeles: American Film Institute, 1984.

Sugar & Spice. Dir. Francine McDougall. New Line, 2001.

Tannen, Deborah. *You Just Don't Understand: Women and Men in Conversation.* New York: HarperCollins, 2001.

Thief. Dir. Michael Mann. MGM, 1981.

Three Thousand Miles to Graceland. Dir. Demian Lichtenstein. Warner Bros., 2001.

The Usual Suspects. Dir. Bryan Singer. PolyGram, 1995.

Vognar, Chris. "Hooked on Heists." *Dallas Morning News* (13 July 2003): G1+.

The Wild Bunch. Dir. Sam Peckinpah. Warner Bros., 1969.

II

CONSTRUCTIONS OF MOTHERHOOD

―――――――――――――――――――――――

Mothers, Daughters, and Sex

FOUR

MODERNIZING MOTHER

The Maternal Figure in Early Hollywood

Heather Addison

In the 1910s and 1920s, Hollywood emerged as a dominant cultural institution that privileged consumerism, physical culture, and youth but maintained a paradoxical relationship with mothers and the practice of mothering. Early Hollywood discourse evinced a high regard for traditional Victorian motherhood and the values of sacrifice and undying maternal love, yet it also titillated audiences with versions of the "modern mother," a youthful, sexual being who loved her children while harboring needs and desires of her own.

MOTHERHOOD IN THE EARLY TWENTIETH CENTURY

Motherhood in the 1910s and 1920s was in a state of flux as the long-standing values of Victorian society were slowly supplanted by an industrial, consumer culture that emphasized youth, sexual display, and personal satisfaction. Women enjoyed greater freedom to make choices and enter public life: after a long struggle, they had won the vote in 1920, and they moved into the workforce in larger numbers. In the wake of World War I, Prohibition, and the popularization of the theories of Freud, manners and morals underwent something of a revolution as boys and girls enjoyed "petting parties" at the movies and in darkened automobiles; girls rolled their stockings, wore makeup, and sometimes competed in the newly established beauty contests; there was a general sense that modernity was preferable to anything old-fashioned. The flapper became the symbol of the youthful woman who was interested in romance and sexual pleasure, but not necessarily marriage and children. According to historian Frederick Lewis Allen:

> Modesty, reticence, and chivalry were going out of style; women no longer wanted to be "ladylike" or could appeal to their daughters to be "wholesome"; it was too widely suspected that the old-fashioned lady had been a sham and that the "wholesome" girl was merely inhibiting a nasty mind and would come to no good end. "Victorian" and "Puritan" were becoming terms of opprobrium: up-to-date people thought of Victorians as old ladies with bustles and inhibitions, and of Puritans as blue-nosed, ranting spoilsports. It was better to be modern—everybody wanted to be modern—and sophisticated, and smart, to smash the conventions and to be devastatingly frank. (112)

Social reformers of the period worked to enshrine motherhood and the home as the centerpieces of civilization. "The degradation of motherhood is the degradation of society," argued Dr. Elizabeth Sloan Chesser in 1913. "It is not by feminine invasion of every field of man's labour that emancipation will be won, but by elevating the work and the duties which have always belonged to women" (4, 250). Well-known reformer Ellen Key denounced the social thinking of suffragettes as "weak," instead praising the untiring women who worked for the "elevation of social morals":

> We find them active in movements for better care of the sick and prisoners, in combating alcohol and prostitution, in improving general conditions of labour, housing, and sanitation. They are working for the protection of motherhood and childhood, for the education and healthful recreation of the masses and of children. They share generously in the care of the poor and aged. . . . Social motherliness has made women's struggles for liberty the loveliest synthesis of egoism and altruism. (58–59)

The social component of motherhood was one reformers gave particular attention, perhaps because it could be used to give motherhood meaning and purpose beyond the raising of one's own children and thus convince women that they were making important public contributions.

A second, more pernicious consideration of these middle- and upper-class female reformers was so-called degenerate motherhood, a threat to the purity of maternity and humanity that was emerging primarily through the faults of the poor and working classes. Using the principles of eugenics, a popular doctrine of the period that held that the human race could be improved by selective breeding to eradicate less desirable traits, these women argued that the best way to elevate motherhood and improve society was to prevent inferior types from reproducing. Even Margaret Sanger, an ardent feminist of the era who has been credited with coining the term "birth control" and who wrote extensively on the subject of voluntary motherhood, accepted the eugenic argument:

> By all means there should be no children when either mother or father suffers from such diseases as tuberculosis, gonorrhea, syphilis, cancer, epilepsy, insanity, drunkenness and mental disorders. In the case of the mother, heart disease, kidney trouble and pelvic deformities are also a serious bar to childbearing. . . . the jails, hospitals for the insane, poorhouses and houses of prostitution are filled with the children born of such parents, while an astounding number of children are either stillborn or die in infancy. (chapter VII)

Degraded parenthood was not viewed specifically in racial terms (indeed, Sanger hoped that all of "racial culture" could be "fused into an amalgam of physical perfection"), but Chesser, Key, Sanger, and many other cultural authorities of their day were unapologetic elitists who considered the highest and best form of motherhood to be one in which educated, healthy, financially secure women (that is, women like themselves) reproduced. Though they did advocate some radical notions such as the greater availability and use of birth control, and the regular payment of wages to stay-at-home mothers, in general these women adopted a classist, reactionary stance toward the institution of motherhood, which they regarded as a de facto "perfect state" of humanity.

Male commentators focused more on what they perceived as women's new concern for their own needs and desires, a shift most clearly manifested in the slim, youthful figure of the flapper. Acerbic journalist H. L. Mencken, who has been called the Mark Twain of his time, noted that there was a significant subset of women who were opting for careers and casual sexual alliances rather than marriage and motherhood. "Women in general may still prefer marriage to work, but there is an increasing minority which begins to realize that work may offer the greater contentment, particularly if it be mellowed with a certain amount of philandering" (183), he quipped in a popular 1918 book. In his 1931 analysis of the 1920s, Frederick Lewis Allen concluded, "The quest for slenderness, the flattening of the breasts, the vogue of short skirts . . . the juvenile effect of the long waist—all were signs that, consciously or unconsciously, the women of this decade worshipped not merely youth, but unripened youth: they wanted to be—or thought men wanted them to be—men's casual and light-hearted companions; not broadhipped mothers of the race, but irresponsible playmates" (109).

FAN MAGAZINE DISCOURSE

The vacillation between notions of sacrifice versus attention to the self that percolated through public discussions of motherhood in the early twentieth century is present to no small degree in Hollywood discourse. Established in sunny California far from traditional eastern centers of civilization, dependent on an intangible visual product that highlighted personal appearance and brought the possibility of substantial largesse, Hollywood quickly began to favor and reinforce the values of consumerism: self-interest, sexual display, satisfaction gleaned through the purchase of appropriate products, and so on. Motion picture stars conspicuously consumed their wealth; exhibited their bodies at swimming pools and beaches; and worked to keep themselves slim, young, attractive, and vigorous so that the "cruel eye" of the camera would not reveal wrinkles or adipose tissue (see Addison, *The Rise of Physical Culture*). Nevertheless, Hollywood's wholehearted embrace of modernity seemed to engender a nostalgia for the symbolic loss it implied—for the perceived halcyon period when self-sacrifice, modesty, decorum, and thrift were the order of the day in many areas of life, including the practice of motherhood.

The total number of silent films that address the subject of motherhood is difficult to ascertain, though the American Film Institute Silent Film Catalog identifies 177 silent, feature-length films that have a substantive focus on "motherhood." Unfortunately, only a small percentage of these are available for screening in archives or on video. The most complete picture of early Hollywood's relationship with the institution of motherhood can be found not in the films it produced but in the fan magazine articles and advertisements that were published during this period. As this discourse demonstrates, Hollywood, in its constant quest to distill and magnify the drama of life, prided itself on its modernity yet also found the practice of looking backward irresistible.

ARTICLES

Hollywood's articulation of Victorian motherhood, though reverent, was closely associated with advanced age and old-fashioned notions. Actresses who frequently played mothers on-screen were like pressed rose leaves: closely admired, but fragile and subject to disintegration. In a 1915 fan magazine article, actress Mary Maurice is hailed as "The Sweet Mother of the Movies." Her successes are duly listed, and the article concludes, "Thousands upon thousands of picture admirers are familiar with the sweet and motherly face of Mary Maurice. It is like a summer day with a clear sky overhead. It beams forth a love and sympathy that hold our closest attention and interest. She is undoubtedly the sweetest old lady who has ever graced the screen" (Brody 42). Ideal mothers, suggests the article, are selfless, kind, accommodating—and elderly.

A 1921 piece on screen mother Mary Carr compliments her for the homely pathos of the aged, suffering mother she portrays in the popular film *Over the Hill to the Poorhouse* (1920). "Mary Carr is beautiful, too, with a beauty that age cannot wither nor time destroy . . . and she has the charity and understanding of all the mothers of the world" (Montanye 38). The impermanence of this maternal veneration became apparent when, ten years later, a *Motion Picture Classic* article considered the difficulties of screen mothers:

Modes and manners change, fashions in clothes and morals alter radically from year to year—but Motherhood, one would think, is

Figure 5. In 1915, actress Mary Maurice appeared as a "little, gray, withered-rose-leaf Mother" in *Mother's Roses*.

one thing that cannot go out of style. . . . Maternity in the movies has flourished like the green bay tree, and the sight of a snowy-haired old lady, languishing over her children, has never failed to reduce an audience to sobs. At least, that has been the accepted creed in Hollywood for many a year. Yet at this very moment four of the most famous mothers in Hollywood [Mary Carr, Mary Alden, Margaret Mann, and Belle Bennett] are jobless; and two of the four are in serious financial straits. (Parsons 32)

Amid a new call for youth, aging mothers were in less demand in Holly-wood, and appearing in a "mother" role could limit one's options for future employment on the screen. "Mary Alden's tremendous success as the mother in 'The Old Nest' was probably the most unfortunate thing that ever hap-pened to her," opines Harriet Parsons. "Casting directors forgot that she was a comparatively young woman and that she had given brilliant performances in scores of widely different roles. Not yet forty, she found herself pigeonholed as an old-fashioned mother type" (32).

Mature mothers did not fade from view in fan magazines, however. Articles on the childhoods of motion picture stars became staple fare, and mothers of stars had valuable insights to share. A typical piece is "The Boyhood of Harold Lloyd," as told to Phyllis Perlman by Harold Lloyd's mother. Mrs. Lloyd reminisces about the "magnetism" Harold demonstrated even as a young child and is pictured embracing her adult son. "It looks as though Mrs. Lloyd is still vitally necessary to her celebrated son's happiness," reads the caption (39). Yet the middle-aged Mrs. Lloyd exists merely as an appendage of her son—a vital influence, but nonetheless simply a part of the support system that allows him to impress the world with his youthful vigor. Indeed, his mother claims that his youthfulness is the cornerstone of his fame: "Harold's pictures are the gay songs of youth immortalized on the motion picture screen. . . . He has hurdled his way to success and into a niche in the heart of all those people who like to feel youth surging in their blood" (40, 89). In a similar article, "A Daughter in the Movies: Sadye Miller Tells What She Did About It," the mother of screen star Patsy Miller somewhat abashedly admits that she still has "old-fashioned" concerns about her daughter's well-being:

I realize that things are changing, that we are constantly going ahead, in ideas and achievement, and that girls today know so much more about the world, and life, than they did when I was twenty. And so they *should* . . . because they are thrown more in contact with it.

But it's like a dash of cold water at first, getting used to the things they know and openly discuss. *Then* it's all right.

Pat says I am not *quite* so bad as I was . . . not *quite* so mid-Victorian.

But I still worry about her. A mother just cant [sic] help it. (103)

For Hollywood, motherhood was an honorable but antiquated institution. Those who practiced it were mature, older women whose appearance tended toward the matronly. "Madge's Mother's Menu," a short article that describes the rich eating style of the mother of screen star Madge Bellamy, notes, "It Tickles the Palate but the Scales Will Give You A-Weigh." Madge herself must eat sparingly, and can rarely permit herself to indulge in food prepared from her mother's recipes: "This young, high-spirited girl must watch her diet or she will soon lose that slim, lithe body of hers" (66). The article implies, however, that her mother need have no such concerns; she can eat generously and find satisfaction in feeding others. Sylvia Ashton, who was dubbed the "Mother of Hollywood" because of her screen roles and her emotional support of many young stars, is described as "tremendously fat—almost incredibly so. . . . And she can cook. Oh, how she can cook!! It's no wonder that Hollywood has adopted Sylvia Ashton as its unofficial mother. She has every one of those God-given propensities that mothers have. And in her heart is the love that passeth all understanding" (Handy 28). Two years later, in 1924, fan magazine writer Gladys Hall reported Mother Ashton's decision to give up acting and open a tearoom in New York City so that she could fulfill her maternal urge to feed the world (46). (Ashton returned to the screen within two years, however.)

Laudable yet removed from the stream of modern life because of their age, their matronly, fleshy figures, and their devotion to old-fashioned morality, mature mothers were left with one key function: providing a convenient route for stars to prove their own virtue. In "So Good to Their Mothers" Gladys Hall declares:

In many a piece of fact and fiction you have heard of the base ingratitude of daughters, sharper than a serpent's tooth. You have heard of profligate sons who have let Mother go over the hill to the poorhouse. But you have never heard of such a happenstance among the movie stars.

It is true that the aforementioned horrors are more or less infrequent. Most children are more or less decent to their progenitors. But the movie stars exceed the bounds of expected decency. They are fanatic. . . . Mother comes first to the movie stars—and let no man or woman think otherwise. (35)

Stars may have been youthful incarnations of modernity, but their morality could not be impugned if they remained close caretakers of the Victorian values of their parents. "So Good to Their Mothers" concludes, "Free of hand and heart [stars] may be, prodigal of life and living, frequently and sometimes rightly subject to criticism. But through their lives runs the silver cord of gratitude and filial love, and surely this argues that the core is sweet and sound" (91). Thus, stars could continue to embrace the values of Victorianism through their relationships with their mothers, even as their screen careers and off-screen exploits often paid tribute to the age of flappers, speakeasies, and conspicuous consumption.

Of course, screen stars were often mothers themselves, and fan magazines did not hide this fact. Articles featuring female stars with their children were as popular as articles in which mothers of stars made revelations about their famous offspring. Because female stars were youthful, sometimes beginning their careers at age eighteen or younger and concluding them after an average of five to seven successful years, articles about stars' maternal activities not surprisingly had as their subjects young mothers of young children. References to matronliness or advancing age were avoided. Such articles also romanticized Hollywood motherhood, suggesting that busy, career-minded female stars were still icons of domesticity and femininity. For example, "With Kings" is a 1921 article that briefly describes screen star Mollie King's life after the birth of Kenneth Alexander Jr., her baby. It features a large photo of King embracing her son; the caption comments, "Mollie King wishes to keep on with her stage and screen work, but her husband would like her to give it up and 'sit on a cushion and sew a fine seam' . . . which Mrs. Alexander will do, it is hard to say" (72). The author, Lillian May, presents King as little more than a girl herself, her youth and slenderness apparently unaffected by her maternity: "Down the corridor a tiny little girl figure waved a welcoming hand. She wore a brown charmeuse frock, very smart and very short" (72).

Older children were less frequently featured in such motherhood articles. The greatest love of screen star Dorothy Phillips, explains a 1924 piece in *Motion Picture Classic*, is her home and baby (Lipman 40). Surprisingly, as one reads the article one learns that the "baby" is eight years old, but, unlike the articles on children under the age of one who are featured in photographs with their mothers, "The Girl Who Is California" has no image of Dorothy Phillips's eight-year-old daughter. "Gloria Swanson, America's Own Marquise" also pays lip service to Swanson's intense maternal feelings: "She was born a mother. The maternal instinct is ninety per cent of her make-up" (Douglas 52). Swanson's two children, ages five and three, are mentioned but not visually represented, though the article assures us that "the best moments the devoted young mother [can] snatch from her work [are] spent in the company of the little ones" (82). "Madonnas of the Movies," a collection of snapshots of Hollywood mothers and children of various ages in loving poses, concludes: "These pictures suggest that motherhood and careers are compatible . . . and that it is not at all necessary to sacrifice one to the other" (24).

In motherhood, as in so many arenas of human experience, Hollywood performed a delicate balancing act of looking backward to move forward. Fan magazines reassured readers that Victorian values were alive and well in the homes of Hollywood stars, who were really charming and domestic despite their public success. Such stars were commended for their accomplishments in motherhood *and* their careers, although praise was reserved chiefly for young mothers: the fact that most popular screen players were youthful meant that most Hollywood mothers were also young and in the early stages of their motherhood. Most commonly, motherhood articles featured mothers and their new babies. Although older children did receive mention, it was less frequent, especially in terms of being photographed with their famous mothers. This may have been because most screen stars faded from public view before their children had advanced beyond their tenderest years; because stars became more protective of their children's privacy as they moved out of toddlerhood; or because having older children dated stars and made it more difficult for them to retain the sheen of youth in the eyes of the public.

Indeed, Hollywood's demand for youthfulness made motherhood itself a kind of calculated risk; being a mother, especially in the long term, was not compatible with Hollywood's idea of youth. As Hall asserts:

> There are Seven Deadly Sins in Hollywood, and the greatest of these is—*children*. They are the bars sinister on the escutcheon of perpetual Youth. They are dead give-aways. They are anathema to Romance. One cannot continue indefinitely to be a sexy maiden of eighteen, if one must admit to the parenthood of a gangling youth or lass. . . .
>
> The studios know this. Some of the best contracts contain "no children" clauses. The hand that rocks the cradle will never rule the Kleigs [studio lights], say they. (28)

Yet many stars took the motherhood plunge, despite the dangers to their careers. Instead of avoiding motherhood, they depended on "modern motherhood" to keep their youth, which could be maintained or recuperated in a number of ways. Clothes, hair, and body shape were monitored or modified, as necessary. "The Return to Youth" documents the odyssey of Mabel Forrest, a youthful star who retired from her career as an extra when she married Bryant Washburn and had children. In 1923, eight years later, she planned to return to the screen:

When Mabel married Bryant, she looked so young the people teased her. So she began to wear matronly clothes and do her hair so that it would give her the effect of added years. But now everything has changed. The two Washburn children have grown up and Mabel—her burnished copper hair bobbed and her form slenderized—has come back to the screen to share honors with Bryant. (Le Berthon 25)

No pictures of Forrest's two "grown up" children (both of whom were less than eight years old) appear in the article about her attempted comeback as a flapper. Interestingly, the article implies that she is only twenty-four years old, but she was actually born in 1894, making her twenty-nine at the time the article was published—an age apparently so advanced for Hollywood that she could not admit she had reached it.

So-called modern mothers were arguably as youthful and fashionable as their daughters, eliminating any distance between them. In 1924, screen star Doris Kenyon argued,

There *are* no mothers any more. That is . . . no mothers of the kind there used to be. Dear souls, with knitting-needles, scarfs about their shoulders and delicate inhibitions.

There are certainly no more grandmothers. No "elders" as you call them.

You cant [sic] expect the sensible modern girl to bend obeisant knee, rise from her chair and otherwise genuflect every time the modern mother enters the room. For that same mother looks as young as her daughter, frequently acts younger and spends most of her time having as good a time as she can manage to achieve. . . .

I believe that a very fine comradeship between the generations, chiefly between mothers and daughters, is going to result from the attitude of this particular generation. Youth will meet youth. (qtd. in Service 25, 86)

Victorian motherhood was old and matronly; Hollywood motherhood embraced the youthfulness of the consumer age. To remain youthful was vital for screen stars, who marginalized their status as mothers in order to prolong their status as flappers. Youthfulness was also recommended for fans; advertisements suggested that lasting youth was no less than the best gift one could give oneself and one's children. The values of love and sacrifice were still enshrined as ideals of motherhood, but they had been superseded by another maxim: youth, always youth. This new maternal imperative was repeatedly articulated in fan magazine advertisements.

ADVERTISEMENTS

"What a tragedy to look old and feel young!" cries a 1927 ad for Helena Rubenstein cosmetics. "So long as you feel young at heart, don't for a single moment permit your face to grow old. The world is ever quick to consign to the background those who cease to look youthful." The call for youth in fan magazine advertising embraced not just mothers, but all readers. Creams, powders, hair dyes, soaps, makeup, pills, exercise and diet plans, and electric tools promised to eliminate wrinkles, renew skin, slenderize bodies, and preserve youth indefinitely, offering protection from the obsolescence of old age. The consumer age demanded youth, both from workers, who were not uncommonly turned out past the age of forty, and from consumers, who were urged to absorb the excess of products factories were able to create. Youthful adults whose buying habits were not yet established were seen as an advantageous audience for advertisements; in addition, youthfulness itself was an ideal bulwark of consumer culture since it was always slipping away and could therefore be pursued on a nearly perpetual basis. Factors particular to Hollywood also predisposed it to favor youthfulness: a location in southern California; dependence on a commercial visual medium that called attention to the body; and concern about the camera's ability to magnify wrinkles or add weight to the body. The word "Hollywood" became nearly synonymous with "youth and beauty" and fan magazine advertising followed suit.

In general, youth ads that targeted mothers argued that remaining fresh and young could ensure the continued love and support of one's husband and children. It was also an important way that mothers could be role models for their daughters. "Which Is the Mother?" asks a 1921 ad for Nature's Remedy Vegetable Tablets that features a small photo of two youthful women. "It is good health which keeps womanly beauty fresh. Cosmetics can only hide the traces of the years in a once pretty face. Mothers who are still young at the age of forty can teach their daughters the value of a good aperient in keeping the blush of youth in their cheeks." Hair dyes were—and are—a common method of hiding one's age, and an ad for Brownatone Hair Dye warned, "Motherhood brings gray hair. . . . Children, as well as many elders, do not discriminate. To them gray hair means age. The devoted mother who would stay young with her children, or any mother who takes pride in her personal appearance, should make her toilette a matter of concern. At the first sign of gray she should call to her aid that magic of modern days—Brownatone."

Body soaps were often promoted on the basis of their youth-enhancing properties, and during the 1920s Palmolive ads idealized youthful motherhood. "Not a Day Older!" trumpets a 1923 example. "Fortunate is the wife and mother whose youthful appearance evokes this compliment on the day of her china wedding [twentieth anniversary]." The ad features a youthful mother surrounded by her adoring family, a husband and two adolescent children. "Stay Young with Your Daughter!" urged Palmolive in 1927. "The present generation recognizes charm only in Youth; with every daughter wishing, in her heart, for *her* mother to retain, above all things, her youthful allure." In 1928, Palmolive addressed the issue of mothers' relationships with their sons: "His first love. . . . What mother's heart but quickens at her small son's adoration? . . . Keep that devotion, mother! Hold that love. Always be, to him, the beautiful princess of fairy book delight. And above all else, keep youth, keep beauty as your most priceless asset[s]." Mothers who remained young were pictured enjoying the embraces of their families, but those same family members, the ads insinuated, could just as easily turn away if Mother showed signs of advancing age.

Figure 6. Advertising implied that women who remained young would receive the praise and affection of their families (*Motion Picture Magazine*, 1923).

Such ads attempted to collapse the distance between generations. As the comments of screen star Doris Kenyon suggested in the previous section, respect for the wisdom of one's elders was on the decline. If everyone was youthful, then no one was in a position to offer advice based on long experience. Indeed, advertisers, eager to develop the brand loyalty of youthful adults, suggested that mothers who wished to be modern would do well to follow the purchasing advice of their modern daughters. Modess, a producer of sanitary napkins, mounted a "Modernizing Mother" campaign in the late 1920s that urged women to discard antiquated notions of female lifestyles. The first of these urges, "Mother . . . Don't Be Quaint—Millions of daughters are teasing mothers back to youth—slamming doors on the quaint ways of the nineties. One by one the foolish old drudgeries and discomforts pass. Living becomes easier, more pleasant—*sensibly modern*." A later ad pictures two women, one presumably a mother and one a daughter, on a roller coaster. " 'Don't You Love It, Mother?' In her play as in everything else she does, the irresistible modern girl demands freedom." A third example features a photograph of two women in a speedboat. " 'Don't Fuss, Mother, This Isn't So Fast'—Speed! Life is all atingle at twenty. This girl of today travels without an anchor. There's too much fun ahead for thought of fear—too many prizes to be won to be satisfied with common things. Do older people really object—are they not just as eager in spirit to escape drabness and drudgery and feel again the thrill of being young?" Middle-aged women, these ads suggested, should feel ridiculous and repressive if they wished to stem the tide of modernity and youthfulness that was flooding American culture.

In addition to cautioning mothers about the importance of maintaining their youth and beauty, fan magazine advertisements also had ample advice about the care of young children. Indeed, advertisers worked to wrest maternal authority and confidence away from individual mothers and convince them that it resided in modern, corporate America, where science trumped the outmoded techniques of old-fashioned motherhood. "A Fly in the Milk May Mean a Baby in the Grave," warned an ad for the Thermos Bottle Company in 1912. "Flies are the most dangerous insects known. They are both in filth, live on filth, and carry filth. . . . Flies are attracted by milk. . . . Thermos keeps infant's milk cold, clean, germ and fly proof." Although a 1914 ad for Nestle's Food does admit that "mother's milk is best" it also exults, "Mothers of the Nation, Be Glad!; fewer babies are dying now that Nestle's is available. [It is] purified milk of healthy cows from our own guarded dairies, scientifically modified, with baby's need of wheat and sugar added." In 1923, Colgate's Dental Cream promised to "Protect Young Teeth From Grit" through the advancements of science: "Modern Dental science has shown that proper care of children's teeth builds eager active minds and sturdy bodies." Science and industry worked in concert to provide a sound foundation for modern motherhood; well-meaning advertisers then made mothers aware of the wondrous new array of products at their disposal. To achieve success as mothers, women had only to follow the wise advice of advertisers, as *Motion Picture Classic* announced in 1927:

> Enter: the baby!
>
> ACCOMPANIED by his faithful stork, the Bitner baby arrived this morning. There was a great deal of rushing around, but things have quieted down now, and advice is pouring in! . . .
>
> ADVERTISING will tell Mrs. Bitner not only which talcum, which blankets, which carriages are best, but it will also give her many helpful hints on keeping her baby happy and healthy. It will suggest toys for his busy hands, shoes for his scampering feet, clothes and foods for his sturdy body, as well as books to set his eager mind to work. And, as the years go by, Mrs. Bitner will keep young, and look young too. . . .
>
> *Read the advertisements. They carry a wealth of sound advice to people who are creating homes.*

Advertising is thus mother's salvation: she no longer has to think or make decisions. She need only read the latest advertisements to execute the duties of her maternal office. While her Victorian predecessors may have struggled to create their homes, modern mothers, gloated the ads, could enjoy a life of relative ease and freedom supported by the products of the consumer age: vacuums, refrigerators, sanitary napkins, infant formula, and so on.

Advertisements for mothers of adolescent children were less common than ads explaining how babies should be fed or toddlers' hair should be cleaned. Most readers of fan magazines were young women, a fact that probably accounts for the predominance of ads for mothers of infants and toddlers. Yet ads for parents of older children did appear, and they constitute a fascinating jumble of modernity (even radical modernity) and mid-Victorianism, suggesting that appropriate methods to parent adolescents were not entirely clear. While Modess dismissed mothers as in need of modernizing via their energetic daughters, Lysol Disinfectant ads praised mothers for passing down the secrets of proper female cleanliness. " 'Mother, what is *feminine hygiene?*' " asks a young woman of her middle-aged mother. The ad notes that Lysol has been a female antiseptic for over forty years and that "the weight of medical opinion is that nothing has been found to take [its] place." Zonite, another antiseptic, also turned to mothers to promote the efficaciousness of its product, offering a free pamphlet: "What is more difficult for a mother than the instruction of her daughter in the facts about feminine hygiene? No matter how scientific and up-to-date her own information may be, it is hard to know just where to begin, and *how*. This little book solves the problem for mother, daughter or wife." Women, this ad suggests, are still important advisers in their daughter's lives, but their duties will be executed much more effectively with the aid of Zonite Products Company. Mothers were presented as a significant but secondary influence; they were the messengers who could make their daughters aware of the repository of hygiene advice and assistance available in modern products and advertisements.

Other ads urged mothers to protect their adolescent daughters through a selection of proper reading, again constructing them as adjuncts to their daughters' education who could serve their children best not by giving them personal advice, but by facilitating their acquisition of appropriate reading materials. One 1911 ad recommended "sanitized" literature that avoided the evil influences of "the society novel and the problem novel" ("Every Girl's Library"), while more progressive ads that appeared in the 1920s made the case that knowledge was less dangerous than ignorance. "Don't 'Talk' To Your Daughter: It's More Convincing to Give Her This Book to Read!" argues an ad for *Never Told Tales*. "The stories grip as only the truth can and carry their message with force and conviction. Never before has such a book been published. The many INTIMATE problems that are constantly confronting men and women are discussed with COMPLETE FRANKNESS." Also frank (or as frank as the 1873 Obscenity Law would allow) was Margaret Sanger's radical volume on voluntary motherhood through birth control, *Woman and the New Race*, which was advertised in *Motion Picture Classic* in 1921. "The Pity of Unwanted Children: This is a delicate subject to put frankly before the public. . . . No woman can afford to be without this knowledge. It is vital to her happiness and to the future of herself, her husband, her children, and all the children that are to be." The best mothering advice for one's self and one's daughters, these ads suggested, could be found not by looking within, but by turning to the products and literature of the modern age.

CONCLUSIONS

In the 1910s and 1920s, the institution of motherhood evolved to accommodate the consumer culture that was flowering as industrial efficiency allowed productive capacity to reach new heights. Victorian notions of domesticity, sacrifice, and thrift were displaced by an exaltation of self-satisfaction consonant with the requirements of continual consumption of new products. Nevertheless, motherhood was not simply ripped from its foundations and cast anew. Much remained of the idealization of mothers as selfless beings devoted to their homes and children. Social reformers who endorsed radical notions such as "free" motherhood through birth control or government wages for mothers stalwartly supported mothers' role as the center of the home and caretaker of society's underprivileged. As Hollywood emerged as an entity distant and distinct from the established values of the East where American filmmaking was born, it gradually eschewed the dictates of

Victorian motherhood for a modern, consumerist, self-centered model. Yet it never completely rejected the ideals of Victorianism, always nostalgically returning to visions of the reverent, altruistic love that mothers should bear their children. Hollywood assured its audiences that the old could coexist with the new; for example, female stars could be screen sirens *and* delicate domestic goddesses.

In terms of motherhood, the most significant social shift of the period was the increasing glorification of youth. Both consumer culture and Hollywood demanded youth, whether it was needed to labor in factories, buy the latest products, display one's body in a swimsuit, or avoid the wrinkles that the motion picture camera was believed to highlight. The values of Victorian motherhood were still embraced, but only on a superficial basis, as they could no longer be practiced by those who were *old* or *old-fashioned*. Mothers were still to be devoted to their children, but they needed to pay close attention to personal hygiene as they did so. It was their maternal duty to remain young and modern so as not to embarrass their children or saddle them with outmoded habits. Maternal authority and experience, argued advertisements, resided not with mothers, but with companies that could offer scientifically proven products and advice. By the late 1920s, Hollywood and America's icon of motherhood was no longer a middle-aged, self-sacrificing woman in a rocking chair but a fashionably dressed modern woman whose devotion to movies and advertising allowed her to raise happy, healthy children while remaining perpetually slender and youthful.

BIBLIOGRAPHY

Addison, Heather. *The Rise of Physical Culture.* New York: Routledge, 2003.

Allen, Frederick Lewis. *Only Yesterday: An Informal History of the Nineteen-Twenties.* New York and London: Harper & Brothers, 1931.

Brody, Allan Douglas Brodie. "Mrs. Mary Maurice, 'The Sweet Mother of the Movies.'" *Motion Picture Classic* (October 1915): 41+.

Chesser, Elizabeth Sloan, M.D. *Woman, Marriage and Motherhood.* London and New York: Funk & Wagnalls, 1913.

Donnell, Dorothy. "Mother's Roses." *Motion Picture Magazine* (March 1915): 58–67.

Douglas, Clement. "Gloria Swanson, America's Own Marquise." *Motion Picture Classic* (May 1925): 51+.

Hall, Gladys. "Man—Woman—Marriage." *Motion Picture Magazine* (April 1921): 49+.

———. "The Mother Complex." *Motion Picture Magazine* (February 1924): 46+.

———. "The Seven Deadly Sins of Hollywood: The Sin of Having Children." *Motion Picture Magazine* (September 1930): 28.

———. "So Good to Their Mothers." *Motion Picture Magazine* (October 1928): 34+.

Handy, Truman. "Mother O'Hollywood." *Motion Picture Magazine* (August 1922): 28+.

Key, Ellen. *The Renaissance of Motherhood.* Trans. Anna E. B. Fries. New York: G. P. Putnam's, 1914.

Le Berthon, Ted. "The Return to Youth." *Motion Picture Magazine* (December 1923): 25+.

Lipman, Jane H. "The Girl Who Is California." *Motion Picture Classic* (January 1924): 40+.

"Madonnas of the Movies." *Motion Picture Magazine* (July 1924): 24–25.

May, Lillian. "With Kings." *Motion Picture Magazine* (March 1921): 72+.

Mencken, H. L. *In Defense of Women.* 1918. New York: Knopf, 1928.

Montanye, Lillian. "Just Folks." *Motion Picture Magazine* (March 1921): 38+.

Palmberg, Rilla Page. "Madge's Mother's Menu." *Motion Picture Magazine* (April 1928): 66+.

Parsons, Harriet. "Are Movie Mothers Starving?" *Motion Picture Classic* (July 1931): 32–33.

Perlman, Phyllis. "The Boyhood of Harold Lloyd." *Motion Picture Magazine* (July 1923): 38+.

Phillips, Henry Albert. "A Spartan Mother." *Motion Picture Magazine* (March 1912): 81–89.

Sanger, Margaret. *Woman and the New Race.* New York: Truth Publishing Company, 1920. Accessed at http://www.interlife.org/woman.html

Service, Faith. "There Are No Mothers Any More." *Motion Picture Classic* (March 1924): 25+.

ADVERTISEMENTS

Brentano's Publishing Company. *Women and the New Race.* "The Pity of Unwanted Children." *Motion Picture Classic* (March 1921): 88.

Brownatone Hair Dye. "Motherhood Brings Gray Hair." *Motion Picture Magazine* (December 1921): 111.

"Enter: the Baby!" *Motion Picture Classic* (June 1927): 7.

Happiness Press. *Never Told Tales.* "Don't 'Talk' to Your Daughter." *Motion Picture Magazine* (April 1928): 114.

Helena Rubenstein Cosmetics. "What a Tragedy." *Motion Picture Magazine* (April 1927): 113.

Lysol Disinfectant. " 'Mother, What Is *Feminine Hygiene?*' " *Motion Picture Magazine* (March 1930): 99.

Modess Napkins. "Mother . . . Don't Be Quaint." *Motion Picture Magazine* (February 1929): 75.

Modess Napkins. " 'Don't You Love It, Mother?' " *Motion Picture Magazine* (August 1929): 95.

Modess Napkins. " 'Don't Fuss, Mother, This Isn't So Fast.' " *Motion Picture Magazine* (September 1929): 97.

Nature's Way Vegetable Tablets. "Which Is the Mother?" *Motion Picture Magazine* (May 1921): 96.

Nestle's Food. "Mothers of the Nation, Be Glad!" *Motion Picture Magazine* (February 1914): 149.

Palmolive Soap. "Not a Day Older." *Motion Picture Magazine* (March 1923): inside cover.

Palmolive Soap. "Stay Young with Your Daughter." *Motion Picture Magazine* (September 1927): inside cover.

Palmolive Soap. "His First Love." *Motion Picture Classic* (September 1928): back cover.

Pearson Publishing Company. *Every Girl's Library.* "Protect Your Daughter." *Motion Picture Magazine* (July 1911): 157.

Thermos Bottle Company. "A Fly in the Milk." *Motion Picture Magazine* (August 1912): 153.

Zonite Products Company. "A Frankly Written Book." *Motion Picture Magazine* (July 1925): 101.

FIVE

"WHOSE BABY ARE YOU?"

Mother/Daughter Discourse in the Star Images of
Mary Pickford and Joan Crawford

Gaylyn Studlar

No girl . . . should leave home to go into the picture business unless her
mother is with her or unless she is well chaperoned.

—Mary Pickford, 1921

I brought myself up.

—Joan Crawford, 1928

Stars have long posed a special challenge to Hollywood's construction—on-
screen and off—of a culturally normative mode of female sexuality. I will
argue that the mother-daughter relationship occupied an important role
in Hollywood's discursive negotiation of female stardom and star sexuality
within the broader social construction of feminine sexuality from the early
1910s, throughout the 1920s, and into the 1930s. While all stars have the
potential to be powerful role models, the influence of female stars whose
roles and star personas resonated with young people was particularly feared
by social reformers throughout the 1920s and into the early 1930s. By the

late 1910s, American society was in the midst of a public debate about the role of women—especially young women—in disturbing the traditional order of gender relations. Females identified with The "New Woman" and the flapper were accused of shattering norms in the sexual sphere. As Paula Fass has noted, "Gazing at the young women of the period, the traditionalist saw the end of American civilization as he had known it."[1]

This cultural debate about the proper boundaries for female sexual behavior was especially important because in the early 1920s Hollywood was also in a crisis around the question of star behavior in general. In September 1921, Roscoe ("Fatty") Arbuckle was accused of committing a rape that led to the death of actress Virginia Rappe during a wild party in a San Francisco hotel room. In an attempt to stave off criticism of Hollywood as a hotbed of debauchery and the censorship of its products, the Motion Picture Producers and Distributors Association of America was established with former postmaster general Will Hays appointed as its head in 1922. He promised both morally upright films and film players. James Quirk, editor of the influential fan magazine *Photoplay*, wrote an open letter to Hays that urged, among other things, the adoption of a morality clause in Hollywood contracts that would allow "the immediate discharge of any actor whose private life reflects discredit on the company."[2] Such a contract clause soon became standard industry practice.[3] Nevertheless, Hollywood continued to suffer from scandal. Coming directly on the heels of the Arbuckle scandal, the unsolved murder of director William Desmond Taylor threw suspicion on two well-known leading ladies, and, in 1923, Wallace Reid, the on-screen epitome of blonde, robust, all-American-nice-guy-ness, died of complications from morphine addiction.

As Richard deCordova has noted, these scandals constituted a watershed moment since they appeared "as a kind of repudiation of the picture of the stars' family lives that had been put forward in the teens."[4] In the years 1909 to 1913, the film industry had begun to publicize the names of its featured actors and learned the financial advantage of exploiting these film actors as "picture personalities." DeCordova has shown how the actor's physical image and personality repeatedly displayed on-screen/in films was extended by Hollywood's publicity apparatus in the 1910s to create a recognizable off-screen, extratextual identity that asserted a "real-life" personality for the actor, one that was, in this originary period, closely aligned with his or her roles.[5] However, in a very short time, Hollywood began to see more value in differentiating between actors and the roles they played and in exploiting audience interest in the off-screen lives of actors through a broad array of venues: fan magazine articles, newspaper interviews, planted news items, and all types of visual and verbal promotion (paid for) and publicity (gratis). As deCordova suggests, this change to a more complex and extensive emphasis on the lives of Hollywood film actors defined the difference between "picture personalities" and "stars," thus marking the emergence of the star system.[6]

Because any process centered on actors had to serve the primary goal of selling films, the discursive construction of stars also inaugurated Hollywood's reliance on a "family discourse." In extratextual discourse in the 1910s, the healthy, morally upright lifestyles of stars were emphasized by frequent positive references to and visualizations of film actors' families, particularly spouses, children, and mothers.[7] Within this discursive framework, the mobilization of the moral power of motherhood quickly became a Hollywood strategy in the discursive construction of stardom, for males and females.

Starting in the 1910s, social controversy swirled around female sexual subjectivity in the wake of the perceived sea change in sexual attitudes that William Marion Reedy dubbed "sex o'clock" in America.[8] Increasingly, public interest in what modernity meant to the social formation of female sexuality led to many Hollywood films that catered to audiences' desire to see uninhibited female sexuality. "Sex o'clock" not only struck, but gonged loudly in Hollywood in the 1920s as actresses such as Clara Bow, Colleen Moore, Sue Carol, Nancy Carroll, Alice White, and Joan Crawford became associated—on-screen—with the excesses of "flaming youth." These actresses regularly portrayed heroines as "modern maidens" who were called upon to deal with the consumer pleasures and sexual temptations of contemporary American society. However, to guarantee the mainstream appeal of Hollywood's modern modes of femininity, films like Bow's It (1927) and Crawford's Our Dancing Daughters (1928) negotiated between approval and condemnation of transgressive aspects of modern femininity by contrasting the heroine's energetic social experimentation (jazzy dancing, drinking, and car dating) with her basic sexual reticence (virginity). In films like these, the threat of female eroticism linked to modernity could be controlled by the last reel conformation of heroines to traditional sexual norms (monogamy and marriage), but off-screen, controversial female sexuality was particularly dangerous when acted out in the "unscripted" actions of women who also happened to be film stars.

Just as female sexual subjectivity had to be regulated on screen to prevent strong public reaction against films that might be perceived as encouraging immorality in impressionable members of the audience, female sexual subjectivity also needed to be regulated in the off-screen personas of Hollywood actresses. Considering the cultural force of gender stereotypes, it may seem somewhat predictable that Hollywood's family discourse would become an important element of defining female stars and controlling their sexuality. But the imperatives of containment that worked to limit the socially and sexually transgressive aspects of stars—especially of young female stars—almost invariably were combined with other elements that resulted in an ideologically contradictory process.

This was especially true in the extratextual discursive construction of youthful female stars. As I will show, Hollywood's selling of female sexuality through the construction of star personas in the 1920s and 1930s often involved enhancing the erotic and identificatory value of female screen idols (their "sex appeal" to women as well as men) through a variety of extratextual means as well as through textual ones. As a consequence, discursive control of star images often invoked a family discourse in which mothers became particularly important to preserving the mainstream "morality" and "normality" of female stars and, consequently, their perceived box-office value. This occurred in a time period when the film industry's attempts to present itself as a representative of mainstream moral values and middle-class sexual norms were frequently threatened by star behavior off-screen or immoral film content on screen.

One might predict the obvious importance of mothers and culturally pervasive notions of motherhood in the construction of child stars of the 1920s and 1930s such as Jackie Coogan, Jackie Cooper, Shirley Temple, and Jane Withers, but mothers also figured significantly in the public discourse surrounding the star personas of certain adult actresses. This chapter will deal with two stars and their mothers who articulated, in different ways, Hollywood's discursive control of the sexual personas of female stars in relation to the figure of the mother: Mary Pickford (born Gladys Smith) and her mother Mrs. Charlotte Pickford, and Joan Crawford (aka Billie Cassin, aka Lucille Le Sueur) and her mother, Anna Le Sueur.

Mary Pickford was one of the first picture personalities to make the transition to the first order of stardom in the 1910s, and her popularity was sustained and then challenged during the 1920s. In this period of intense social commentary about American women's changing social and sexual subjectivity, her popularity as an exemplar of childlike feminine beauty and innocence became eclipsed by stars such as Joan Crawford, who represented young womanhood as sophisticated and modern. Pickford retired in the early 1930s, but Crawford, who began acting in films in the mid-1920s, saw her star power increase during the industry's transition to talkies, a period in which the industry's representation of female subjectivity reflected the uneasy transition from the ethos of the Jazz Age to the preoccupations of Depression-era America. The latter is often regarded as a time of retrenchment for both traditional gender alignments and cultural values, but, in the early 1930s, the film industry came under increased criticism for its depiction of sexually and socially transgressive femininity, which Lea Jacobs has characterized as the "self-consciously 'modern' American types: flappers, gold diggers, chorines, [and] wisecracking shopgirls."[9] These types were often central to "Cinderella Stories" that depicted women who rose up the class ladder through "sexual degradation and decline."[10]

Archetypal of these was the heroine of Metro-Goldwyn-Mayer's *Possessed* (1931), played by Joan Crawford. Marian Martin (Crawford) leaves a life of drudgery at a paper box factory in a small town to go to the city. Her purpose is, as a male acquaintance characterizes it, "to meet a rich man and let nature take its course." She meets a wealthy politician, Mark Whitney (played by Clark Gable), and becomes his mistress. To provide a cover for their illicit relationship, she calls herself "Mrs. Moreland," and pretends to be a wealthy divorcée. Marian is content until she finds out that Mark's advisors see her both as an impediment to his career and only one step above a prostitute. When Mark runs for office, her name is used by the opposition to stir up scandal, but she proves her loyalty, and he proves his love.

No wonder that then chief moral regulator for the film industry, Jason Joy, commented to a colleague that once the film industry decided that gangster films were no longer effective in attracting audiences to "the talkies," the only thing Hollywood appeared to know how to exploit was sex.[11]

"OUR LITTLE MARY" AND HER MOTHER, MRS. CHARLOTTE PICKFORD

Mary Pickford started as a child actress on stage and first appeared in the movies in 1909, in one-reelers for American Biograph. Known as "Our Little Mary," Pickford became popular during the film industry's shift to relying on the actor as a personality for enticing audiences into regular moviegoing. The bond between Mary Pickford and her mother, the long-widowed Charlotte Pickford (formerly Smith), was an important part of the development of the star persona of "America's Sweetheart" in the 1910s and 1920s. In 1918, it was used to deflect sexual scandal and ten years later, shortly after Charlotte's death, it was called upon to justify some of the actress's questionable career choices.

Pickford started out playing a wide range of roles for American Biograph and then other studios, including children (*The Lonely Villa* [1909] and *Little Red Riding Hood* [1912]), adolescents (*The New York Hat* [1912] and *Cinderella* [1914]), and adults (*For Home and Honor* [1912]). It was not just her acting but the appeal of her on-screen personality that drew audiences. As one article noted in 1916, "The popular success of Miss Pickford . . . has been a thing apart from her dramatic triumphs. . . . [her] chief attributes have been her tender human sympathy, her utter sweetness, her steadfast sincerity."[12] In films like *Rags* (1915), her appeal as a hoyden—her signature feminine type—was defined by cuteness, innocence, and spunk. In 1918, the industry trade magazine *Motion Picture News* defined "the 'typical' Pickford picture" as showing "her in rags and curls, in situations both humorous and dramatic."[13] One reviewer of her film *M'Liss* (1918) noted: "All dressed up and in a beautiful garden she is lovely, but in funny tattered little garments, with curls flying, she is—well, just 'our Mary.' "[14] By the late 1910s, Pickford was widely recognized as "the most popular motion picture actress in the world."[15]

Pickford's screen characters assumed signs of childishness that made her womanly aesthetic perfection and erotic potential safe for her audiences.[16] As her career developed in the late 1910s, the diminutive actress began to specialize in playing children and adolescents in films like *The Foundling* (1916), *Rebecca of Sunnybrook Farm* (1917), *The Little Princess* (1917), and *Pollyanna* (1920). Her films were especially popular with women and children and were regarded as the essence of wholesome family fare. In 1918, an article in *American Magazine* declared that "the biggest single factor of Mary Pickford's success as a screen star is her total abstinence from all forms of questionable photoplays. Mary Pickford has never appeared in a picture that the whole family couldn't see and enjoy."[17] The actress continued to rely on her juvenated screen persona in those films she made under her own control at United Artists after 1919. These included *Tess of the Storm Country* (1922 remake), *Little Annie Rooney* (1925), and *Sparrows* (1927). Well into the era when the flapper and sophisticate had emerged to become film favorites, Pickford's on-screen femininity continued to be characterized by childlike sexual innocence.

Figure 7. Mary Pickford in costume as a child for *The Little Princess*, 1917 (courtesy of the Academy of Motion Picture Arts and Sciences).

Whether portraying a child or adolescent, Pickford's masquerade of juvenated femininity extended beyond the screen to how she was portrayed in extratextual discourse. This extension implicitly promoted the actress as an antidote to the perceived crisis in feminine sexual behavior represented by the flapper and the New Woman. In late 1917, a horoscope reading of Mary published in *Photoplay* characterized her as evidencing "great love for her mother and religion" and concludes by suggesting, "If everybody were as pure minded as she, there would be no sin in this world."[18] An advertisement of that same year for Pompeian night cream shows her in a flowing (but decidedly demure) nightdress. She looks up and away in a pose that refuses acknowledgment of the viewer. Flowers spring up by her feet. The advertising text does not suggest that she uses the product, but, instead, describes her as "gentle, sincere, unselfish, clever and with a girlish charm and beauty that make her adored in every civilized country."

In articles, interviews, and editorials in general interest and fan magazines as well as newspapers, Pickford was the subject of a juvenating discourse that associated her with a working-class, female-centered family headed by her widowed mother, Charlotte Pickford. Extratextual discourse suggested that Mrs. Pickford was a hardworking survivor, a widow with three children who worked on the stage to support her brood before her eldest daughter's acting talent was discovered. Charlotte Pickford was also frequently depicted as being a formidable businesswoman who protected her daughter's financial interests. In 1918, Edwin Carty Ranck wrote that even though Mary Pickford was married to actor Owen Moore, it was her mother who was the actress's "practical business manager."[19] Ranck's article also absolved mother Charlotte of being a stereotypical stage mother who forced her child into work. He recounts how, in the days before she took the stage name of Pickford for her entire family, Mrs. Smith, the "sole support of three little Smiths," played stock company roles. One day she attended rehearsal accompanied by her eldest, Gladys, aged five. Gladys (Mary) volunteered for the role of Bootle's baby in a play. Ranck recounts the moment: " 'I'll do it,' she piped up." Gladys/Mary is described as standing in "patched and worn shoes, her legs encased in intricately darned stockings—eyes bright and serious."[20] The result, says Ranck, was that "those who saw Gladys Smith in the role of Bootle's baby say . . . that she 'ate up the part.' "[21] The daughter's success on stage becomes, as the informed reader knows, the key to relieving the family's poverty. Ranck's description of Gladys's clothes inscribes that poverty but also manages to register the mother's care of her child through attention to the little girl's "intricately darned" stockings. Such details serve to suggest that Charlotte was not a stage mother grasping for power and fame in the public sphere, but a caring, albeit struggling, young mother. The fortuitousness of her child's own eagerness to act absolves Charlotte, as a mother, of an inappropriate desire to force her daughter to work.

In the late 1910s and into the 1920s, it was the relationship between Mary and Charlotte that formed the core of the Pickford family discourse, to the exclusion of Mary's husband, Owen Moore, and even, to a lesser extent, to that of her second husband, superstar Douglas Fairbanks. In fact, Pickford was married from 1911 to 1919 to Moore, but one would hardly know that since they were rarely if ever depicted in photographs together and little mention was made of him as her husband.[22] While *Photoplay* made brief mention of the marriage in December of 1912, in fact, the juvenating discourse in fan and general interest magazines regularly gave fans of the actress the distinct impression that she was too young to be married.[23] For example, in "An Actress from the Movies," Pickford (then twenty-one) is described as a teenager, "an unsophisticated believer in fairies, whose "golden blonde curls and big wistful violet eyes and budding girlish figure are also her real self."[24] In keeping with this juvenating discourse that sought a convergence between the on-screen "Little Mary" and the off-screen "real self" of Mary Pickford, numerous pictures circulated of Mary and Mrs. Pickford throughout the 1910s and 1920s; they were shown both at repose at home and in negotiation together with studio executives.[25] In one such picture, Mrs. Pickford sits between director Ernst Lubitsch and Mary in discussion,

Figure 8. Pickford with her mother Charlotte and niece Gwynne (1921) (private collection of the author).

no doubt regarding Mary's role in *Rosita* (1925). Mary, by virtue of both her high-necked, lace-collared dress and her unauthoritative body language, seems to signal a displacement of her own often acknowledged business acumen onto her mother.[26]

During the 1910s, both Mrs. Pickford's displacement of Owen Moore as the most important family member in Mary Pickford's life as well as her displacement of Mary (and Moore) as her daughter's chief representative in the movie business extended the juvenating discourse of the star's films into print and extratextual visual media. However, there were occasional moments when tensions in the Pickford family discourse were acknowledged. In January 1916, *Photoplay* discussed at length (to ultimately dismiss) the rumors that Charlotte Pickford "has been an obstacle in the path of the Moore-Pickford domesticity."[27] The fan magazine article noted how, out of love and concern, Charlotte did object initially to the marriage because, "familiar with her daughter's every thought since babyhood she, perhaps alone of all who knew or had seen her, felt keenly the tremendous career impending, and did not wish the girl's best interests jeopardized." The article recounts a story of Charlotte Pickford's maternal heroism on behalf of her daughter's marriage. Without her daughter's knowledge, she is able to marshal "all of the force of a rugged and unafraid personality" to save the "life of the son-in-law she has been falsely accused of hating."[28] Charlotte's rescue of Moore from a Cuban jail proves that she is not the stereotypical "stage mother" who perversely turns from domesticity to the entertainment business in order to live out her own ambitions through her child, but a woman who loves her daughter so much that she will move heaven and earth to fight for her happiness.[29]

Mother Charlotte was frequently depicted as setting boundaries for her adult daughter in ways that made Mary Pickford seem like a child. In a first-person article "written" by Mary for *Ladies' Home Journal* in 1915, the twenty-three-year-old actress notes that "mother will not let [her] eat candy."[30] In other articles and news items, Charlotte is described as a perpetual presence at the studio; her desire is to attend to her daughter's needs, but also to give professional advice. A newspaper report in 1921 detailing such a situation starts with Mrs. Pickford quizzing Mary (now married to her second husband) as to whether she is drinking boiled milk: "Her mother, as usual, was with her in the studio, looking after her comfort and her health, and also giving advice as to the filming of the picture. . . . As for the drinking of milk at the L. A. studio, this incident is recorded as showing better than a string of generalities that Mary Pickford, although twenty-eight years old, with a home of her own, and world-famous as she is, remains her mother's girl."[31] Mary's juvenated screen image of spunky innocence and her equally juvenated but more refined visualization in publicity materials as a delicately beautiful traditionalist were both well-served by this family discourse.[32] For many years, it helped create a seamless and unchallenged convergence between her on-screen childishness and her juvenated off-screen personal life as an adult.

Through such extratextual means, Pickford's star image was constructed to stand as an exemplar of traditional feminine values, but at one moment in her career, in 1918, reports of the actress's scandalous sexual behavior demanded an intervention that involved placing her relationship with her mother in a different light. The strategies used to do this reflect the imperative to curb negative public reactions against Pickford as a female star whose sexual behavior off-screen suggested not just the modern phenomenon of women's desire, but sexual scandal involving adultery and divorce. Such scandal threatened the fundamental veracity of Mary Pickford's established star persona.

In 1918, superstar Douglas Fairbanks separated from his socialite wife, Beth Sully, the mother to his nine-year-old son, Douglas Fairbanks Jr. Rumors flew that Pickford, who had joined Fairbanks and Charles Chaplin on Liberty war bond tours, was the cause of his marital breakup. Mrs. Fairbanks reported that her husband was involved with an actress.[33] When queried by the press to make a statement concerning the separation of Mr. and Mrs. Fairbanks, Pickford's response was noncommittal but coy: "Of that I have absolutely nothing to say. . . . Maybe later on . . . but the right time has not come."[34] The love affair with Fairbanks was the type of scandal that could ruin both their careers. Pickford was threatened with being named a corespondent in Mrs. Fairbanks' divorce suit, and after her own divorce from Owen Moore, she was accused by Leonard J. Fowler, attorney general of Nevada, of collusion and falsifying her Nevada residency. Fowler brought suit to annul the Pickford/Moore divorce.[35]

The breakup of Fairbanks's marriage, the messy divorce from Moore, and Pickford's hasty remarriage to Fairbanks threatened to link her to transgressive sexual articulations of the modern woman. These, of course, were completely in opposition to her established star persona of desexualized, childlike femininity. Mary Pickford's adulterous relationship with Fairbanks not only threatened her carefully constructed image of juvenated feminine innocence, but was the kind of female sexual behavior that was believed to threaten the primacy of the family. It was a transgression that dovetailed with broadly held cultural fears about female sexual subjectivity. Modern women, it was believed by social conservatives, were trying to live "the codeless existence of the male."[36] They were overturning accepted standards of female sexual restraint through sexual experimentation and undermining the foundational structure of the family. In Current History, philosopher Will Durant wrote that history would look back on women in the 1920s and observe how marriage, "[an] institution which had lasted ten thousand years, was destroyed in a generation."[37]

Simultaneous to Fairbanks's announcement of his separation and divorce from Beth Sully, a new twist to the Pickfordian family discourse emerged to rearticulate Mary's relationship with her mother. It performed the functions of (1) eliciting sympathy for Mary Pickford and (2) providing justification for her seeking romantic happiness with a married man. In other words, fundamentally, this rearticulation of the mother-daughter relationship necessitated a revision of the discursive image of Charlotte Pickford in order to realign her daughter with an ideologically conservative—and sympathetic—view of working-class femininity.

Suddenly the discursive construction of Mary Pickford was as a dutiful daughter to an emotionally supportive but financially dependent mother. This revision of Charlotte's formerly dominant role with her daughter is apparent in an article in *American Magazine* in May 1918 that claimed: "we all didn't know until recently that Mary Pickford was a breadwinner at the stupendous age of five."[38] Mary's childhood relationship to her widowed mother who struggles to raise three children becomes crucial in realigning Pickford with an ideologically conservative view of femininity.

This virtual simultaneity of the Fairbanks separation and the change in the Pickford family discourse suggests a possible conscious move by Pickford's publicity machine to displace the specter of scandal by amplifying the sense among the filmgoing public that Mary Pickford had suffered as a child on behalf of her family, indeed, on behalf of her mother, and thus deserved the public's sympathy. This approach became standardized in articles about Pickford from 1918 and throughout the 1920s. In one newspaper interview from March 1921, Pickford says, "Even childhood is a terrible thing. I had one of the dearest mothers in the world, but I was an unhappy child."[39] In another from around the same time, she is quoted: "Think of what I missed. I've been acting since I was five years old. I'm glad I was able to help my mother. We had no man to look after us, but I missed all the sweet things of childhood that other people have to look back on. . . . It's rather a cruel life for a child."[40] In Pickford's autobiography, serialized in *Ladies' Home Journal* in 1923, the actress condemns the practice of children working in films, but she makes her own work as a child actress a different order of experience based on her loving relationship to her mother and her childhood poverty: "I had to give up my own childhood, but it was necessary in my case—either work or be separated from my mother."[41] Mary is a dutiful working-class daughter who kept her family together through sacrificing her childhood.

In fact, Mary Pickford's portrayals of girlhood were often attributed in the 1920s to her need to relive, on-screen, the normal childhood she had missed because of work. Pickford says of her childhood in an article in 1922: "One deep-seated grudge I held against the world. It had cheated me out of my youth. . . . I had never been a real child."[42] A newspaper article of

1923 continues this aspect of the Pickford family discourse when T. Roger Lewis writes: "You may note a somewhat wistful look in her eyes as she tells you that among other things that she has missed in life was a REAL CHILDHOOD. Constant engagements . . . and the weekly struggle to make both ends meet, gave her hardly a nodding acquaintance with childhood as most of us have known it."[43] Mary Pickford was a star, such articles implied, who was to be admired for her talent, her lifetime of hard work, and for the sacrifices she had made in support of her mother and siblings. The proof of her deprived childhood could be seen on the screen, in her wish-fulfilling portrayals of girlhood.

For a woman whose responsibilities to her mother and siblings meant she never knew happiness as a child, Mary's rather scandalous remarriage to Fairbanks in 1920 was discursively regulated to become her reward for years of service as a dutiful working daughter. This sentiment was expressed in the *Los Angeles Times*: "No one, I'm sure, speaking humanly, who sees these two together could possibly wish to take their happiness from them—Mary, especially, perhaps, with her years of conscientious, hard labor, when as a mere child, she was mother to all her family, Jack, Lottie, even her own mother."[44] Mary, childless though she is, becomes the mother to her own family, even as later articles emphasized how she was called upon to mother the childish Douglas Fairbanks.

Although they were denounced on occasion for giving divorce respectability it had not had previously, their marriage was accepted, somewhat surprisingly, by the majority of their audience.[45] Somehow it seemed appropriate that the most famous and famously juvenated actress in the world had become the wife of the most famous and famously juvenated actor in the world. To support this, the Pickford family discourse moved in yet another direction. Writing in *Photoplay* in 1927, Adela Rogers St. Johns compared the couple to Wendy and Peter Pan. St. Johns asked readers: "What more natural than that eternal motherhood and eternal youth should make a perfect mating?"[46] Whether or not it was "natural" to mate "eternal motherhood and eternal youth" is a more complicated (and creepy) question than St. Johns allows. What is clear is that now, as Pickford was striving to attain a belated adulthood on-screen in the late 1920s, her once scandal-provoking relationship to Fairbanks emerged as an extratextual avenue for turning Mary herself into a sympathetic mother figure. She becomes a paragon of traditional feminine sexuality—a married woman who mothers her husband.

In the case of Mary Pickford and Charlotte Pickford, the discursive construction of this, one of the first widely publicized Hollywood mother-daughter bonds, was used for over a decade to encourage a favorable view of a star who momentarily transgressed normative standards of female sexuality and the boundaries of her star image. That transgression threatened the "truth" of Mary Pickford's star persona, but the extratextual discursive control of the mother-daughter bond helped deflect a potentially career-ending scandal for "America's Sweetheart" in the years 1918 to 1920.

A very different discursive construction of the mother-daughter bond was mobilized again in 1928 to account for why Mary Pickford bobbed her hair, an iconic action of feminine modernity indicative of the star's attempt to update her screen image and maintain her popularity. In a lengthy article by Adela Rogers St. Johns for *Photoplay*, published soon after Charlotte's death, the earlier image of Charlotte as a mother who lovingly dominates her daughter is revived. Now the mother-daughter relationship is articulated as a public one in which the mother is accorded unusual power to shape her daughter's career. Through her "loving and miraculously suc-cessful domination," says St. Johns, Charlotte literally created Mary as a star: "Their relation to each other was more than that of a loving mother and daughter. It was that of a sculptor and his masterpiece." But, St. Johns continues, Mary succumbed to her mother's judgment in the 1920s, "to follow the old formula, to retain the curls and all that went with them."[47] Thus, Charlotte "held Mary back, held her to the things that had made her famous"—Mary's curls chief among them. Mary's attempts to grow up on-screen were undermined by those curls that her mother loved, but that served as the "constant reminder" to her audience of her child roles. The result, says St. Johns, was that, for five years, "Mary the artist sacrificed herself to Mary, the daughter."[48]

In this account of the Mary/Charlotte relationship, Charlotte not only exercises power in the public sphere, but she accomplishes a major feat—creating the biggest female star in a system supposedly unsuited to maternal contributions. Here, Charlotte's maternal role allows her to be-come powerful, influential, and career-shaping, but the dangers in being a stage mother catch up to her: her judgment fails and her influence over her daughter is too great. Even though Mary was one of the founders of United Artists, it is Charlotte who is blamed for keeping Mary attached to an anachronistic screen persona in the 1920s. Once again, as in the oft-repeated, rather melodramatic accounts of her childhood, Mary Pickford is inscribed as a dutiful, sacrificing daughter. The star's love for her mother is so great that she only can bear to cut off her curls, so dear to Charlotte, "when it could no longer wound her mother."[49]

This article sets the stage, as it were, for the change in Pickford's screen roles after Charlotte's death on March 21,1928, and justifies the star's previous on-screen adherence to a childish, asexual femininity.[50] In 1929, Pickford assayed her first all-talkie film role by playing a Southern belle whose irresponsible flirtations lead to tragedy in *Coquette* (1929). The film was advertised as offering "a modern, grown-up Mary Pickford—with chic bobbed hair . . . lovelier than ever before, as an alluring little flirt, breaking hearts, playing with love!"[51] The advertisements made Pickford's role sound somewhat more daring than it was, but the film generated more money than any previous Pickford vehicle. Venturing even more against type, Pickford next took on the role of a French chorus girl with a yen for a married man in *Kiki* (1930). *Kiki* flopped at the box office. One reviewer suggested that the star had made the naughty chorus girl into another Pickford "hoyden," the kind of "young imp of her early films," and that Pickford had "influenced Kiki a good deal more than Kiki has influenced her."[52] Thus, the film reviewer recognizes what the St. Johns article of 1928 works so hard to disavow through its discourse on mother love gone wrong: Pickford's complicity in the sustained childishness of her portrayals in the 1920s.

In 1932, Claire Booth Brokaw (later Luce) wrote of this phase of Pickford's career: "You cannot stay a child too long without paying the penalty of a devitalized maturity."[53] As William Everson and other film scholars have acknowledged, representations of female sexuality aligned with social modernity and sexual experimentation coexisted with, then appeared to eclipse, the older, Victorian-indebted femininity represented most famously by "America's Sweetheart," Mary Pickford.[54] In fact, in 1929, a poll taken by the trade magazine *Exhibitors' Trade Herald and Moving Picture World* named quintessential modern girl Clara Bow as the year's "most popular film actress," with archetypal flapper Colleen Moore in second place. Mary Pickford ranked sixth.[55] Pickford had become an anachronism, still beloved by many, but displaced in box-office power by those ubiquitous Jazz Age "dancing daughters" and "modern maidens" of the screen. *Photoplay* noted that "fans are young and the new stars are young."[56] As I have argued elsewhere, controversial aspects of modern female behavior such as flapperdom, bobbed hair, careers for women, and destruction of the sexual double standard were often exploited as subject matter of mainstream commercial filmmaking in the 1920s to increase box-office interest.[57]

Pickford had retained her curls and her anachronistic little girl roles past the time when, in the words of Adela Rogers St. Johns, "an entirely new generation had evolved an entirely new type of girl."[58] One of the prime representations of that "new generation" and among the most popular of the screen's modern maidens was Joan Crawford. Yet even in the discursive construction of the sexual persona of Crawford, one of the most famous film flappers of the era, the figure of the mother—dispersed across a number of different mothers—became key in measuring (and regulating) the sexuality of a highly eroticized female star persona. Joan Crawford's connection to motherhood may now be framed almost exclusively through the unflattering lens of *Mommie Dearest*, the tell-all best seller authored by one of her adopted daughters, but, in the 1920s and 1930s, mothers and the concept of mothering had a different relationship to the young Joan Crawford.[59] Her own mother and others, most particular, the mothers (and even stepmother, in one instance) of men with whom she was romantically involved, functioned in extratextual discourse to situate Joan Crawford—not always comfortably—in relation to controversial cultural values attached both to modern feminine sexual subjectivity and to working-class women.

THE SELF-MADE STAR: FROM SLAVEY TO HOLLYWOOD PRINCESS

Motion Picture Classic noted in 1924: "No topic of the day . . . is so eagerly pursued as that of the Modern Girl: what she is doing and why she is doing it; and what she is thinking, if at all; and why she is as she is."[60] Despite public ambivalence if not outright condemnation of modern modes of young womanhood, in the 1920s, the flapper became the most recognizable public image of the modern girl. In various incarnations she was featured as the heroine of numerous films such as *The Adventurous Sex* (1925), *Bare Knees* (1928), *The Exalted Flapper* (1927), *Flapper Wives* (1924), *It* (1927), *Modern Daughters* (1927), *Nice People* (1922), *Our Dancing Daughters* (1928), *The Painted Flapper* (1924), *The Plastic Age* (1925), *Prodigal Daughters* (1923), *Sinners in Silk* (1924), and *Wild, Wild Susan* (1925), among others.[61] Box-office trends suggested that audiences reveled in the excitement of modern women on-screen and in the eroticized stars who played them. These films traded on the appeal of adventurous, energetic, and erotically charged modern femininity, even if they most often pulled in the reins on youth in the final reel to reaffirm traditional sexual values attached to marriage. Even if they remained virgins in the final film reel, modern women with sex appeal were in, good girls aligned with old-fashioned innocence were out.[62]

In the midst of a national debate over changing sexual and social expectations for women, Hollywood was accused of encouraging a new, dangerous model of female sexuality. In "What the Films Are Doing to Young America," sociologist Edward Alsworth Ross represented a vocal segment of public opinion when he wrote that the movies were making young women (as well as young men) more "sex-wise, sex-excited, and sex-absorbed than . . . any generation of which we have knowledge."[63] Sociologist Herbert Blumer interviewed young people and confirmed the widespread belief that the imitation of young female stars was having a deleterious effect on the behavior of America's young women. One young woman told Blumer: "I have learned from the movies [and Clara Bow] how to be a flirt, and I have found out that at parties and elsewhere the coquette is the one who enjoys herself the most."[64]

In the late 1920s, Crawford emerged as another screen exemplar of the flirt as well as a rising star that embodied the vivacious modern girl in films like *Our Dancing Daughters* (1928), *Our Modern Maidens* (1929), *Our Blushing Brides* (1930), and *Dance, Fools, Dance* (1931). In "Friendly Advice from Carolyn Van Wyck on Girls' Problems," Diana, Crawford's character in *Our Dancing Daughters*, was used as an example of why the "innocent, sweet girl" who may be "the life of the party" needed to appear less modern in some ways, for "the girl who has the reputation of being a flirt," Van Wyck advised her inquiring readers, "sometimes has a hard time convincing a man that she really loves him."[65] Crawford's heroines suggested new sexual direct-ness, but also the restlessness and uncertainty attached to the image of the "modern maiden." As one newspaper article noted, "Slowly, sophistication came in, as the mode and the mood of films changed. Before you realized it, Joan was the modern young woman at her best on the screen."[66]

Thus, on-screen, Crawford's heroines of the 1920s often were marked as highly erotic eye candy, but for all their sexualized display (and behavior) her heroines remained "virtuous." The Crawford vehicle *Our Blushing Brides* foregrounded this contradictory Hollywood assertion of modern femininity. A review in *Photoplay* noted of Crawford's role in this second sequel to *Our Dancing Daughters*: "Joan is the fashion model that holds out for the wedding ring. She gives a beautiful performance as the girl who sticks to the straight and narrow. You must see her in those lace step-ins!"[67] Looking back on films like this, Harry Evans remarked in *Life* magazine in 1931 that "Joan first stepped into screen prominence by stepping out of her clothes . . . MGM's idea of a jazz mad gal being one who slinks about in fancy underwear and pretends it's all in fun."[68]

In the 1920s, Crawford's life was thought to parallel her on-screen identity as a key representative of "flaming youth" and modern young femi-ninity, but in that life, despite the publicity machine of MGM, there was no definitive last reel confirmation of her morality. As a rising star, she was publicized across newspaper articles, MGM promotion, and fan magazine articles, which all provided a discursive construction of her as a goodtime girl whose behavior earned her nicknames like "Hey-Hey Girl" and the "Whoopee Girl." During this period, Crawford was, in the words of Adela Rogers St. Johns, "the harum-scarum favorite of the night spots."[69] Crawford's publicity photographs were everywhere in the late 1920s, often featuring her in provocatively "come hither" poses and skimpy dance costumes, lingerie, or bathing suits. However, even at this point, there is often the suggestion, as in *Our Dancing Daughters*, that Crawford's public frivolity is a mask. A fan magazine article of 1927 alludes to a childhood that, in Crawford's words, "wasn't as pleasant as it might have been" and that has left her with "awful moods" that often drive her from "the midst of a party."[70]

Hollywood's construction of Crawford's star image wasn't always as a jazz baby, even one whose dancing hid the fact that "she never had a dancing heart."[71] In 1925, *Movie Weekly* featured a photo of a solemn, big-eyed girl in velvet wrap and pearls, and asked, "What Name Do You Think Suits This Girl?" The girl's name, "Lucille Le Sueur," it was noted, was "not suitable for the screen because it is difficult to pronounce and hard to remember and spell." Therefore, Metro-Goldwyn-Mayer Studios were sponsoring the contest

Figure 9. Joan Crawford as chorus girl, 1922 (private collection of the author).

to "help Miss Le Sueur to carve her place in the cinema niche of fame."[72] The contest described her as having "dark brown hair, large, deep-sea blue eyes, a fair complexion"; she was, *Movie Weekly* claimed, "eighteen years of age . . . a girl of culture" [who] deliberately deserted the debutante ranks of society to enter theatrical life because she is energetic and ambitious."[73]

Following theatrical precedent, and attempting to overcome prejudice against actors as denizens of the lower class (and, thus, people who did not know how to behave), *Movie Weekly*'s description of Lucille Le Sueur as a "girl of culture" embraced the tendency to invent affluent, socially inflated backgrounds for actors and actresses. For both genders, extratextual discourses that supported Hollywood stardom frequently emphasized the pursuit of artistic ideals and professional adventure rather than an escape from drudgery and deprivation. In keeping with this trend, early studio publicity asserted that Lucille Le Sueur was a Kansas City "socialite" who had left the life of a debutante to be a chorus girl and Hollywood hopeful.[74]

But Hollywood soon abandoned this socially elevating tact with the newly named "Joan Crawford," for *Movie Weekly*'s contest was not the first time the M-G-M contract player being groomed for stardom had had her name changed. One newspaper article of 1929 described Crawford as "The girl who scarcely knew her own name when a child."[75] Why didn't she know? This process of renaming had occurred, said the article, throughout her childhood. In this, one of many such accounts of Crawford's early life that appeared in the late 1920s, Joan Crawford's name had been whatever her current father's happened to be, and not only did she not have a name that securely belonged to her, but she had had no definite knowledge of who her father was or if he were alive. The story related in numerous newspaper and fan magazine articles and interviews told how little Billie Cassin found out from her brother that the man she thought was her father was not, and that her name was actually Lucille Fay Le Sueur, not Billie Cassin.[76]

As Crawford recounts to Ruth Biery in a *Photoplay* interview of 1928, the person to blame for this was clear: her mother, Anna Thompson Le Sueur Cassin. Crawford's recounting of her early life points to lower-class instability: secrets, lies, and family dysfunctionality all centered on a mother who valued male companionship over her relationship with her daughter. Crawford tells Biery that after Henry Cassin, the man she originally thought was her father, was sent to prison for embezzlement, her mother failed at running a cheap hotel.

Unlike the image of Mary Pickford working to stay with her mother, Crawford is depicted as being constantly sent away from her mother, of being arbitrarily abandoned to drudgery and even abuse. A newspaper account suggests the instability of her early life: "One day the mother picked up and moved to Kansas City. Joan, or Lucille, went along and was placed in a school where she worked, as a general slavey, for her board and such education that she got."[77] Crawford was there to be cheap help, a child waiting on other children, one, she claims, who was beaten and kicked almost daily. She ran away, but couldn't return to tell her mother of her mistreatment, for when she would go "home" to her mother's laundry agency "in one of the poorest districts of Kansas City," she would face rejection: "as soon as I'd get in the door she'd tell me to watch the laundry. Then she'd go out with somebody."[78] Crawford's miserably lower-class upbringing as Lucille Le Sueur, aka Billie Cassin, was portrayed as the impetus for a rags to riches story in which a neglected, penniless girl born in Texas (or Kansas City or Oklahoma depending on the reporter) uses her dancing abilities to climb up the ladder from the backrooms of a laundry to nightclubs to revues to Hollywood.

Apparently, the multipart series in *Photoplay* was a strong enough rebuke of her mother that it may have played a role in an estrangement between mother and daughter.[79] But Anna Le Sueur could not escape her daughter's version of their history together as publicity wrote and rewrote this story of Joan Crawford's upbringing, giving differing emphases to childhood deprivation and maternal neglect. In one newspaper article, Joan is quoted as remarking: "I ought to make a grand actress. I've had every hardship; so many disappointments my heart's been torn out of me. I'm numb with tragedies." The reporter asks how she was brought up. The response: " 'I brought myself up,' Joan declared."[80] The star's bitter frankness defies the usual careful Hollywood treatment of star family discourse. Instead, the reportage on Crawford's life continually suggests that her own mother was a source of discomforting emotional and sexual instability, moving as she apparently did, from a relationship with one "husband" to another (for a total of three) with little concern for the impact on her child. Contrary to the Hollywood "Cinderella" formula, men led Anna Le Sueur down the class ladder rather than up.

Yet, in keeping with the Mary/Charlotte Pickford saga of familial devotion, Crawford is presented as a dutiful daughter who, even while driven to run away from home to join show business, still financially supports her mother. Like Pickford, Joan is depicted as attempting to relive her childhood, not in this instance, on-screen, but off-screen in her special playhouse lined with dolls: "The room was eloquent of Lucille LeSueur's starved childhood . . . she was washing, dressing, cooking for a hundred or

Figure 10. Young Crawford with her mother, 1914 (joancrawfordma.tripod.com).

more juveniles in that awful boarding school where she earned what little education she got."[81] Yet the defining difference between the two tales of mother-daughter bonding is the sexual history of the mother, and, consequently, the sexuality of the daughter. Unlike Charlotte Pickford, who never remarried after she was widowed, and who was never seen on the arm of a man other than her son Jack or son(s)-in-law, Anna Le Sueur is depicted as a self-centered woman who puts her sexual desires ahead of her child's needs. Going from man to man, with each abandoning her, she ends up financially dependent on a daughter who denounces her mother's past in public.[82]

Crawford's relationship to her mother, like that of Mary to Charlotte Pickford, served its purposes in regulating the actress's sexuality as a star image, but Crawford's sexuality was constructed very differently. Just as Anna Le Sueur was never portrayed as decent and respectable, ironically, the charge of sexual promiscuity also haunted Crawford's star image in the late 1920s, and fed into (or off) assumptions about modern as well as working-class women. Because of her lower-class origins, Crawford's association with jazz and nightlife threatened to mark her as vulgar rather than sophisticated. For example, in *Motion Picture Magazine*, a series of photos of her demonstrating "The Black Bottom" dance suggest the kind of vulgar physicality associated with popular dance that few (with the exception perhaps of Irene Castle) could escape.[83] The latter was something Mary Pickford had evaded through the happy convergence of her on-screen innocence and her family discourse, with its continual emphasis on hard work, careful maternal oversight, and seriousness of purpose.

The positive mediation of the sexuality of Crawford's on-screen characters was easily provided by screenwriters, but newspaper reports of Crawford's nightclubbing and her social climbing via romantic liaisons with men eluded such easy solutions. The question of Crawford's off-screen deployment of her sexuality, as well as the implications of her lower-class origins on her femininity, were potentially trouble for the budding star and her home studio, MGM. As a result, images of other mothers—the wary mothers of Crawford's beaus and lovers—circulated in newspaper coverage as a counterdiscourse to Hollywood's normative standards of family discourse. In contrast to Crawford's catch-as-catch-can childhood and adolescence outside of the watchful gaze of a respectable mother, the image of protective middle-class (if not upper-class) mothering was put into play as something that was employed to protect young men from Crawford as an oversexualized, gold-digging, and society-climbing ex-chorine who was "born south of the tracks."[84] This was certainly the case when Crawford garnered unfavorable publicity through her very public romantic involvement in 1926 with Michael Cudahy, the polo-playing scion of a Chicago meat-packing family.

Cudahy's mother pointedly warned the actress through statements in the press that she was the legal guardian of her eighteen-year-old son, and that "his marriage would be annulled if he ever did decide to marry this girl."[85] The implication was that Crawford was beneath naming, a social-climbing nobody, and the kind of predatory woman that vigilant mothers protected their sons against. In June 1926, Crawford announced the dissolution of her engagement to Cudahy.[86] Five years later, Katherine Albert would defend Joan, and characterize Cudahy as "a handsome young cad who danced with Joan . . . and dragged her name along with his own, over the scandal sections of the newspapers."[87] In the interim, Cudahy's mother had made a public spectacle of her underage son's attempt to marry another social nobody.[88]

In 1929, Crawford, then at least twenty-three (though reported to be as young as eighteen), married nineteen-year-old Douglas Fairbanks Jr., son of superstar Douglas and stepson of none other than Mary Pickford. That marriage into Hollywood's "royalty" put considerable pressure on her "Hey-Hey Girl" image, and on the public treatment of Joan Crawford's sexuality in relation to her originating social classes and her previous romantic entanglements. Fairbanks and Crawford were engaged for a two-year period during which there was continual speculation about their marital status (were they or weren't they—she wore a wedding ring). Finally, in June 1929 they eloped on a trip to New York City. As in her romance with Mike Cudahy, it was her lover's mother whose approval counted. "Mother's blessing, congratulations from dad, and a few friends for witnesses" reported the *Cleveland News* on June 9, 1929.[89] Doug Jr.'s mother, Mrs. Beth Sully Fairbanks Evans, was in attendance, but another newspaper report from Los Angeles noted that "the marriage ceremony [came] as a surprise to the friends of the couple here and to the mother of the bride."[90] The story of the marriage was publicized widely, through very similar accounts in both newspapers and fan magazines. One news item included a brief interview with the star and her new husband. Joan is described as sitting down, "penning a letter to her mother which, she said, started with, 'Dear Mother, it is an hour since. . . .' "[91] This reads like something out of a nineteenth-century novel, and Crawford's concern with telling her mother of the marriage by letter in the face of instantaneous press coverage of the event is comical. Mrs. Le Sueur, reported several newspapers, was completely taken by surprise by the elopement since she had been planning her daughter's wedding for some time. One newspaper account registered the mother's pathetic inability to understand exactly what had happened: "Both Doug Sr. and Mrs. Anna Le Sueur, parents of the couple, expressed surprise last night when told that the wedding had taken place. Mrs. Le Sueur was unable to understand why they elected to be married in a Catholic church. 'We've never been Catholics and I don't think the Fairbankses are either,' she said."[92] This was the only news story that suggested that Doug Sr. did not give his prenuptial blessing to his son's marriage. Another report noted: "Joan's mother said last night in Hollywood that the marriage was a surprise to her as she had been helping her daughter prepare her trousseau and was making plans for the wedding here. 'I received a wire from Joan,' she said, 'telling of her marriage and it certainly was news to me . . . I am only sorry that I wasn't there to witness the ceremony. But I am happy for them. He is such a nice boy.' "[93]

Anyone familiar with fan magazine and newspaper accounts of the relationship between the star and her mother might wonder if this elopement was a strange imitation or "acting out" of Crawford's many public accounts of her mother's surprise announcements of new husbands and the frequent unexpected moves that peppered her daughter's childhood. Here, of course, the daughter was marrying "up," not down. As one newspaper noted, "The girl who scarcely knew her own name when a child married into the Fairbanks dynasty, became a princess in filmdom's royal family."[94] Certainly, the elopement's function as a kind of retaliatory gesture was hard for knowledgeable fans to miss.

The theme of the marriage in Hollywood's family discourse became self-improvement, both of Crawford and of her husband, who, in the words of one fan magazine writer, became "Hollywood's gaga-est lovers."[95] Crawford was no longer the wild "Hey-Hey Girl" who let herself be drawn into divorce suits and bad publicity centering on her sexual escapades. She puts those escapades in perspective now that she was part of Hollywood's first family. In "Lessons in Love," Crawford tells readers of *Motion Picture Classic* that the modern girls who "are not put away in moth-balls to wait for some Prince Charming to come along," who are "thrust up against life early in life," have to have the courage to tell their true love about "past love ghosts." While this may seem a particularly modern attitude, the article, while hinting that Crawford was not a virgin, suggests the fundamental traditionalism of the star when she claims that all of her romantic adventures were never true love.[96] The difference between Crawford before marriage to her "Dodo" and Crawford after the union was likened to the difference between Will Rogers and Mahatma Gandhi.[97] Now Crawford had a marriage that had brought her "a home (she never had a real one before), and love (what did her sleek-haired playboys know of love?), and companionship."[98]

What did Joan do for her husband? Joan made a man of him: "Fine woman, Beth Sully, but you know what a mother is prone to do when she is bringing up a boy without a father! Before Doug fell in love with Joan he was lazy, mentally and physically, a dilettante . . . a dreamer," suggested one newspaper article.[99] In "What Marriage Has Done to Young Doug," Charles Grayson quoted one of Doug Jr.'s friends as saying that " 'Joan brought the outside world to him. . . . She transmuted some of her strength, her force of character, to Doug.' " Joan is the realist, the woman of common clay who weans him away from the sheltered life of a "hot house plant."[100] She had earned her place in the rarefied atmosphere of the Hollywood elite because she guided him into improvement in his acting. Through her influence, a boy who was "far from successful when Joan took him in hand" had evolved from "a rather awkward young juvenile into an actor of talent" who had become a star by virtue of his effective performances in films such as *The Dawn Patrol* (1930).[101] Her mother-in-law, Mary Pickford, the woman who "had been unable to retain her title as America's Sweetheart but was finding consolation as queen of the motion picture world," needed only to discover that Douglas's new wife "was clever as well as beautiful, [with a] capacity for self-improvement [that] would leave her rivals incoherent with wrath."[102]

Thus, Joan Crawford was constructed as being able to do the one thing that her mother could not: change her life's patterns and those of her mate's. She became half of a "Perfect Couple," a woman who defied, by strength of will, those who wanted to judge her by her past, both as a jazz baby and as the neglected child of a slatternly mother. Joan's life story was made to be of interest to her public almost at the beginning of her screen career. Both Mary Pickford and Joan Crawford were presented as self-made stars who suffered greatly as children and as young women who were raised in poverty. The difference with Crawford was that she was affiliated with a female-centered family that was portrayed as dysfunctional because of the deployment of the mother's sexuality. While publicity disassociated Joan from that sexuality through her accounts of her unhappy childhood, her reported life as a chorus girl and then as a nightclubbing "Whoopee Girl" in Hollywood continued the theme of untrammeled female sexuality that her films managed to regulate. Nevertheless, as in her films, marriage allowed her to recuperate her image as a woman worthy of imitation. After her marriage to Douglas Fairbanks Jr., she was portrayed as an extraordinary person whose sexual reification (through marriage) and social improvement (through the embracing of better things) had both come as a result of her discovery of true love. Having found true love, Joan could even forgive her mother, who became a benign figure at the margins of her daughter's new life, "silent on the sidelines" as one newspaper article remarked of her appearance on the set of her daughter's then-current film.[103]

CONCLUSION

By the late 1930s, the power of the mother-daughter relationship in managing the sexual personas of female stars, not only that of Pickford and Crawford, but also that of Jean Harlow and Lana Turner, was an important tool in Hollywood's arsenal of discursive star management. It was used to manage potentially negative responses to the emergence of modernity in the United States, and, in particular, modernity linked to female sexuality. In the discursive management of the mother-daughter relationships implicated in the star personas of Mary Pickford and Joan Crawford, positive cultural notions attached to traditional ideals of motherhood, as well as negative stereotypes of the mother (including the slattern and the stage mother), were mobilized to regulate ideologically transgressive aspects of female sexuality.

What does this prove? It shows that Hollywood's exploitation of the controversy over changing female sexual subjectivity was continually marshalled to support the industry's primary task of selling the movies. The industry incorporated controversial female behavior into films and allowed its expression in stars' lives as constructed by extratextual discourses that were generated to sell individual films and to further stars' careers. Within that network, the role of the mother in regulating the image of female stars could play a powerful part in shaping public sentiment toward women stars, whether they were old-fashioned mother's girls who had trod the boards or jazz babies who danced their way from the wrong side of the tracks into Hollywood fame.

NOTES

The Douglas Fairbanks Jr. personal scrapbooks are two unpaginated, professionally assembled scrapbooks previously in the author's personal collection. They include personal, handwritten notes by Fairbanks, snapshots, and telegrams to Crawford and Fairbanks from family members that suggest strongly that the volumes were once in the ownership of Fairbanks and Crawford. Ownership of these volumes was transferred to the Academy of Motion Picture Arts and Sciences in 2009 so that they will be available to all scholars.

1. Paula Fass, *The Damned and the Beautiful: American Youth in the 1920s* (New York: Oxford University Press, 1977) 2.

2. James Quirk, "Open Letter to Will Hays," *Photoplay* (April 1922): 52, qtd. in Richard de Cordova, *Picture Personalities* (Urbana: University of Illinois Press, 1991) 134.

3. deCordova 134–135.

4. deCordova 136.

5. deCordova 86–88. DeCordova says the extratextual discourse devoted to screen actors and actresses originally emerged in the form of "explicitly posing or revealing a secret" but articles that "promised to reveal what the players were really like merely reproduced the representations of personality already produced in films" (87). There was actually little if any reliance on unveiling the actors' off-screen private lives (82).

6. deCordova 105.

7. deCordova 102–105. DeCordova sees this as, in part, a "backlash against the theatrical model" of stardom: "The discourse on the star involved a work that disassociated the film star from this aspect of the theatrical tradition" (102). DeCordova notes that "most claims about the healthiness of the players' lives referred to this notion of domesticity and focused specifically on the family lives of the players"(105).

8. "Sex O'Clock in America," *Current Opinion* (August 1913): 113. U.S. women were, the article suggests, asking for "the same promiscuity that society tacitly grants to the male."

9. Lea Jacobs, *The Wages of Sin* (Berkeley: University of California Press, 1995) 11.

10. Jacobs 11.

11. Jason S. Joy, in Tino Balio, *Grand Design: Hollywood as a Modern Business Enterprise, 1930–1939* (Berkeley: University of California Press, 1991) 52.

12. *Photoplay* (February 1916): 50.

13. Review of *M'Liss*, *Motion Picture News* (11 May 1918), Scrapbook 31, Ms. Collection U-6, Mary Pickford Collection, Academy of Motion Picture Arts and Sciences, Fairbanks Study Center, Beverly Hills, CA (hereafter cited as Pickford Collection, AMPAS).

14. Virginia Dare, "News of Filmland: Moving Pictures," *Chicago Journal* (16 May 1918): n.p. Scrapbook 31, Pickford Collection, AMPAS.

15. Edwin Carty Ranck, "Mary Pickford—Whose Real Name Is Gladys Smith," *American Magazine* (May 1918): 34–35.

16. It is interesting to note that her endorsement of Pompeian night cream and appearance in advertisements for the product were marked by the imperative to women: "Grow Beautiful!"

17. Ranck 34–35, 75.

18. Ellen Woods, "Stars of the Screen and Their Stars in the Sky," *Photoplay* (October 1917): 82.

19. Ranck 34.

20. Ranck 34.

21. Ranck 34.

22. One exception to this in early star discourse on Pickford is a 1914 article that focuses on D. W. Griffith, but tells a story from the Biograph company involving Owen Moore, who "was engaged to Miss Pickford." See Edward Mott Woolley, "The $100,000 Salary Man of the Movies," *McClure's* (September 1914): 112.

23. *Photoplay* (December 1912): 100, cited in deCordova 105.

24. "An Actress from the Movies," *Cosmopolitan* (July 1913): 265.

25. Not only female-centeredness of the Pickford family discourse, but its tight entwining of this discourse around Mary and Charlotte to the exclusion of other family members is recorded in "The Family Album" photo by Nelson Evans that appears in an undated issue of *Motion Picture Classic* (ca. 1920) that shows Mary sitting, book in hand, at her mother's feet, while Charlotte, also in formal wear, holds the child of her other daughter, Lottie. This child, Gwynne, was adopted by Charlotte and renamed Mary. The caption calls the child "Mary II." Undated clipping, Clipping file, AMPAS.

26. It should be noted that Mary's business acumen was often commented upon or implied by acknowledgment of her tremendous salary (over $100,000 a year in 1917).

27. "Mary Pickford," *Photoplay* (January 1916): 43.

28. "Mary Pickford," *Photoplay* (January 1916): 43.

29. Hollywood tended to tread lightly on this subject so as not to paint a negative portrait of stars' mothers, but, inevitably (with Shirley Temple being the only exception I have found), former child stars or young actresses with prominent "stage mothers" always conclude in interviews that they would never let their children become actors. See, for example, an account of Helen Mack and her mother in Julie

Lang Hunt, "Not A Minute of Childhood," *Photoplay* (October 1934): 38, 84. Mrs. Charlotte Pickford and Mrs. Elizabeth Lloyd are credited with the idea that resulted in the formation of the "Motion Picture Mothers of America" in "Movie Star Mothers Hold Cocktail Fete," *Los Angeles Times* (20 August 1939): D5. Exactly what the mothers do (other than "hosting cocktail parties") is not clear from the article.

30. "The Most Popular Girl in America," *Ladies' Home Journal* (January 1915): 9.

31. "Mary Pickford, Daughter of Toronto," *Toronto Star Weekly* (12 March 1921): n.p., Scrapbook 29, Pickford Collection, AMPAS.

32. Vachel Lindsay comments on (and laments) the difference between the Mary as presented on screen as a hoyden and her Botticelli-like beauty in "Queen of My People," *New Republic* (17 July 1917): 280–281.

33. Gary Carey, *Doug and Mary* (New York: E. P. Dutton, 1977) 62.

34. "I'll Not Retire, Says Little Mary Pickford on Return," untitled Oakland California newspaper clipping (12 May 1918): n.p. Collection U-6, Pickford Scrapbook 31 of 48, AMPAS.

35. *New York Times* (4 April 1920): 1. See also Carey 77–78.

36. Gaylyn Studlar, "The Perils of Pleasure? Fan Magazine Discourse as Women's Commodified Culture in the 1920s," *Wide Angle* 13.1 (1991): 6–36. For negative views of women's changing sexual desires, see Joseph Collins, "Woman's Morality in Transition," *Current History* 27 (1927): 33–40; Edward Sapir, "The Discipline of Sex," *American Mercury* 16 (1929): 413–420; Will Durant, "The Modern Woman: Philosophers Grow Dizzy as She Passes," *Century Magazine* (February 1927): 421; and H. McMenamin, "Evils of Woman's Revolt Against the Old Standard," *Current History* 19 (1927): 30–32.

37. Durant 421.

38. Ranck 34.

39. Evelyn Wells, "Big Film Role, 4 Babies, Pickford Wish," *San Francisco Call* (22 March 1921), clipping in Scrapbook 29, Ms. Collection U-6, Pickford Collection, AMPAS.

40. *San Francisco Daily News* (28 March 1921), Pickford Collection, AMPAS.

41. Many articles emphasize how hard Mary continued to work as an adult in the motion picture business. One newspaper article tells readers: "Think of Mary's sacrifices and then decide if you really want to become a star." "Following Mary Around the Clock," *Chicago American* (19 February 1921): n.p. in Scrapbook 29, U-6 Collection, Pickford Collection, AMPAS.

42. Mary Pickford, "The Greatest Business in the World," *Collier's* (10 June 1922): 22–23.

43. T. Roger Lewis, "A Character Study of the Real Mary Pickford: Woman and Genius," *New York City Success* (June 1923), Scrapbook 39, Pickford Collection, AMPAS.

44. Grace Kingsley, "Europe Again Calls Star Duo," *Los Angeles Times* (3 March 1921), clipping in Scrapbook 29, Ms. Collection U-6, Pickford Collection, AMPAS.

45. On denunciations of them, see Carey 99. On the surprising public acceptance of their marriage, see deCordova 123.

46. Adela Rogers St. Johns, "The Married Life of Doug and Mary," *Photoplay* (February 1927): 35.

47. St. Johns 128.

48. St. Johns 128.

49. St. Johns 129.

50. Some mourned the passing of the Pickford curls. An editorial in the *New York Times* suggested that while the popular notion of "sex appeal" might be "very much minus" in Mary Pickford, they liked her anyway because she was "as comfortable as an old shoe." Qtd. in Gary Carey 181–182.

51. "Mary Pickford's Voice Comes to the Screen," advertisement for Gala World Premiere at the Rivoli, untitled newspaper clipping (5 April 1929): 29, Clipping file, AMPAS.

52. Mordaunt Hall, "*Kiki*," *New York Times* (6 March 1931): 29.

53. Clare Boothe Brokaw, "Mary Pickford: the End of an Era," *Vanity Fair* (August 1932): 53.

54. Cynthia Felando, "Hollywood in the 1920s: Youth Must Be Served," *Hollywood Goes Shopping*, eds. David Desser and Garth Jowett (Minneapolis: University of Minnesota Press, 2001) 97.

55. "Clara Bow Leads Film List," *Los Angeles Times* (3 January 1929): A3. Joan Crawford was ranked tenth.

56. Qtd. in Felando 97.

57. Gaylyn Studlar 18–20.

58. Adela Rogers St. Johns, "Why Mary Pickford Bobbed Her Hair," *Photoplay* (September 1928): 33.

59. Crawford died on May 10, 1977. One of four children whom Crawford adopted, Christina Crawford, accused her mother of child abuse in her book *Mommie Dearest*, published in 1978. The film version of the book was released in 1981. Another of Crawford's three daughters, Cathy, spoke in defense of her mother: "Christina committed matricide on Mother's image." "Was She Devil or Doting Mom? 'Dearest' Stirs a Row Among Joan Crawford's Adopted Kids," *People Weekly* (19 October 1981): 58.

60. Qtd. in Studlar 6–36.

61. On the flapper pro and con see, for example, Freeman Tilden, "Flapperdames and Flapperoosters," *Ladies' Home Journal* (May 1923): 16–17, 157–158; Ruth Biery, "Judge Ben Lindsey Defends Flapper Movies," *Photoplay* (November 1928): 29; and Margaret Reid, "Has the Flapper Changed?" *Motion Picture Magazine* (July 1927): 28–29, 104.

62. See Ruth Biery, "Judge Ben Lindsey Defends Flapper Movies" 29, and Margaret Reid, "Has the Flapper Changed?" 104.

63. Edward Alsworth Ross, *World Drift* (New York: Century, 1928) 179.

64. Herbert Blumer, *Movies and Conduct* (New York: Macmillan, 1933) 52.

65. "Friendly Advice from Carolyn Van Wyck on Girls' Problems: Appearance May Deceive," *Photoplay* (January 1929): 16.

66. In her obituary, May 11, 1977, in the *Charlotte Observer*, the Associated Press noted: "No one epitomized the decade's high living era of short skirts and hip flasks marked by the excesses of 'flaming youth' more than Joan Crawford." 1A.

67. "The Shadow Stage: A Review of the New Pictures," *Photoplay* (September 1930): 52.

68. Harry Evans, "Movies" review of *This Modern Age*, *Life* (9 October 1931): 18.

69. Adela Rogers St. Johns, "Joan Crawford: The Dramatic Rise of a Self-Made Star," *Photoplay* (December 1937): 70.

70. "Moods to Fit the Occasion," *Motion Picture* (November 1927): 89.

71. "Don't Believe All You Hear About Dietrich and Other Stars," *Motion Picture* (May 1932): 76.

72. "What Name Do You Think Suits This Girl," *Movie Weekly* (4 April 1925): 14.

73. "There Is Still Time to Enter the $1,000 Name Contest," *Movie Weekly* (11 April 1925): 17. The results were announced in September 1925 in *Movie Weekly* and publicity extended to a news item in "Cognomen of Actress Discarded," *Los Angeles Times* (5 September 1925): A18.

74. Hollywood loved to discuss "Why Rich Girls Leave Home" as in its explication for why one Elinor Patterson abandoned afternoon teas with the Junior League in favor of stage and screen in "Her Parents Don't Understand" by Lynn Fairfield in *Motion Picture* (September 1927): 37. There is one half-hearted reversion to this original insistence on Crawford's middle-class origins in a MGM "In Action" flyer from the early 1930s that says of Crawford: "She left home against her parents' wishes and secured a part as a dancer in a Chicago review." One article of 1927, "She Doesn't Use a Lipstick in Public," shows a very revealing publicity shot of Crawford from *The Unknown*, but claims that the "mysterious" young leading lady, despite her modern look and vigorous dancing, "is femininity before the Nineteenth Amendment." This attempt to make Crawford old-fashioned as well as modern was a typical discursive strategy attached to many popular constructions of youthful femininity in the 1920s, both in women's magazines as well as in Hollywood's extratextual venues, such as fan magazines. See Studlar 36.

75. Clipping, *Boston Globe*, no date [ca. 1929], Douglas Fairbanks Jr. personal scrapbook, author's private collection. See also Alma Whitaker, "How They Manage Their Homes," in which Crawford claims she supported her mother and her grandmother after she came to Hollywood. *Photoplay* (August 1929): 101, 102.

76. Joan Crawford as told to Ruth Biery, "The Story of a Dancing Girl," *Photoplay* (September 1928): 34–35, 122. The spelling of the last name "Le Sueur" alternates with "Le Seuer" in newspapers and articles throughout the 1920s and 1930s.

77. Helen Hurd, "Missouri CINDERELLA Who GOT HER Prince," *St. Louis Post-Dispatch* n.d. [ca. 1931], Douglas Fairbanks Jr. personal scrapbook.

78. Biery 123.

79. A very public "quarrel" is referred to by Katherine Albert in "Why They Said Joan Was 'High Hat,'" *Photoplay* (August 1931): 65.

80. Mayme Ober Peak, " 'Doug Junior's' Wife—Maybe," untitled Boston newspaper clipping, n.p., ca. 1929, Douglas Fairbanks Jr. personal scrapbook, private collection of the author. See also: "From Billie Cassin to Joan Crawford," *Boston Globe* clipping, n.d; Robert Moorefield, " 'Flaming Youth,' Brought Fame to Joan

Crawford," *Des Moines Sunday Register* 22 May 1932, clipping in Douglas Fairbanks Jr. personal scrapbook.

81. "Throne of Garbo" unidentified, undated newspaper clipping, Douglas Fairbanks Jr. personal scrapbook.

82. Peak, ca. 1929, n.p. Crawford is quoted as saying that her mother and brother "had always more or less depended on her," a theme reiterated in other accounts.

83. "The Black Bottom: In Ten Lessons, by Hollywood's Expert, Joan Crawford," *Motion Picture Magazine* (March 1927): 59.

84. "The Joan Crawford No One Knows," *Los Angeles Times* (21 May 1939).

85. "Young Cudahy's Mother Warns of Annulment," *Los Angeles Times* (6 May 1926): 18.

86. "Love Knot Untied by Fair Joan," *Los Angeles Times* (8 June 1926): A1.

87. Katherine Albert, "Why They Said Joan Was 'High Hat,' " *Photoplay* (August 1931): 65.

88. "Michael Cudahy Jailed," *Los Angeles Times* (5 January 1927): A1.

89. Untitled clipping, *Cleveland News* (9 June 1929), Douglas Fairbanks Jr. personal scrapbook.

90. Untitled, undated, clipping, Douglas Fairbanks Jr. personal scrapbook.

91. "Young Doug Weds Joan," *Los Angeles Times* (4 June 1929): 1.

92. "Joan and Doug Jr. Married by Rector of St. Malachy's," *Daily News* (4 June 1929), clipping, Douglas Fairbanks Jr. personal scrapbook.

93. "Young Doug Weds Joan," *Los Angeles Times* (4 June 1929): 1.

94. Helen Hurd, "Missouri CINDERELLA Who GOT HER Prince."

95. Harry Lang, " 'Young Doug': A keen pen portrait of 'Boy' Fairbanks, who wants his own kingdom," *Photoplay* (November 1930): 65. On their excess displays of affection and silly behavior, see Elisabeth Goldbeck, "Swopell: Dodo and Billy Play Just the Cutest Games Together," *Motion Picture Classic* (July 1929): 55, 79, 85.

96. Dorothy Manners, "Lessons in Love: You Can't Hold a Man Says Joan Crawford If You Hide Your Past," *Motion Picture Classic* (September 1929): 16–17, 95. Crawford is quoted as saying: 'How many women have hesitated over that age-old question, 'Will he love me if he knows?' " (16).

97. On the Will Rogers/Mahatma Gandhi comparison, see Albert, "Why They Said Joan Was 'High Hat,' " 112. For similar remarks on her change, see Ruth Biery, "From Jazz to Gentility: Joan Crawford Is Going to Be Demure If It Kills Her," *Motion Picture* (May 1930): 66, 122.

98. "The Girl on the Cover," *Photoplay* (March 1930): 10.

99. Unidentified clipping, ca. 1929, Douglas Fairbanks Jr. personal scrapbook.

100. Charles Grayson, "What Marriage Has Done to Young Doug," *Motion Picture* (August 1931): 56.

101. Henry F. Pringle, "Joan and Doug," *Collier's* (16 January) 1932: 19, 38.

102. Pringle 38.

103. Lang 146. A contest in *Photoplay* in January 1931 asks readers to identify "baby" pictures of various stars. One shows a picture of Crawford, supposedly at age five, with her mother. They are both well dressed and posed in a tender scene,

with the pretty, rather wistful daughter resting her head against her mother's bosom. "Whose Baby Are You?" *Photoplay* (January 1931): 70. See also "Albert, "Why They Said Joan Was 'High Hat,' " in which the author remarks: "It is natural that she should . . . leave home, then return to find companionship with her mother" (112). In "Producers Sigh With Relief as 'Stage Mothers' Reform," this mention is made of Anna Le Sueur: "Joan Crawford's parent is seen at Metro-Goldwyn-Mayer only once for every picture the star makes. She was a visitor, silent on the sidelines, the day 'The Gorgeous Hussy' went into production." *Los Angeles Times* (13 May 1926): 17. See also "Film Stars' Mothers Bid to Luncheon," *Los Angeles Times* (10 September 1941): A8.

SIX

"YOU JUST HATE MEN!"

―――――――――――――――――

Maternal Sexuality and the Nuclear Family in *Gas, Food, Lodging*

ELAINE ROTH

Toward the end of independent writer and director Allison Anders' film *Gas, Food, Lodging* (1992), a single scene brings together many formal, thematic, and political characteristics of the melodrama genre. Focusing on women's lives in a domestic setting, complete with heightened emotions that result in tears, the scene raises weighty cultural issues that no film can possibly resolve. Set in a kitchen, an argument between a single mother and her teenaged daughter escalates into hysterics. At the climax of the scene, the daughter blames the mother for the family's failure to accord to conventional standards and screams that her sexually active, heterosexual mother "just hates men." Many topics and emotions central to melodrama circulate in this scene, including the desire for a normative nuclear family, longing for an absent patriarch, and ambivalence about maternal sexuality. This chapter uses a close reading of *Gas, Food, Lodging* to argue that the film's explicitly feminist representation of maternal sexuality breaks new cinematic ground, offering a corrective to the otherwise widespread demonization of the sexual maternal figure.

In many Hollywood films, mothers recede from the lives of their adult children at an alarming rate; when they do remain on the scene, they often struggle to balance their own desires with those of their adult children. Frequently this struggle involves maternal sexuality, which is typically depicted as destructive to the mother and child relationship. *All That Heaven Allows* (1955), for instance, follows a rupture between mother and adult children in response to the mother's desire to date again after the death of her husband, although this film offers a fairly sympathetic portrait of the mother. While romantic longing is a familiar theme in many Hollywood films, and melodramas in particular, the possibility of a sexual mother poses a crisis in representation. In opposition to this long-standing pattern, *Gas, Food, Lodging* allows the mother, Nora, to participate in both maternity and sexuality without being vilified.

The condemnation of maternal sexuality has many sources, including Christianity and capitalism. (The Virgin Mary, for instance, exemplifies the opposition between maternity and sexuality.) As Kathleen Rowe Karlyn has noted, "Our culture likes its mothers 'immaculate' and maternal sexuality unacknowledged and unrepresented" (paragraph 50). Capitalist principles similarly seek to regulate and eliminate nonreproductive female sexuality, since uncontained, unproductive female pleasure serves no economic function and, as such, warrants reproach.

In keeping with these cultural preoccupations, cinema has a long history of either glorifying or denigrating mothers, often in the same film. In an examination of the "woman's film" of the 1930s and 1940s, a subgenre of melodrama, Linda Williams argues that the "device of devaluing and debasing the actual figure of the mother while sanctifying the institution of motherhood is typical" ("Something Else" 308). Actual mothers make easy targets for what Peter Brooks has called melodrama's "moral occult," a secular system of judgment that naturalizes sympathy and punishment, and corresponds well with melodrama's investment in the clear distinction between good and evil. For instance, it takes just one moment to code the mother, Michelle (played by Catherine Keener), in *Lovely and Amazing* (2001) as immature and negligent. A brief shot shows Michelle seated watching television on the couch; when her young daughter, off-screen, asks her mother to come read with her, Michelle responds without getting up by encouraging her daughter to come watch cartoons instead. This short exchange generated outraged gasps of horror in the theater audience, a clear example of how efficiently the moral occult can indicate a mother's shortcomings. At the same time that melodramas punish mothers, however, they also typically depend on the notion of ideal motherhood. This contradictory dynamic plays out in a film such as *Now, Voyager* (1942), in which Bette Davis's character demonstrates her newfound allegiance to normative femininity by longing for a child of her own, despite the fact that every actual mother in the film is failed or monstrous (LaPlace 163).

If the particulars of perfect motherhood vary according to their historical moment, the impossibility of achieving them remains constant. Thus, the suffering of the eponymous protagonist in *Mildred Pierce* (1945) reflects post–World War II anxiety about women's participation in the workforce, while a film such as *Raising Helen* (2004) responds to early twenty-first-century anxiety about white middle-class women delaying having children.

Rather than allowing the maternal figure to be a sexually desiring subject, in much of Hollywood cinema, the best way for a mother to be sanctified as a mother is through death; in this way the mother figure ceases to be an actual mother and signifies instead, in her absence, an institution. Psychoanalytic theory helps account for this lethal trajectory, in that the mother raises her child into the symbolic order and then capitulates to that order by receding in significance and power. This process appears in mainstream Hollywood cinema in the figure of the passive, marginal good mother, or, taken to its logical extreme, an entirely absent or dying good mother. These characters abound in Hollywood films, including good passive mothers such as the character simply called Mother Bartlett in D. W. Griffith's 1920 *Way Down East*, who makes no effort to protect the protagonist Anna from the patriarchal wrath of Squire Bartlett, who censures Anna's sexual history. Another appears in *Norma Rae* (1979) in the good passive mother who mutely suffers at her factory job but makes no attempt to protect herself or her daughter Norma, who also works at the factory, from the job's dehumanizing conditions. Good mothers who die also appear regularly in films, from *Imitation of Life* (1934 and 1959), to *Gone with the Wind* (1939), *Terms of Endearment* (1983), *Steel Magnolias* (1989), *Stepmom* (1998), *One True Thing* (1998), *Finding Neverland* (2004), and *The Family Stone* (2005). In each, the good mother's characteristics correspond to her historical moment. Anxiety about working mothers shapes both versions of *Imitation of Life*, while the dying domestic figures in 1980s and 1990s films constitute a virtual elegy for the white middle-class stay-at-home mom.

In his examination of 1950s family melodramas, film scholar Thomas Schatz notes, "The strategy of these films, generally speaking, is to counter the heroine's role as mother-domesticator with that of sexual partner" (158). Evidently, then, the quickest route to mobilize the moral occult against a maternal figure in a film melodrama is to depict her as an agent of sexual desire. In *Stella Dallas* (1937), for example, the mother's relationship with her boyfriend helps destroy her connection to her daughter, while in *Mildred Pierce*, the mother's younger, more innocent daughter dies the moment her mother begins a postmarital sexual liaison. Contemporary independent films have maintained this logic: in *Laurel Canyon* (2002), the mother's sexual activities threaten her relationship with her grown son and his girlfriend; similarly, in *Thirteen* (2003), the return of the mother's boyfriend undermines the mother and daughter's previous closeness and triggers the daughter's self-destructive behavior.

In its depiction of a single mother's bind between her roles as a sexual partner and mother-domesticator of adolescent daughters, *Gas, Food, Lodging* reveals the ideology that makes maternity and sexuality incompatible. Herself a single mother of teenaged daughters when she directed the film, Anders sympathetically follows the maternal figure's attempt to reconcile maternity with sexuality (Espinoza and Wang). This significant departure in representations of maternal sexuality challenges the limits traditionally placed on the mother figure. Furthermore, *Gas, Food, Lodging*, which might be called a contemporary "woman's film," manages neither to valorize motherhood in general nor devalue the actual mother it portrays.

The story of *Gas, Food, Lodging* is as follows: single mother Nora (played by Brooke Adams) lives in the bleak town of Laramie, New Mexico, where she works as a waitress at a truckstop diner and struggles to raise her two teenaged daughters while living beneath the poverty line in a trailer home. Trudi (Ione Skye), the older daughter, is sexually promiscuous, while Shade (Fairuza Balk), the younger, nurses explicitly cinematic fantasies of finding her long-lost father, who left the family years earlier. Over the course of the film, the audience witnesses two of Nora's relationships, neither of which is culturally sanctioned. She has recently ended an affair with a married man, foreclosing on this primarily sexual liaison out of concern for her daughters, despite their obliviousness of the affair. Nora then begins a relationship with a slightly eccentric, if doting, younger man. Meanwhile, Trudi becomes pregnant out of wedlock and gives her child, a daughter, up for adoption, while Shade finally meets her father, and begins a relationship of her own.

In 1977, Chuck Kleinhans noted presciently that "melodrama, the genre made earlier by men for women, is now taken over and changed by women filmmakers" (202–203). In many ways, *Gas, Food, Lodging* demonstrates that appropriation. The film carefully builds audience identification with the three women, attempting to elicit sympathy for their dilemmas and avoid directing moral outrage at them. Audience members are meant to support Nora's desire; to feel horrified by Trudi's account of surviving a gang rape; and to worry that Shade's hopefulness about her father's return will be futile. Although each narrative follows a familiar pattern of female suffering and powerlessness, the film resists mobilizing audience antipathy in traditional ways, such as against sexually active women, and particularly sexually active mothers.

As a family melodrama, the film focuses on the familiar themes of family, motherhood, and sexuality, but in this case in unusual, provocative, and progressive ways. A fan of Hispanic melodramas starring a fictional diva, Elvia Rivero, Shade is galvanized through spectatorship into efforts to transform her single-parent household into a traditional nuclear family (she declares: "It was Elvia who first gave me the idea"). Shade hopes that by finding a man for her single mother, her family will conform to traditional standards and metamorphosize into one that can participate in "dumb normal stuff like regular families." As Thomas Schatz notes, "at the narrative-thematic core of family melodramas is a metaphoric search for the ideal husband/lover/father who, as American mythology would have it, will stabilize the family and integrate it into the larger community" (160). Ultimately, Shade's attempt to reconstruct this mythic male presence, to fill the gap his absence creates, ends in failure. The film figures the power of cultural myths, in which the patriarch has the ability to rescue the family, and the inevitable disappointment such myths produce, such as when Shade's father does appear but can provide little help.

Anders dramatizes the impossible demands placed on the patriarch and the nuclear family by including Shade's family's home movies in the film. This self-referential gesture blends the conventions of melodrama and realism, and blurs the boundaries between the fictional and the real. Joining family melodrama with an ostensibly realist film form illustrates the common narrative impulses that shape both forms. Accompanied by melancholy piano music, the sequences of home movies offer a nostalgic glimpse of the former unity of the nuclear family, showing a young father playing with two small girls. Significantly, Nora, the mother, is presumably behind the camera, indicating the shaping hand of the woman artist throughout this film. By situating family movies—the "real"—within melodrama, Anders foregrounds the myths and desires that make up both film traditions. In a discussion of a documentary that includes home movie footage, Valerie Smith observes, "The use of these materials enables the film to address at once the psychopathology of this particular family as well as the nature of the oppressive cultural weight that the image of the nuclear family bears" (384). Anders similarly suggests the intersection between Shade's particular family and the myth of the nuclear family that Shade desires. The images of the home movies are preceded with a shot of the same movie theater Shade attends to view melodramas, revealing that Shade is screening home movies in that very space, presumably aided by her boyfriend, who works as a projectionist. Having established the site as one receptive to melodrama, *Gas, Food, Lodging* first shows a projection of the home movie and then cuts to Shade observing intently, mirroring the film's opening sequence, in which Shade watches Elvia Rivero star in a melodrama. Anders thereby creates a parallel between the reception of the overwrought, excessive melodrama and the "realist" home movies, suggesting that the home movies also function as melodrama, and that the desires brought to bear on their images are every bit as irreconcilable as those generated by the most over-the-top melodrama. The melodrama, in turn, has its roots in the dominant and widespread expectations about the nuclear family found in home movies. *Gas, Food,*

Lodging thus formally and thematically prompts its viewers to recognize that Shade brings the same hopes of unity and closure to both films, asking them to perform weighty, ultimately impossible cultural tasks.

Anders begins her film with an explicit acknowledgment of melodrama's effect on spectators. During one of the first shots, a single, unmoving take of a trailer home, Shade declares in a voice-over, "If it weren't for Elvia Rivero, this story wouldn't even be worth telling." The image of the trailer home, not unlike Shade's own domicile, suggests that screen icon Rivero has the ability to shape domestic lives and transform those lives into stories worth telling. Importantly, Shade has learned the value of her own identity from melodrama.

Shade's pronouncement underscores one of melodrama's primary progressive functions: it can give narrative and visual significance to the lives of those not typically deemed worthy of narration. Linda Williams has argued that "the sexual, racial, and gender problems of American history have found their most powerful expression in melodrama" ("Melodrama Revised" 82). Directly tackling the topic of the sexual behavior of mothers and teenagers, the film also allows for the depiction of a family that, while increasingly common in the United States, still receives only minimal representation in mainstream media. Formally, Shade does not even exist until melodrama legitimates her voice; not until Shade has explained the effects the melodramas have on her does she actually appear on screen as a spectator in a theater transfixed by an Elvia Rivero movie. She is thus prefigured and generated by her belief in melodrama and her emotional response to the genre. The female voice-over, the allegiance to melodrama, and the unembarrassed representation of spectatorship all work to locate this film as a progressive feminist melodrama. Family melodrama is thus the ideal mode for Anders's film. It clearly demonstrates the failure of both the nuclear family and the genre of melodrama to fulfill the demands placed on them, while simultaneously illustrating the power they nonetheless maintain.

Gas, Food, Lodging registers the failure of the nuclear family to bear the weight of cultural expectations, but it does not sacrifice the mother figure to do so. This contemporary melodrama cannily finesses the seeming impasse between maternity and sexuality, allowing the mother to enjoy a conventional happy ending. The film thus rejects a model of passive, self-sacrificing maternity. In doing so, it debunks the myth that maternal figures remain entirely dedicated to their adult children, a fantasy perpetuated by a film like *Stella Dallas*. When Stella facilitates the success of her daughter by reluctantly agreeing not to participate in her life, the daughter remains unaware of her mother's sacrifice, instead imagining incorrectly that Stella valued her own interests and romantic prospects. Film spectators, however, recognize that Stella never truly desires her male companion and actually continues to devote herself to her child's well-being. The film thus reassures viewers, particularly adult daughters, that their mothers never had interests outside their daughters' happiness, and certainly no investment in maternal sexuality.

In opposition to this familiar lack or renunciation of desire, *Gas, Food, Lodging* portrays a mother intent on personal satisfaction, while also attempting to nurture her daughters. The film grants Nora a happy ending, but this victory is not accomplished without some compromises, such as the daughters' emotional hardship and the invocation of heterosexual romance as a necessity for happiness. In a sense, the film privileges Nora by shifting melodrama's suffering onto her daughters.[1] Nonetheless, it offers a nuanced depiction of maternal sexuality, a significant cinematic achievement.

In the scene mentioned at the beginning of this chapter, Nora and her younger daughter, Shade, meet up in the kitchen in the morning. Although Shade remains unaware, the audience knows that Nora consummated a relationship with her young suitor, Hamlet Humphrey, the night before. (Hamlet's name suggests the awkwardness, as well as the whimsy, of this relationship.) Nora thus enters the kitchen in a dreamy postcoital state. Shade, on the other hand, has recently experienced several traumas, one sexual and one familial, of which the audience is again aware but Nora is not. At a girlfriend's party the previous evening, Shade and her friend became targets of an attempted assault by several older boys. Later, we learn that Shade's older sister, Trudi, was in fact the victim of a gang rape years earlier, suggesting a pattern of vulnerability. In a coincidence typical of melodrama, the rape threat against Shade is deflected by a delivery man who turns out to be her own father, whom Shade has not seen for years. Despite his heroic entrance, complete with cowboy hat, the audience recognizes the intensity of the expectations Shade has for the figure of the patriarch and suspects that her fantasies will end in disappointment.

Rather than drawing upon any of melodrama's more stylized representations of conflict and desire, forgoing even a close-up, Anders plays the scene out in a two-and-a-half minute long take, keeping the camera at an emotional distance and moving it very little. Although she orchestrates emotion at other moments in the film with a non-diegetic soundtrack, this explosive scene unfolds without any sound prompts. In drawing upon a range of traditions, including the conventions of melodrama, Anders intersects with the formal characteristics of other independent films from the same time period, such as *sex, lies, and videotape* (1989). Her film links various cinematic traditions, creating a quirky, personal independent movie that acknowledges melodrama's commitment to representing female desire.

The costuming choices made for this scene reflect each character's previous evening and illustrate how alienated the two are from one another. Nora has returned to the sexy lower-middle-class ensemble she wore for her date the night before. Shade, who has a thrift-store aesthetic, has combined a chaste, floor-length black dress with a black cowboy hat that mirrors her father's, arming herself with an emblem of patriarchal power against possible future assaults.

The sexual and familial desires circulating in this mother-and-daughter scene clash quickly. When Shade burns herself on a piece of toast, she explodes, blaming Nora for the dissolution of the nuclear family. Despite the fact that the father abandoned the family and has essentially been a deadbeat dad ever since, Shade operates in accordance with a cultural prevalence to blame the mother, screaming: "It's all your fault. . . . We don't have a family—you just hate men." While Shade is unaware of Nora's sexual liaison the night before, her accusation resonates ironically for the audience. At the same time, however, the proximity of this scene to Nora's sexual encounter punishes Nora to some extent.

Shade's angry charge reveals the mutually exclusive terms of maternity and sexuality. While Nora clearly does not hate men, her position outside of a traditional nuclear family makes her a target for condemnation. If Nora's nascent relationship with Hamlet Humphrey would seem to refute the charge that she hates men, in fact her sexuality, uncontained by social conventions, constitutes a threat to patriarchal institutions. Nora thus has no avenue with which to defend herself. Because the film encourages sympathy for Nora, this moment reveals the logic whereby single mothers are blamed for their own marginal social status.

When Shade screams at Nora, she exemplifies a moment Freud identified as a crucial step in an adolescent girl's repudiation of the mother in

Figure 11. In a climactic scene, Shade (Fairuza Balk) blames her mother for the family's lack of a patriarch (*Gas, Food, Lodging*, 1992).

favor of the father. E. L. McCallum's astute reading of Freud suggests that "the girl first develops penis envy as a necessary stage for her giving up her attachment to her mother" (74). At this moment, according to Freud, the girl feels anger toward her mother for "sending her into the world so insufficiently equipped" (189). Clearly Shade blames her mother for what she conceives of as her family's inadequacy, or insufficient equipment, due to its lack of a patriarch. Freud theorizes that the girl goes on to substitute her penis envy with a desire for a child. Through this lens, Shade's earlier search for a mate for her mother registers as a search for a phallus. When this quest fails, Shade holds her phallus-less mother responsible. While, in accordance with social and Freudian logic, Shade eventually finds a heterosexual mate of her own, she also abandons her desire to find her father. While this might be viewed in Freudian terms as Shade's healthy and necessary transition from penis envy to an eventual desire for a child, Anders' film accomplishes this transition by depicting the patriarch as lacking both financially and emotionally, thereby shifting the burden of failure from the mother to the father.

After presenting a familiar melodramatic scenario featuring a missing father, Anders challenges the possibility that the paternal figure can resolve familial dilemmas. John, Shade's father, neither remains an off-screen fantasy, nor does he offer any real help when he finally makes an appearance. After a fairly macho entrance, his mythic potential almost entirely evaporates. "I ain't shit, but I'm your old man," he announces by way of introduction, explicitly acknowledging his inability to provide Shade or her family with any miraculous aid. The paternal presence ultimately offers some heroism, some letdown, and almost no resolution. John recedes from the movie soon after his return, and the three women continue to drive the film's narrative. Anders avoids demonizing John, instead locating him as a disenfranchised drifter unable to transform anyone, including himself. Fundamentally, the most acute problem faced by Shade's family, as well as John's current relationship, is not the emotional aftermath of divorce but the lack of adequate financial resources, and the film offers no possibilities for resolving that dilemma, while sympathetically portraying the family's economic difficulties. As Chuck Kleinhans has noted, "melodrama locates . . . problems in the area of the family, precisely where many of the issues raised cannot ever be solved" (203). The failure of Shade's quest to rescue her family by finding her father demonstrates the unreasonable demand placed upon the nuclear family, particularly the patriarch, to solve what are essentially economic problems.

After the scene of crisis in the kitchen, which ends without resolution, the film "solves" the problem of Nora's sexuality by establishing her in a relationship with Hamlet. The film thus evades some of the judgment directed at the figure of the sexually active single mother, albeit through containment in the heterosexual romance plot. Nonetheless, to reinforce the connection between Nora as a mother and Nora as a lover, Hamlet Humphrey tells Shade that her mother resembles Elvia Rivero, Shade's beloved melodramatic matinee idol, thereby creating a significant link between the maternal and the romantic. In moments like these, the film combines the binary oppositions of melodrama, allowing Nora to function as a mother-domesticator as well as a sexual partner, providing a new representation of cinematic maternity.

Gas, Food, Lodging first refuses to devalue Nora for her sexuality and then explodes the institution of motherhood entirely when Trudi, Shade's older sister, gives her illegitimate child up for adoption. With this act, Trudi sacrifices her child to save herself, posing yet another challenge to the figure of the self-sacrificing mother. Although adopted children appear throughout melodrama, adoption tends to function as a temporary separation on the way toward an inevitable family reunion, not the final, bureaucratic rift Anders portrays. In melodramas such as Orphans of the Storm (1922), or Peyton Place (1957), orphans ultimately discover their real, benevolent, usually wealthy parents. In contrast, Anders denies the possibility of the organic wholeness of the family unit. Her representation of adoption and divorce suggests that families are constructed, not biological. This portrayal of the nuclear family is both culturally subversive and entirely melodramatic. Although Trudi's predicament as a pregnant unwed teenager seems dismal, Shade notes in a voice-over that "still, it was her choice" to allow her child to be adopted. This invocation of female agency within a narrow range of options operates similarly to the genre of melodrama in providing a limited space for female autonomy.

Jane Gaines, in revisiting Ernst Bloch's notion of utopia, has suggested that because cultural and film critics have focused on locating "resistance" in texts, rather than "utopianism," "the origins of the understanding of ideology as tempered by the aspiration for something better in popular forms are in danger of being forgotten" (107). If critics have ignored the ability of genre films to provide fantasies and dreams that are not inherently complicit with dominant ideology, directors such as Allison Anders have continued to create film melodramas with utopian possibilities. Gas, Food, Lodging in fact contains both moments of resistance as well as invocations of utopianism. It challenges conventionally negative depictions of maternal sexuality, but it also offers a romantic ending for the maternal figure. Trudi and Shade's endings are somewhat less stable. Trudi, recently delivered, is left abject in tears, while Shade ventures a positive note at the film's close in a voice-over. Melodrama, in representing the painful problems faced by sympathetic protagonists under dominant culture, implicitly suggests a better world, or what Shade calls "the future the way you want it to be." This possibility of a better future offers one of melodrama's most powerful and progressive weapons against dominant ideology. Accordingly, in the final scene of the film, Nora drives off into the desert landscape with her younger, wealthier boyfriend. Against traditional configurations of motherhood, the nuclear family, and female sexuality, *Gas, Food, Lodging* rewards the maternal figure, offering a challenge to the terms of melodrama as well as the cultural binds the genre reflects.

NOTES

1. This pattern is true also of *Terms of Endearment* (1983), although with more lethal consequences for the daughter.

BIBLIOGRAPHY

Brooks, Peter. *The Melodramatic Imagination: Balzac, Henry James, Melodrama, and the Mode of Excess.* New Haven: Yale University Press, 1995.

Elsaesser, Thomas. "Tales of Sound and Fury: Observations on the Family Melodrama." *Home Is Where the Heart Is: Studies in Melodrama and the Woman's Film.* Ed. Christine Gledhill. London: British Film Institute, 1992. 70–74.

Espinoza, Galina, and Cynthia Wang. "Nightmare Revisited." *People* 56 (9) (2001).

Freud, Sigmund. "Some Psychological Consequences of the Anatomical Distinction between the Sexes." *Sexuality and the Psychology of Love.* Ed. Philip Rieff. New York: Macmillan, 1963.

Gaines, Jane. "Dream/Factory." *Reinventing Film Studies.* Ed. Christine Gledhill and Linda Williams. London: Oxford University Press, 2000.

Gas, Food, Lodging. Dir. Allison Anders. IRS Media, 1992.

Gullette, Margaret Morganroth. "Wicked Powerful: The 'Postmaternal' in Contemporary Film and Psychoanalytic Theory." *Gender and Psychoanalysis* 5 (2000): 107–139, 149–154.

Karlyn, Kathleen Rowe. "*Scream*, Popular Culture, and Feminism's Third Wave: 'I'm Not My Mother.'" *Genders* 38 (2003).

Kleinhans, Chuck. "Melodrama and the Family under Capitalism." *Imitations of Life: A Reader on Film and Television Melodrama.* Ed. Marcia Landy. Detroit: Wayne State University Press, 1991. 197–204.

LaPlace, Maria. "Producing and Consuming the Woman's Film: Discursive Struggle in *Now, Voyager.*" *Home Is Where the Heart Is: Studies in Melodrama and the Woman's Film.* Ed. Christine Gledhill. London: British Film Institute, 1992. 138–166.

McCallum, E. L. "Mother Talk: Maternal Masquerade and the Problem of the Single Girl." *Camera Obscura: A Journal of Feminism, Culture, and Media Studies* 42 (1999): 71–94.

Neale, Steve. *Genre and Hollywood.* New York: Routledge, 2000.

Schatz, Thomas. "The Family Melodrama." *Imitations of Life: A Reader on Film and Television Melodrama.* Ed. Marcia Landy. Detroit: Wayne State University Press, 1991. 148–167.

Smith, Valerie. "Telling Family Secrets," in *Multiple Voices in Feminist Film Criticism*. Ed. Diane Carson et al. Minneapolis: University of Minnesota Press, 1994. 380–391.

Williams, Linda. " 'Something Else Besides a Mother': Stella Dallas the Maternal Melodrama." *Imitations of Life: A Reader on Film and Television Melodrama*. Ed. Marcia Landy. Detroit: Wayne State University Press, 1991. 307–330.

———. "Melodrama Revised." *Refiguring American Film Genres*. Ed. Nick Browne. Los Angeles: University of California Press, 1998. 42–88.

III

HORRIFIC MOTHERS AND THE
MOTHERS OF HORROR

SEVEN

HOLLYWOOD'S "MOMS"
AND POSTWAR AMERICA

Mike Chopra-Gant

Beneath this aurora of pitiable weakness is mom, the brass-breasted Baal, or mom, the thin and enfeebled martyr whose very urine, nevertheless, will etch glass.

—Philip Wylie 187

This young man, you had to feel sorry for him. After all, being dominated by an almost maniacal woman was enough to drive anyone to the extreme of, oh, well, let's go in.

—Alfred Hitchcock, trailer for *Psycho* (1960)

In an article examining representations of motherhood in Alfred Hitchcock's films, Bernard F. Dick suggested that *"for reasons that will always elude us,* Hitchcock wanted to explore the mother-child relationship" (239, my emphasis). One explanation frequently proffered for Hitchcock's persistent interest in the mother-child relationship is the director's experiences with his own mother.[1] But the force that motivated Hitchcock's interest in examining the mother-child relationship—and, more specifically, a particular kind of relationship between mothers and their children—need be neither as elusive as Dick suggests nor explained by this rather simplistic link to the personal history of the auteur director. Early in the period in which Hitchcock directed some of his classic explorations of the mother-child relationship—*Notorious*

(1946), *Psycho*, *The Birds* (1963), *Marnie* (1964)—a discourse about a particular kind of mother began to gather a momentum that would propel an allegorical maternal figure, the "mom," to a key position in postwar U.S. popular culture's conceptions of motherhood. In adopting the particular representational mode he used in constructing the mother figures in his films, Hitchcock registered not only the supposed traumas[2] of his own childhood but also these powerful discursive currents circulating throughout American culture in the postwar period.

According to Geoffrey Gorer's *The Americans: A Study in National Character*, the development of the figure of the "mom" can be traced back to the publication of Sidney Howard's play *The Silver Cord* in 1927. Since that time, according to Gorer, "many books and plays have been written in which she is the villain" (45). But the key moment in the passage of this figure into the popular imaginary came during World War II with the publication, in 1943, of Philip Wylie's *Generation of Vipers*. Although it was not the origin of discourses about momism, Wylie's book played such a central role in the development of these discourses and particularly in aiding their passage into the popular consciousness that it has frequently been treated as such both by Wylie's contemporaries (for example, Strecker) and by subsequent generations of scholars (see, for example, Cohan and Fischer). The reasons for this are not difficult to discern. Describing Wylie as "the 'superwriter' of the Forties and Fifties" (3), Clifford Bendau argues that Wylie became the "voice of America" (3) during the period. Wylie had been a successful writer since the late 1920s, working in advertising, public relations, and journalism as well as publishing science fiction novels and completing several screenplays that were made into movies. Even this background of literary success, however, gave little hint of the degree of influence that would be achieved by *Generation of Vipers*. As Bendau indicates, the book "was a blockbuster. The reception was nothing less than phenomenal" (25). When Farrar and Rinehart published Wylie's book in January 1943, they believed that the initial print run of four thousand copies would be too large (Keefer 102). It sold out in a week. By 1954, despite only being available in hardback, *Generation of Vipers* had sold one hundred and eighty thousand copies and continued to average five thousand sales per year (102). According to Keefer, Wylie became the "seer, prophet, and scourge-bearer of the Western World" (102). The extent of Wylie's influence on Hollywood's creative community in general, and Hitchcock in particular, is more difficult to assess, although it is inconceivable that this community would have been immune to the extraordinary impact of *Generation of Vipers*, and Wylie's vocation as a Hollywood screenwriter may have afforded him more direct access to Hollywood's filmmakers, enabling his ideas to spread in more subtle ways.[3] I would argue that the construction of female characters in the films I discuss here provides compelling evidence that Wylie's influence on Hollywood was considerable.

Wylie conceived the "mom" as a relatively new development that arose from an easing of the burdens of women in modern society. Previously, the strains of women's lives had either shortened those lives or led to the development of a strong character in those women who survived into old age, which militated against the development of momish tendencies: "until very recently, mom folded up and died of hard work somewhere in the middle of her life. Old ladies were scarce and those who managed to get old did so by making some remarkable inner adjustments and by virtue of a fabulous horniness of body, so that they lent to old age not only dignity but metal" (186). Modern life had, according to Wylie, changed the conditions for women, relieving them of many of the burdens they had borne in earlier times and, in the process, transformed them into voracious consumers who now imposed a new and infinite burden on men by expecting them to fulfill women's capricious consumer desires (186). Wylie was in no doubt that the power of this new generation of "moms" was a legacy of their earlier status as "Cinderellas" (184): men surrendered power to young women by placing them on a pedestal and worshipping them only to find that in middle age these "Cinderellas" retained this power, dominating their husbands and doting on their male children to such a degree that they produced generation after generation of infantilized men, incapable of breaking free from the "apron strings" and the "silver cord" (185) the "mom" used to bind her children to her. As Wylie put it: "Men live for her and die for her, dote upon her and whisper her name as they pass away, and I believe she has now achieved, in the hierarchy of miscellaneous articles, a spot next to the Bible and the Flag, being reckoned part of both in a way" (185–186). Notably, Wylie's rhetoric tends to focus on the dangerous aspects of the relationship between mom and son, rather than mom and daughter.

Film theory has tended to focus on another figure—the *femme fatale*—in considering the representation of women in the early postwar period, and has treated that figure as a distillation of a vague set of anxieties ranging from material concerns about the displacement of returning veterans from their jobs by the women who entered traditionally male areas of employment in aid of the war effort, to psychosexual anxieties about male castration provoked by the image of the sexually powerful female. While the "mom" has been relatively neglected by film studies in comparison with this figure, there are good reasons for thinking that, in historical terms, the "mom" was a representational figure of at least equal significance. First, while the *femme fatale* has been linked to a rather vague set of anxieties, the "mom" is rooted in a traceable set of historical discourses that were demonstrably significant during the period. Second, while the *films noir* in which the *femme fatale* characteristically featured have now been promoted by the canonizing activities of film scholars to a privileged position in which the films are understood to capture a sense of the postwar *zeitgeist*, examination of the rental revenues achieved by films in the years following the end of the war reveals that few *films noir* are to be found among the highest earning films of the time. In contrast, "mom"-like representations of women appeared in a number of the highest earning movies. Thus, the "mom" was a figure who enjoyed wider circulation in the popular movies of the time. Finally, the figure of the "mom" has proven to be an enduring one; as late as the mid-1970s, writers such as Hans Sebald still characterized momism as "The Silent Disease of America." While it is true that images of sexually powerful women may have been equally persistent, there have been clear changes of attitude toward such representations of women, while discourses about momism survived into the late twentieth century in a relatively unchanged form: the "mom" remained a *bête noire* of postwar American popular culture in a way that the *femme fatale* did not.

In the context of the immediate postwar period, it was certainly possible to discern a strong connection between discourses about momism and the immediate social situation, taking the form of a concern about the infantilization of men. Both momism and the military milieu were thought to produce overly dependent, infantilized men. Wylie was quite certain that "war is a demonstration of infantilism in man. It is a reduction of all his efforts, schemes, ideals, aims, hopes, faiths, purposes, plots and possessions to the nursery level. . . . There is no other way to look at war than as the final proof of the infantilism of man—the revelation of . . . his failure to achieve adulthood" (256). Edward A. Strecker took this argument even further in his book, *Their Mother's Sons: The Psychiatrist Examines an American Problem.* Strecker identified the existence of other relationships characterized by the same dynamics as that between a "mom" and son. Styling these as "mom surrogates," Strecker argued,

> The army is so structured that it could become a mom surrogate. . . . In a good army, there is a close dependence-relationship between soldiers and officers. The right kind of officer feels responsible for his men and in some sense regards them affectionately and protectingly as his children. . . . The stage would seem to be set for "child-soldier" "mom-officer" relationships, dangerously promoting immaturity. (117–118)

This conflation of military service with the male infantilization associated with unfettered momism illustrates the particular adaptation of discourses about momism to the sociohistorical circumstances of the immediate postwar period in America. Unsurprisingly, then, some of the most popular films released shortly after the war also feature easily recognizable images of momism, and, perhaps not surprisingly, focused on mother-son relationships.

The character of Madame Sebastian (played by Leopoldine Konstantin) in *Notorious* (1946) provides a particularly striking image of momism. Konstantin's performance perfectly captures some of the distinctive characteristics of the "mom" as this figure was constructed by Wylie and other contributors to discourses about momism, combining extreme overprotectiveness toward her son, Alex (Claude Rains)—amounting to a desire to bind him to her in a relationship of dependency—with extraordinary hostility toward anyone she perceives as representing a threat either to him or to the continuance of maternal domination of the son, particularly women who interest him romantically.

Madame Sebastian's momish proclivities are apparent from her first appearance in the film, manifested in the aura of palpable menace that Konstantin's remarkable performance creates. The scene begins with the arrival of Alicia Hubermann (Ingrid Bergman)—a woman working as an undercover agent for the American government and charged with the mission of infiltrating a cell of Nazis operating in Brazil—at Alex's mansion. Alicia has succeeded in gaining access to the group by playing on Alex's infatuation with her and in this scene she has been invited to the mansion for a dinner in order to meet Alex's mother and associates for the first time. The butler opens the front door and shows Alicia into an anteroom, where she waits for Alex. As Alicia waits, Madame Sebastian appears toward the rear of the shot, at the top of the imposing staircase, and begins to descend, filmed in a long shot from approximately Alicia's point of view. The editing of this scene, which shows Madame Sebastian's descent on the stairs and passage across the hallway toward Alicia, and the interposed shots of Alicia's nervous reaction, creates a feeling of intense dread about the meeting between the two women. Right before the two women meet, Madame Sebastian moves through a shadow before finally emerging into the light to greet Alicia. During their conversation, Konstantin's facial expressions—her smile which is not a smile; the cold, unflinching glare of her eyes—undermine her polite, solicitous words, investing the scene with an almost unbearable tension between the superficial level of the women's engagement with one another and the deeper reality of Madame Sebastian's feelings toward a woman she clearly perceives as a threat to her own relationship with her son. Their conversation does not last very long before this concealed level begins to rupture the conventions of polite conversation, when Madame Sebastian begins to call Alicia's political sympathies into doubt by questioning the real reason why Alicia's father—a Nazi activist working in the United States, shown being sentenced to imprisonment for treason in the film's opening scene—had not called her to give evidence at his trial. Open conflict between the two women is only avoided by the arrival of Alex in the room, which deflects his mother from her interrogation of Alicia.

Two later scenes make explicit both Madame Sebastian's dislike of Alicia and her intense desire to control Alex. In the first, Alex and his mother sit together in a box at the races waiting for Alicia to return to them. As Madame Sebastian observes, in a tone that combines both contempt and suspicion, that "Miss Hubermann has been gone a long time," Alex wonders whether his mother could try to "be a little more cordial to her." His suggestion that Madame Sebastian might attempt to smile at Alicia is met with her rebuke, "Wouldn't it be too much if we both grinned at her like idiots?"

In the second scene, Alex and his mother argue about his intention to marry Alicia. Madame Sebastian questions whether Alicia is a gold digger seeking to "capture the rich Alex Sebastian for a husband." When Alex dismisses this possibility, Madame Sebastian's response—"we will discuss it more fully tonight"—reveals the degree to which this Hollywood "mom" expects to control her son. Alex's rejection of this suggestion fully exposes the momish nature of the relationship between mother and son: "All these carping questions are just an expression of your own jealousy, just as you've always been jealous of any woman I've ever shown any interest in."

Figure 12. Alex's arrival momentarily suppresses his mother's hostile "momish" tendencies toward Alicia Hubermann in *Notorious* (1946).

Alex rejects his mother's attempts to control him by marrying Alicia without his mother's approval, but soon turns to his mother again for help when he discovers that his wife is an American agent. Late in the film, the scene in which Alex reveals his discovery to Madame Sebastian provides a remarkable display of domineering motherhood. As Alex tells her that there is a problem in his relationship with Alicia, Madame Sebastian allows herself a self-satisfied smile on hearing of her son's disenchantment with his new wife, assuming that this is a result of the latter's infidelity. She evinces disgust at Alex's tender memories of his relationship with Alicia, dismissing his thoughts of Alicia's "clinging kisses" as "foul memories" and, even as she comes to understand the true magnitude of the danger faced by her son as a result of his intimate relationship with an American spy, nevertheless takes the opportunity to reinforce her power by belittling him: "You're protected by the enormity of your stupidity." Finally she reasserts her dominant position, taking control of their plan to gradually poison Alicia in order to kill her without arousing the suspicion of their Nazi associates.

In *Generation of Vipers* Wylie presents an image of the "mom" as a masculinized type of womanhood: "mom, however, is a great little guy. Pulling pants on her by these words, let us look at mom" (189). Konstantin's performance in this scene employs several mannerisms that conform to this impression of the inversion of normative gender roles. When told of Alex's suspicions, Madame Sebastian reaches for a cigarette box beside her bed, tosses it onto the bed and takes out and lights a cigarette. Madame Sebastian's evident lack of concern about the need to maintain a normatively feminine appearance, revealed by her manner in throwing the box onto the bed, and apparent in the very masculine image she projects while sitting in bed with a cigarette dangling from her lips, contribute to the strong impression the scene creates of this character's façade of genteel motherliness being removed, and Madame Sebastian's true, masculinized, momish quality being revealed. Toward the end of this scene, the relative positioning of Alex and Madame Sebastian within the frame reveals the dynamics of dominance and subservience in their relationship. Still smoking her cigarette, Madame Sebastian stands alongside Alex, who sits hunched on the end of her bed with his head in hands, while she dictates how the pair will go about poisoning Alicia.

The same dynamics are evident in a later scene. One of the group of Nazi conspirators, Dr. Anderson (Rheinhold Schünzel), mistakenly picks up Alicia's poisoned coffee cup. As Alex and his mother react with alarm at the prospect that their associate might unwittingly take the poison intended for Alicia, there is a cut from a close-up shot of the cup to a close-up of Alicia's face as she realizes that the illness she has been experiencing is the result of Alex and his mother's progressive poisoning. Alicia looks from the coffee cup across the room at each of her poisoners in turn. As she does so, there is a cut to a shot in which the camera zooms into a close-up of Madame Sebastian's face, defiantly returning Alicia's look with her own chilling, unflinching glare. This is followed by a return to a close-up of Alicia's face and then a further cut to a shot zooming into a close-up of Alex's face, his eyes averted toward the newspaper he is reading. The defiance of Madame Sebastian's withering glower—returning Alicia's own look and revealing Madame Sebastian's plea-sure in Alicia's awareness of the plot against her and, in particular, her own role in that plot—juxtaposed against the conscious avoidance of eye contact in Alex's averted gaze signals the power dynamic between mother and son. Madame Sebastian is in control. She is poisoning Alicia while Alex merely follows her murderous instruction. This scene and the one that follows, in which Alex and Madame Sebastian are cast into black silhouettes, distorted by Alicia's increasingly hallucinatory perception, provide one of postwar Hollywood's most sinister and unsettling vision of demonic momism and its potentially awful consequences. As Bernard Dick rightly observes, "Mrs. Bates of *Psycho*, Lydia Brenner of *The Birds*, and Bernice Edgar of *Marnie* were models of motherhood compared to Madame Sebastian" (239).

In *Notorious*, Hitchcock provides us with a sustained and particularly extreme vision of momism. While Dick's mystification over the reasons why Hitchcock revisited the dynamics of mother-child relationships implies that these relationships were particular to that director's films, in reality the figure of the domineering mother was central to discourses about momism in a much wider range of postwar Hollywood films. In *The Green Years* (1946), another of the most popular films released the same year as *Notorious*, the figure of the "mom" is both less central to the film's plot and less sinister, but it nevertheless illustrates some of the distinctive characteristics of momism identified by Wylie and other contributors to discourses about "moms."

Observing that "megaloid momworship has got completely out of hand" (185), Wylie suggests that "our land, subjectively mapped, would have more silver cords and apron strings crisscrossing it than railroads and telephone wires" (185). This image of "silver cords" and "apron strings" used to bind children to their "moms" is a recurring trope in the discourses about momism. Strecker devotes a chapter to "Mom and her silver cord," in which he employs an image of umbilical dependence to characterize the relationship between a "mom" and her children:

> A mom does not untie the emotional apron string—the Silver Cord—which binds her children to her . . . [Moms] have one thing in common—the emotional satisfaction, almost repletion, [they derive] from keeping [their] children paddling about in a kind of psychological amniotic fluid rather than letting them swim away with the bold and decisive strokes of maturity from the emotional womb. (30–31)

In *The Green Years*, the character of Grandma Leckie (Gladys Cooper) plays the role of the "mom" and provides another striking image of domineering womanhood, especially in one particular scene that owes a great deal to the sort of imagery provided by discussions of "apron strings" and "silver cords." *The Green Years* presents the story of a young orphaned boy, Robert Shannon (played by Dean Stockwell), who is sent from Ireland to live in his maternal grandparents' home in Scotland following the death of his parents. Also living in this home are Robert's grandmother's father, Alexander Gow (Charles Coburn), and his grandfather's mother, Grandma Leckie, who occupy separate rooms at the top of the house. In the early parts of the film the household appears to be dominated by Robert's grandfather, Papa Leckie (Hume Cronyn), a petty official—assistant sanitation officer—who compensates for the insignificance of his occupation by attempting to exercise authority within the home, keeping tight control over household finances, and constantly belittling his wife through unrestrained expressions of disdain for her family and criticizing her efforts to run the household. He makes no secret of the fact that he resents the presence of his wife's father in the house. For the first few days after his arrival, Robert sleeps in his great-grandfather's bed and is entrusted to the old man's care during the daytime. The return of Grandma Leckie to the home after a few days radically changes the power dynamics within the house and the arrangements for Robert's care.

Grandma Leckie is a domineering matriarch who does not hesitate to overrule decisions made by her son concerning Robert's schooling, insisting that he should attend "The Academy," a more expensive and prestigious institution. Grandma Leckie then assumes responsibility for Robert's care and upbringing, overriding Grandpa Gow's objections, and insisting that the boy should sleep in her room and share her bed. Her most overtly momish action occurs, however, when she decides that Robert's only clothing is unsuitable to wear to his new school. Grandma Leckie decides to make him a new suit and, having taken the boy's measurements, opens her wardrobe and begins looking through dresses for an appropriate material from which to make the suit. Finding nothing suitable, she removes the skirt she is wearing and begins to scrutinize its many petticoats, removing one after another until she finds what she considers an appropriate material, a green cloth with a floral pattern. Despite Robert's objections, Grandma Leckie insists on making the suit from this material.

It is difficult to imagine a more explicit example of the "apron strings" discussed by Wylie, Strecker, Gorer, and other commentators than this suit, cut from a decidedly inappropriate fabric for a young man that literally envelopes the boy in his great grandmother's petticoat. Furthermore, this bright, patterned fabric threatens to feminize Robert in much the same way that Gorer suggested that the influence of American mothers over their children produced men with a feminized conscience:

> The idiosyncratic feature of the American conscience is that it is predominantly feminine. Owing to the major role played by the mother . . . far more aspects of the mother than of the father become incorporated . . . for the son, the American male, the situation is . . . complicated and confusing. He carries around, as if it were encapsulated inside him, an ethical, admonitory, censorious mother. (39)

Robert eventually rejects Grandma Leckie's suffocating care. His new suit marks him as an object of ridicule and target for bullying when he arrives at school, providing a visual reminder of his difference from his fellow pupils, not only because of his nationality and religion, but also because of the extraordinary dominance of Grandma Leckie over him, to which his flowery, colorful garment attests. A montage sequence shows the repeated bullying to which Robert is subjected at school. Desperately unhappy, the boy turns to Grandpa Gow for help. His great-grandfather advises that the boy must take on the most respected boy in the class in a fight, and instructs Robert in the pugilistic art. The ensuing scrap wins Robert the respect and friendship of his adversary and the other boys at the school. More importantly, however, his suit is destroyed in the skirmish, thereby severing Grandma Leckie's symbolic "silver cord." The remains of this symbol of matriarchal power are finally thrown onto the fire by Grandpa Gow. Encouraged by his great-grandfather, Robert begins to stand up to Grandma Leckie, insisting that he should be allowed to worship in his own faith and returned to the care of his great-grandfather. Although the image of domineering womanhood provided by Grandma Leckie amounts to only a relatively brief interlude in the film, its inclusion does have a particular resonance with the concerns about momism in the wider culture and demonstrates that these concerns were reflected in a much wider range of postwar Hollywood films than have generally been considered by film scholars.

While Madame Sebastian and Grandma Leckie may be the most notable major characters that exhibit momish characteristics in the most popular films released just after the war ended, several other contemporary movies featured more marginal characters that shared the distinctive features of the "mom." The gendered dynamics of power in the relationship between its main protagonists, Clint Maroon (Gary Cooper) and Clio Dulaine (Ingrid Bergman), are the central narrative concern of Saratoga Trunk (1945), but it is two relatively minor characters, Mrs. Bellop (Florence Bates) and Clarissa Van Steed (Ethel Griffies), who actually demonstrate the successful acquisition and maintenance of power by women, and both characters are constructed in ways that clearly conform to contemporary discourses about momism. Both are mature women, and both have risen to positions among the highest echelons of the social milieu that they inhabit. Clarissa

Van Steed conforms to the characteristics of the "mom" that typify both *Notorious* and *The Green Years*: she is an intimidating presence who expects to be able to exercise absolute control over her son, Bartholomew (John Warburton), and exhibits considerable hostility toward Clio, as a result of the latter's attempts to woo her son.

Mrs. Bellop presents a rather different case, however. This character does not conform to the common pattern of representations of momish women discussed so far: she is not intimidating or overtly domineering. Her character does, however, resonate with discourses about momism in other ways. Wylie described the "mom" as "a middle-aged puffin with the eye of a hawk that has just seen a rabbit twitch far below. She is about twenty-five pounds overweight, with no sprint, but sharp heels and a hard backhand which she does not regard as a foul but a womanly defense" (189). And, according to Wylie, the "mom" was not only sharp-witted, but also possessed a remarkable ability to live a life of ease on the back of the efforts of men:

> Nowadays, with nothing to do, and all the tens of thousands of men I wrote about in a preceding chapter to maintain her, every clattering prickamette in the republic survives for an incredible number of years. . . . The machine has deprived her of all social usefulness; time has stripped away her biological possibilities and poured her hide full of liquid soap; and man has sealed his own soul . . . by handing her the checkbook and going to work in service of her caprices. (186)

With her corpulent figure and self-confessed ability to live a life of considerable luxury through her sharp wits, despite having no wealth or income of her own, Mrs. Bellop's character exhibits a clear conformity with Wylie's image of the "mom."

Although relatively few in number, the films discussed here were all among the highest earning films released in the United States in the year after the end of World War II. With rental revenues amounting to $5.1 million, *Saratoga Trunk* was the fifth highest earning American movie in 1946. *Notorious* was sixth, with revenues of $4.9 million, while *The Green Years*, with earnings of $4.2 million, took fourteenth place among the top earners of the year. Images of momish women were, therefore, central features of some of the most popular movies of the time. Clearly, as the nation moved from war to peace, there was considerable concern within American culture about women and their position within the postwar social order, and both the figures of the "mom" and the *femme fatale* resonate with contemporary discourses about femininity. However, in devoting as much attention as it has to the figure of the *femme fatale*, film scholarship has tended to overlook or underestimate the significance of the "mom." The explanation that links the presence of momish women in Hitchcock's movies to the director's own childhood represents a clear instance of this, giving the figure a unique, personal connection to the biography of the filmmaker that completely ignores the pervasiveness of the "mom" figure throughout the culture as a whole.

While there is no denying the possibility that a director like Hitchcock may have had intensely personal reasons for his explorations of the dynamics of maternal domination, *Notorious* and the other films in which he continued to examine domineering motherhood (*Psycho*, *The Birds*, *Marnie*) also registered the concerns expressed in the discourses about momism circulating in the wider cultural context. For compelling evidence of the broader influence of these discourses on Hollywood's filmmakers and other cultural producers in postwar America, it is only necessary to look to performances of motherhood such as that offered by Ma Jarrett (Margaret Wycherly) in *White Heat* (1949) and Mrs. Stark (Ann Doran) in *Rebel Without a Cause* (1953), both of whom, in their construction of mature female characters, clearly continue the representational tradition to be found in the films discussed here. This distinctive mode for representing women arguably even extends to the performance of motherhood captured in the character of Endora (Agnes Moorehead) in the television series, *Bewitched* (1964–1972). While the generic conventions of the situation comedy rob this particular construction of motherhood of the more obviously sinister overtones of the mother figures found in the movies I have discussed, the same themes that dominate in the construction of those momish characters—particularly her possession of "unnatural" power over men—persist in the construction of this character who carries the discourses about momism not only into the late part of the twentieth century but also into a new medium, one which dominated that historical period in much the same way that film dominated the early postwar mediascape. As these examples illustrate, the "mom" provided a versatile representational figure that was historically persistent and transcended the boundaries of oeuvre, genre, and medium to articulate some of the fears and anxieties provoked by the idea of empowered femininity in the popular cultural productions of postwar America.

NOTES

1. Many of the numerous biographies of the director recount an intensely close relationship between Hitchcock and his mother. In *The Life of Alfred Hitchcock: The Dark Side of Genius*, Donald Spoto paints a vivid picture of a doting but also stern and controlling mother whose influence over Hitchcock persisted long into his adult life. In a similar vein, in her monograph on *The Birds*, Camille Paglia at one point describes the director as "the mother-bedevilled Hitchcock" (47).

2. Despite a general sense in the biographical literature of a childhood molded by a strict Catholic father and a doting but controlling mother, details of

specific traumatic instances are vague. Certainly Hitchcock's experiences at school seem to have been unpleasant (see Taylor 28–30) and memories of feelings of terror and abandonment when his parents once left him in the care of a maid while they went for a long walk seem to have left a deep impression in Hitchcock's memory of his childhood (see Spoto 18–19), but throughout the biographical literature there is a consistent sense that this and other incidents (such as being briefly locked in a police cell at his father's behest following some minor misbehavior) may have been embellished over the years by a man who was, above all, a master storyteller.

3. Among others, Wylie co-wrote the screenplay for *King of the Jungle* (1933), *Island of Lost Souls* (1933), *Under Suspicion* (1937), and *Charlie Chan in Reno* (1939). His 1930 novel, *The Gladiator*, was made into a movie in 1938 and was the inspiration for Superman, who also made his first appearance, in Action Comics, in 1938.

BIBLIOGRAPHY

Bendau, Clifford. *Still Worlds Collide: Philip Wylie and the End of the American Dream.* San Bernardino: Borgo Press, 1980.

Cohan, Steven. *Masked Men: Masculinity and the Movies in the Fifties.* Bloomington and Indianapolis: Indiana University Press, 1997.

Dick, Bernard F. "Hitchcock's Terrible Mothers." *Literature/Film Quarterly* 28.4 (2000): 238-249.

Fischer, Lucy. "Mama's Boy: Filial Hysteria in *White Heat*." *Screening the Male: Exploring Masculinities in Hollywood Cinema.* Ed. S. Cohan and I. R. Hark. London and New York: Routledge, 1993. 70-84.

Gorer, Geoffrey. *The Americans: A Study in National Character.* London: Cresset Press, 1948.

The Green Years. Dir. Victor Saville. MGM, 1946.

Howard, Sidney. *The Silver Cord.* New York: Scribner's, 1927.

Keefer, Truman Frederick. *Philip Wylie.* Boston: Twayne, 1977.

Notorious. Dir. Alfred Hitchcock. RKO Radio Productions, 1942.

Paglia, Camille. *The Birds.* London: BFI, 1998.

Rebello, Stephen. *Alfred Hitchcock and the Making of Psycho.* New York: St. Martin's Griffin, 1990.

Sebald, Hans. *Momism: The Silent Disease of America.* Chicago: Nelson Hall, 1976.

Spoto, Donald. *The Life of Alfred Hitchcock: The Dark Side of Genius.* London: Collins, 1983.

Strecker, E. A. *Their Mother's Sons: The Psychiatrist Examines an American Problem.* Philadelphia and New York: J. B. Lippincott, 1946.

Taylor, John R. *Hitch: The Life and Work of Alfred Hitchcock.* London and Boston: Faber and Faber, 1978.

Wylie, Philip. *Generation of Vipers.* New York and Toronto: Farrar and Rhinehart, 1943.

EIGHT

ALFRED HITCHCOCK AND THE

PHOBIC MATERNAL BODY

_____

Mun-Hou Lo

What's that old Oscar Wilde thing? "Each man kills the thing he loves. . . ."
That I think is a very natural phenomenon, really.

—Alfred Hitchcock, to Ian Cameron and V. F. Perkins, 1963

In the pantheon of our dearest Hollywood mommies, Mrs. Bates, mother to
Norman from Alfred Hitchcock's *Psycho* (1960), must surely hold a prominent
place. This despite the fact that she is never actually present in the film—as
Norman puts it, in a line that comes close to being a camp classic, mother
"isn't quite herself today"—except as a dead body, and in the form and figure of her cross-dressed son. If in this sense Mrs. Bates is pure construction,
then she has also seemed to some critics like a construction whose function
is pretty transparent and barely worthy of comment. In an essay entitled
"Unveiling Maternal Desires: Hitchcock and American Domesticity," Elsie B.
Michie undertakes a fine reading of "the way the mother is the vehicle for
but also resists . . . an idyllic image of the domestic sphere"; the Hitchcock
films Michie analyzes are *Shadow of a Doubt* (1943) and *The Man Who Knew
Too Much* (1956), because in them "the mother is represented not critically,
as in films like *Psycho, Notorious* (1945), *The Birds* (1963), and even *North
by Northwest* (1959), but positively" (29). As the brevity of Michie's mention
of *Psycho* suggests, there seems little else to say about Mrs. Bates, aside from
registering how she is obviously portrayed in a negative, "critical" fashion,

139

and the film, the implication goes, therefore does its cultural work simply through a straightforward vilification of the mother figure.

Far from being the equivalent of shooting fish in a barrel, however, a more sustained consideration of how the mother functions in *Psycho* is needed because that function is by no means simple. I want to begin by arguing that Hitchcock uses—"critically," indeed—the figure of Mrs. Bates to mark, within the filmic text, the homosexuality of Norman, but I will also move on to suggest, more importantly, how Hitchcock deploys this mother figure "beyond" the text to destabilize the sexual identities of its male spectators, a process that the film then confirms through its staging of spectatorial identifications. Furthermore, *Psycho* does not stop at such a "homosexualization" of its male viewers. Instead, the film constructs what I will show is a paranoid position for its viewers to occupy. While this might be said—indeed, has been said—to be true of thrillers and even film in general, *Psycho*, I will argue, is systematic in the construction of this position, and, further, even enforces an occupation of that position by inscribing into the movie the symptoms of paranoia for the viewer to "experience." In so doing, Hitchcock schools his male viewers from identification into a repudiation of homosexuality, a phobic reaction that depends on violence toward the maternal body.

As that outline of my argument suggests, I will therefore focus chiefly on the psychic male spectator, and the ways this figure is, we might say, subjected by the film—especially through its representation of the mother—and its surrounding discourses. This statement, and the assumptions behind it, deserve elaboration on three fronts. The first has to do with the notion of the film's "psychic spectators." In "When Women Look: A Sequel," one of her several essays on the reception of *Psycho*, Linda Williams usefully points out that "the conventional distinction that often gets drawn [in film studies] is between hypothetical spectators addressed by films (psychic subjects constructed by the institution of cinema and individual film texts) and 'real' viewers (actual people who make up audiences, possessing certain shared social identities in addition to unique histories)" (paragraph 5). However, Williams continues, it is impossible to speak of the hypothetical spectators that a film constructs without the category also including actual viewers; "real people," she points out, "do not escape being addressed by texts and addressed by ideology" (paragraph 5), and indeed, we might say that if a film is "successful" in producing the viewing positions it wants, then the two "kinds" of viewers will coincide perfectly. Whether or not this coincidence occurs in the case of *Psycho* does not concern me, interested as I am in what the film attempts to do, and less in its success; because of this, I will mostly speak of the film's "psychic" or "hypothetical" spectators. Second, it should already be clear that I am most interested in the male viewers of the film—in contrast, for example, to Williams's essay, which strives to "speak, as much as possible, of the *actual experiences* of the women who saw the film on its initial release in 1960" (paragraph 5) and would thus be a good place to look for another side to the story. I do this because I believe that that is where the film concentrates its energy, and because an examination of how the film manages its male viewers through its construction of the mother figure seems to me a rich way of thinking about the intersections of sexuality and gender in the film. Which leads to a final point: because I am examining the more performative aspects of *Psycho*, focusing on the way the film tries to produce certain kinds of identifications and reactions, this chapter may seem especially speculative, not to say paranoid, in places; but by analyzing the film and its surrounding discourses (Hitchcock's statements about the film, critical reactions to it), I hope to shed new light on the cultural work done by the movie, which is, after all, a horror picture whose *raison d'être* is precisely to have an impact on its audience.

When his badly received remake of *Psycho* was released in 1998, Gus Van Sant sat down for a chat with Paige Powell for *Interview* magazine. "What character," Powell asks at one point, "do you identify with most in *Psycho*? I was surprised you didn't cast yourself as Norman Bates." It is a queer notion, given that Van Sant has never appeared as an actor in his films, or any film, but the thinking behind Powell's question becomes clearer as the interview proceeds. After Van Sant replies that he "probably identif[ies] less with the Norman Bates character than with how Anthony Perkins [the original Bates] appears physically," and that he is "not sure [he] relate[s] to Norman's living with his mother and working at a motel in the middle of nowhere," Powell follows up with a query whose relation to the first was embarrassingly obvious: "Do you think Hitchcock had anything off-screen in mind when he cast Perkins as the schizophrenic, possibly gay Norman Bates?" Why, of course: Norman Bates is "possibly gay"; Hitchcock cast Perkins because he suspected the actor might be gay; Van Sant is openly gay and thus identified with Norman, and really should have just gone ahead and played the role already.

Powell is hardly the first—although, in her baiting of Van Sant, she may be among the clumsiest—to allude to Norman's "possible homosexuality." Many years earlier, the much more influential critic Robin Wood had wondered in "The Murderous Gays," a chapter of his *Hitchcock's Films Revisited*, "which, in fact, *are* Hitchcock's gay characters?" (345) Noting that no "inconvertible evidence" can be found for the homosexuality of candidates such as Norman, Wood remarks that a case can only be made if we relied on "heterosexist mythology" (336). In pre-1960s Hollywood, Wood points out, "homosexuality had to be coded, and discreetly, and coding, even when indiscreet, is notoriously likely to produce ambiguities and uncertainties" (346). Implicitly elaborating on Wood's point, D. A. Miller, in a seminal reading of Hitchcock's *Rope* (1948), has argued that both "the famously hardass [Hays] Production Code in force" (until October 1961), as well as "the cultural surround of legal, social, psychic, and aesthetic practices (that last including those of spectatorship) that tolerate homosexuality only on condition that it be kept out of sight" meant that the "representation of homosexuality" in classic Hollywood films such as Hitchcock's—and arguably beyond—must always be "consigned to connotation" (123).

And what a consignment we have in *Psycho*, chock-full as it is with second-order signs—what Wood might call "heterosexist mythology"—of Norman's queerness, his "homosexuality" (albeit one that is largely based, and not inconveniently either, as it will turn out, on a model of gender inversion). To rehearse just a few of the most amusing, we might recall, for example, the suggestively named "fruit cellar" to which Mrs. Bates is relegated, or remind ourselves of Mrs. Bates's supposed quarrel with her son: "As if men desire strangers! Ah! I refuse to speak of disgusting things, because they disgust me! Do you understand, boy?" Not only do these lines conjure up the specter of anonymous gay male sex, but they simultaneously present the classic trope of "unspeakability" for which the love that dares not speak its name is famous. But to focus on these instances of winking puns and allusions might be to miss the forest for the trees, since Norman's queer sexuality is most strongly connoted by his relationship to his mother. Near the end of the film, the court-appointed psychiatrist Dr. Simon goes on about how "Mrs. Bates was a clinging, demanding woman, and for years the two of them lived as if there was no one else in the world." This faux-medical verdict confirms what viewers will have already suspected by that point: that Norman is a "mama's boy," a major player in the by-now familiar drama of the homosexual as the son who never outgrew, or can never outgrow, his mother.

How did this stereotype of the gay mama's boy arise? I have elsewhere tried to sketch out a brief genealogy (Lo 441–443), but even there, as is the case here, I am much less interested in providing a history of this associa-tion of the maternal and male homosexuality, and much more intrigued by the uses to which this linkage has been put. That history, however, would certainly feature Freud, who in "Leonardo Da Vinci and a Memory of his Childhood" (1910), suggests that the "psychical genesis of homosexuality" can be understood once we notice how "in all our male homosexual cases the subjects have had a very intense erotic attachment to a female person, as a rule their mother, during the first period of childhood, which is afterwards forgotten; this attachment was evoked or encouraged by too much tenderness on the part of the mother herself, and further reinforced by the small part played by the father during their childhood" (98–99). But, more significantly, we might look to Freud's popularizers, foremost among whom is Irving Bieber. In 1962, Bieber and his team of researchers, assuming that homosexuality is an acquired illness to be cured, published a study (reissued as an affordable paperback a few years later) that contained the insight that the " 'classical' homosexual triangular pattern is one where the mother is CBI [i.e., Close Binding Intimate] and is dominant and minimizing toward a husband who is a detached father, particularly a hostile-detached one." "From our statistical analysis," Bieber concluded, "the chances appear to be high that any son exposed to this parental combination will become homosexual or develop severe homosexual problems" (172). The Bieber study is usually credited—if we can call it credit—with popularizing and providing "scientific" support for the connection between male homosexuality and maternity in American culture, but *Psycho*, two years earlier, might have been even more effective at scapegoating mothers for their son's homosexuality.

What is powerful about this cultural tactic is that no one can ever be sure that a mother is not already too *much* of a mother. Who is to say, after all, where is the line that separates "appropriate" from "excessive" mothering? How much "tenderness" is "too much," and how can a mother ever be sure that she has not "evoked or encouraged" that supposedly extravagant tenderness? Further, given how universal mothers are, who can claim with confidence that they do not have someone in their lives who is ready to turn, or has already turned, them gay? In his essay, Miller reports a conversation from a Barbara Pym novel that makes this point. "He strikes one as the kind of person who would have a mother.—Well, everyone has or had a mother. But I see just what you mean" (qtd. in Miller 120). In Pym's novel, the conversation no doubt alludes to the shaky sexuality of one character in question, but in reminding us that "everyone has or had a mother," the sly exchange also drives home the point that every man is *always* in some danger of having a mother who is a little much. Because every man has a mother, every man is always already at risk of being overmothered.

Against this backdrop, Hitchcock, presenting a film about a man and his "clinging, demanding" mother, to some degree must have raised for his male viewers the specter of their own relationships to their mothers. If in *Psycho*, therefore, Norman's homosexuality is connoted by means of his "dysfunctional" relationship to his mother, then this is a method whose expediency is not limited to on-screen theatrics. In other words, the mother is used in *Psycho* not just to connote diegetically the possible homosexuality of Norman, but also, extradiegetically, to question its male spectators. That is what makes it a potent signifier: most male viewers may be able to distinguish themselves from Norman's cross-dressing, and still more may be able to safely distance themselves, say, from having something so strange as a "fruit cellar"—but not a single male audience member can be absolutely sure that he is not in some ways like Norman in *having a mother*. I am not suggesting, of course, that *Psycho* is a film that has had massive and untempered success in making its male viewers question their sexualities. (Although we have on record at least one man who appeared to have been successfully rattled. Faced with what he calls Norman's "takeover by this fantasmal mother," critic Keith

Cohen nakedly confesses: "it leaves me quaking with sexual undifferentia-tion" [159].) Instead, I am merely noting that we can discern, in and beyond the film, signs—whose systematic nature I want to point out—of such an investment in toying with its audience this way.

Hitchcock in fact has a well-documented fondness for playing with his viewers, often seeming to enjoy what goes on beyond the screen more than he does what is on it, and *Psycho* brought out this peccadillo espe-cially strongly. "*Psycho* has a very interesting construction," Hitchcock has said, "and that game with the audience was fascinating. I was directing the viewers. You might say I was playing them, like an organ" (qtd. in Truffaut 269).[1] Quite. Or again:

> My main satisfaction is that the film had an effect on the audiences, and I consider that very important.... It wasn't a great message that stirred the audiences, nor was it a great performance or their enjoyment of the novel. They were aroused by pure film.... I also know that the construction of the story and the way in which it was told caused audiences all over the world to react and become emotional. (qtd. in Truffaut 282–283)

Hitchcock's desire to reach out and "arouse" his audience is further reflected in one of the two additions that Hitchcock made to Saul Bass's storyboard-ing of the shower sequence. He wanted an "impression of a knife slashing, as if tearing at the very screen, ripping the film" (Spoto 419), as if the force of the film's aggression is not so much directed at Marion as it is at the audience.

Still, any film's effort to destabilize its male spectators' sexual identities simply through the figure of the mother is likely to be a game of chance. To increase its odds, *Psycho* works harder, playing out for us a drama of what it might mean to feel or see like a homosexual. At the center of the film lies a puzzle that Hitchcock has managed to render resolvable, and thus make seemingly inconsequential and invisible *as* a puzzle. *Psycho* is the picture famous for "kill[ing] its star in the first third of the film" (Truffaut 269)—and here we should understand "star" as meaning both *within* the picture (Marion, the apparent protagonist) and *outside* of it (Janet Leigh, the biggest name)—in a shower slashing that has become classic. Hitchcock himself has mostly passed off this move as only serving a suspenseful, and never an ideological, function. But explaining this murder purely in terms of a desire to shock, as Hitchcock does and many others also do, can serve to obscure the more disciplinary aspects of the movie.

These aspects begin to come to light when we look past the obvious shock value of the slashing and instead consider it from the perspective of identification. Hitchcock characterizes "the first part of the story [as] a red herring."

> That was deliberate, you see, to detract the viewer's attention in order to heighten the murder. We purposely made the beginning on the long side, with the bit about the theft and her escape, in order to get the audience absorbed with the question of whether she would or would not be caught. . . . The more we go into the details of the girl's journey, the more the audience becomes absorbed with her flight. (qtd. in Truffaut 269)

Despite its continued adherence to the party line ("to heighten the murder"), Hitchcock's comment does also demonstrate his wish to get the audience "absorbed" in Marion's adventures; this has provided the cue for astute critics to understand the sudden slashing in terms of audience identification. In his chapter on *Psycho*, Wood, for instance, saw the murder as constituting

> an alienation effect so shattering that (at a first viewing of the film) we scarcely recover from it. Never—not even in *Vertigo*—has identification been broken off so brutally. At the time, so engrossed are we in Marion, so secure in her potential salvation, that we can scarcely believe it is happening; when it is over, and she is dead, we are left shocked, with nothing to cling to, the apparent center of the film entirely dissolved.
>   Needing a new center, we attach ourselves to Norman Bates, the only other character (at this point) available. We have been carefully prepared for this shift of sympathies. (146)

As Wood details, the film does much to encourage our identification with Norman, beginning with the careful way in which the film gives us no real choice, seeing as how Norman is "the only other character" around when Marion meets her grisly end. That identification, we might further notice, is sealed shortly after the slashing. Norman has carefully removed all traces of the murder and placed Marion's body in the car, and we then see him push the car into a swamp; in a series of countershots, we watch Norman watch it sink. But there is a sudden stop to this sinking, a stop marked by a halt in the sound effects that had (unrealistically) been a bubbling noise. At this point, "when the car stops sinking for a moment," Hitchcock explains, relishing the notion that his audience now roots for a murderer, "the public is thinking, 'I hope it goes down!'" (qtd. in Truffaut 272). This moment—or rather, what Hitchcock desires of this moment—most strongly endorses Wood's argument of the intended switch in audience identification.

"Switch" is the operative word here: what Hitchcock wants and strives for, it would seem, is a certain trajectory of identification. In killing off Marion, Hitchcock pushes the male spectator to shift his identification from a woman to a man—despite or rather because this "man" will turn out to be only half a man, or maybe even no(r)-man at all. The important thing about what Raymond Bellour twice calls the "substitution" (314, 320) of Norman for Marion is not just that we *end up* identifying with Norman; rather, it is that we *move* from (being pushed into) identifying with Marion, to identifying with Norman. After all, if what is important is simply identification with Norman, Hitchcock could have introduced Norman from the start, made him the more obvious and immediate central character.

That it is the switch and not the final identification that is crucial can be gleaned from Hitchcock's famous insistence that "the audiences be kept out of the theaters once the picture had started, because the latecomers would have been waiting to see Janet Leigh after she had disappeared from the screen action" (qtd. in Truffaut 269).[2] This explanation for why we need to be along for the *entire* ride is not really adequate. After all, despite the killing, no one would miss Leigh unless he or she walks into the theater an hour late, and in any case, it is slightly incongruous to find this director, famed as he is for cameo appearances that the audience always has to work to spot, worried about our missing a promised star. What Hitchcock's spiel really suggests is how important it is to him that an audience *first* identifies with Marion, and *then* with Norman. By attempting a segue from Marion's perspective to Norman's, the film solidifies, and more importantly, *enacts* a definition of homosexuality as gender inversion, by configuring the woman and the homosexual as interchangeable, as "substitutes." Watching *Psycho*, a male spectator might be forgiven for thinking about his own relationship to his mother and wondering how he ended up seeing things through the eyes of women and homosexuals.

Often recognized as "the quintessential horror film" (Modleski 102) or the "immediate ancestor of the slasher film" (Clover 192), *Psycho* possesses a horror that is particularly Gothic. The film's Gothic style is not hard to notice: the decision to shoot in black and white, the perpetually dark-and-stormy-night setting of the film, and the look of the Bates mansion—which Hitchcock described as "California Gothic" ("I felt that type of architecture would help the atmosphere of the yarn," the director notes [qtd. in Truffaut 269])—all help to give the film its recognizably oppressive feel.

Psycho does not merely follow the Gothic *style*, but adheres as well to the genre's *themes*, foremost among which may be an interest in paranoia, and, concomitantly, its relation to a specific kind of sexuality. In her classic study *Between Men* (especially chapters 5 and 6), Eve Kosofsky Sedgwick argues that we first see a thematization of homophobia in the English Gothic novel through its plots of paranoia. Because paranoia, as Jean Laplanche and J. B. Pontalis bluntly remark, "is defined in psychoanalysis, whatever the variations in its delusional modes, as a defence against homosexuality" (297), what such Gothic novels present are portraits of men whose para-noia always seems to be a fear of how their sexuality might turn out. And such paranoia, in the Gothic, often attaches itself to a specific figure: the mother. In a preface to the revised edition of her first book, more properly devoted to the Gothic, Sedgwick outlines what she sees to be the structure of Gothic novels, noting that they predictably feature a "classic paranoid" as the male protagonist, and a "classic hysteric" as his female counterpart. " 'Hysteria' and 'paranoia,' " Sedgwick observes, "as psychoanalytic entities, are kept distinct by, among other things, insistent gender markings." Critical treatments, Sedgwick points out, therefore tend to either concentrate on either "the feminocentric or hysterically-oriented" plot, or the "masculocen-tric or paranoiacally-oriented" aspect; a typical slogan for the first kind of reading might be the Barbara Johnson title "My Monster/My Self," while a dictum for the second focus might be "it takes one to know one" (*Coher-ence* vii–viii). However, as Sedgwick's subsequent work in *Between Men*, on male homosocial desire, makes clearer, "arguably in most Gothic novels, the male paranoid plot is not separate from the maternal or monstrous plot; instead, there is articulated within the text a male paranoid *reading* of maternity" (*Coherence* ix).

What Sedgwick calls a "male paranoid reading of maternity" certainly prevails in *Psycho*, where the male paranoia is about being transformed *into* the monstrous mother. At the conclusion of the film, Norman sits isolated in a cell, wrapped in a blanket; as the camera tracks and draws him into the center of the frame, we hear Mrs. Bates's voice "[speak] the words that condemn her own son," concluding with repeated assertions: "they are probably watching me . . . I hope they are watching, they will see." The fears of persecution and surveillance that Norman here exhibits are usually held as exemplary of paranoia—held, for one, by Freud, whose case study of Dr. Paul Schreber might just as easily be a study of Norman. Accord-ing to Freud, for example, the "idea of being transformed into a woman was the most salient feature and the earliest gem of [Schreber's] delusional system" ("Psychoanalytic Notes" 117), and by the end of *Psycho*, Norman "no longer exists," having been taken over by his mother. Further, if we believe the film's psychiatrist when he tells us that Norman "murdered his mother and her lover [because] it seemed to Norman that she threw him over for this man," then "Mrs. Bates's" eventual murder of Marion appears to be the result of projection: Norman's delusional jealousy of his mother (and her new lover) becomes transformed into *her* jealousy of his potential new lover, Marion. For Freud, this kind of delusional jealousy, whereby your jealousy of someone mutates instead into his or her jealousy of you, "rightly takes its position among the classical forms of paranoia" ("Some Neurotic Mechanisms" 225).

But Norman isn't the only one constructed by the film as paranoid—or specifically, paranoid about monstrous maternity—though the film does seem to go out of its way to map, even clumsily, such a psychological schema onto Norman's tale. What is more remarkable is the way we have a horror film depicting paranoia that is also dependent on something quite akin to it. Earlier, I pointed out Hitchcock's oft-stated desire to make a visceral impact on his audience, but that statement of his desire was more generic than it should have been. To be more specific, the emotion that Hitchcock wanted to engender in his spectators might most properly be considered "paranoia," and this becomes clearer in light of two remarks he made. First: "fear, you see, is an emotion people like to feel when they know they are safe" (Spoto 39). And then, more specifically, a comment about *Psycho*: "The showing of a violent murder at the beginning was intended purely to instill into the minds of the audience a certain degree of fear of what is to come. Actually in the film, as it goes on, there's less and less violence because it has been transferred to the minds of the audience" (Rebello 121). These comments make clear the fact that Hitchcock—or perhaps horror films in general—encourage and depend on a kind of internalized spectatorial paranoia. For, without losing sight of the Freudian definition of paranoia as a defense against homosexuality, we should also remember that "paranoia" is of course much more encompassing a term. Etymologically meaning a "disorder of the mind," the Greek word "paranoia," Leo Bersani tells us, "has had an extraordinarily complex medical, psychiatric, and psychoanalytic history. . . . [Not only could it mean] something like unfounded suspicions about a hostile environment, but the fear of persecution is only one aspect of a symptomatological picture that has included such things as delusions of grandeur, schizophrenic dissociation, and erotomania" (179). The one thing that *is* constant about the history of the word, however, is that paranoia is always delusionary, a description that applies to the experience of film, and the horror film in particular. For the "horror" of a flick like *Psycho* always relies on our fears and fearful expectations that something is about to happen—so much so that when nothing does, it can also be a profound shock. In that sense, watching a horror film may be always already an experience of paranoia, encouraged as we are endlessly to expect something to happen, and endlessly ridiculed for our sometimes groundless expectations (or perhaps "always groundless," since we are more than likely to leave the theater in one piece).[3]

For a male spectator, that paranoia may be especially profound. Culturally, of course, paranoia, but also fear and nervousness in general, tend to be associated with women. (This is not contradicted by Freud's linkage of paranoia with male homosexuality, since this connection depends on a conceptualization of homosexuality as feminine, as Mary Ann Doane has observed: "Because Freud defines a passive homosexual current as feminine, paranoia, whether male or female, involves the adoption of a feminine position" [129].) As a consequence of the feminization of passive fear, as Williams also remarks intuitively, a man "has to make it a point of honor to look [at images of horror], while little girls and grown women cover their eyes or hide behind the shoulders of their dates" ("When a Woman Looks" 83). This point is in fact quietly inscribed in *Psycho*, via the difference between two of Lila Crane's intrusions into fearful spaces. When she searches the motel room with Sam Loomis, the camera makes no explicit attempts to induce fears in the audience that Norman would arrive on the scene. In contrast, Lila's solo sojourn into Mrs. Bates's room is filmed using lots of countershots that either loom menacingly (for instance, the close-up of the bronzed hands), or withhold information (as when Lila picks up and opens a book, and then recoils in disgust, but we are denied a view of its contents). It is as if the very presence of a man helps the viewer feel a little less paranoid. The paranoia that *Psycho* engenders is therefore not only psychoanalytically feminine, but diegetically inscribed as such.

Furthermore, in *Psycho*, that inscription is engendered forcefully. Hitchcock has gone so far as to claim that Marion's sudden murder was pretty much the *only* reason why he wanted to do the film. "I think," he said, "that the thing that appealed to me and made me decide to do the picture was the suddenness of the murder in the shower, coming, as it were, out of the blue. That was about all" (qtd. in Truffaut 268–269). The coup that Hitchcock pulls off via the shocking slashing of Marion works precisely to impeach the male viewers, like Marion, for not being paranoid *enough*. From then on, if we weren't already paranoid, it would seem as if we had every reason to be: just because you're paranoid, after all, doesn't mean they're not out to get you.

What *Psycho* does, therefore, goes beyond depicting a paranoid man with fears of turning into his mother; instead, it puts viewers into a position of paranoia. But finally, the film even enforces a kind of occupation of that position by supplying the symptoms of such spectatorial paranoia for viewers to "experience." We can begin to appreciate this when we consider the way the film showcases certain murders. For all its shock value, Marion's murder may not be, in the logic of the film, the most traumatic. Rather, the one murder that is unrepresented—unrepresentable—is Norman's matricide. Notwithstanding the issue of suspense (which the film could always circumvent—say, by showing the matricide in flashback), the omission of this scene marks it as the repressed primal scene. For Norman, this is literally the case. In the film, the sheriff hints at this, initially believing that "Mrs. Bates poisoned this guy she was—involved with, when she found out he was married—then took a helping of the same stuff herself." His wife then chips in: "Norman found them dead together. In bed." As it turns out, it may have been more the case, according to the psychiatrist, that Norman "murdered his mother and her lover . . . it seemed to Norman that she threw him over for this man. Now that pushed him over the line and he killed them both." Presenting two explanations that are not exactly commensurate, the film leaves open the possibility that Mrs. Bates and her lover were not found "dead together, in bed" by Norman, but perhaps found "in bed," and then "dead together."

The primal scene, according to Doane, building on the work of Guy Rosolato, may be considered the scene in which paranoia is first constituted:

> The fixation to the primal scene elucidates the paranoiac's activation of sound and image as the material supports of the symptom (the obsessions with "hearing voices" and "being watched"). For the young child watching and listening to its parents in the primal scene must itself remain unseen, unheard. As Rosolato points out, sound has a double polarity at the level of this originary fantasy. For it can potentially "betray" not only the parents but the little voyeur as well: sound would expose the parents for their act and the child for its desire to see that act. Sound exists, in this context, as a betrayal of the desire to see. (132)

Certainly for Norman and his paranoia, Doane's theorization would seem to apply; after all, in the concluding sequence of the film, with Mrs. Bates's skull and her voice-over, he fears "being watched," and "hears voices." But, once again, I want to shift the focus away from Norman to his spectators. If the primal scene was witnessed by Norman—who, if we follow Doane, is thereby formed as paranoid by this witnessing—then why would the film conversely deny the scene to us, the spectators?

I want to suggest that the presiding scene is cinematically absent because only its absence will allow for its reconstruction—its reconstruction by a spectator, that is. The usual understanding of Freud's primal scene, whereby the child observes his parents in the act of intercourse, is that it is a memory after the fact. For instance, Kaja Silverman argues that "the primal scene occurs not so much in 'reality' as in fantasy. . . . It is a construction after the fact, subsequent to an event with which it is by no means commensurate. The primal scene, in other words, never actually 'happens' as such, but is either constituted through a deferred action . . . or constructed as a fantasy on the basis of some remembered detail. It is consequently 'marked' as an image" (164). By avoiding a direct representation of the primal scene in *Psycho*, Hitchcock allows, even demands, that his spectators, working from several discrete conversations, piece together the scene themselves. Hitchcock thereby places his spectators in the exact position of needing to reconstruct and remember what in fact we never saw at all. This process of (re)construction, in fact, might be exemplary of what Lee Edelman would term "(be)hindsight"; indeed, for Edelman, the very practice of psychoanalysis can be construed in terms of such (be)hindsight, that is, "in terms of metalepsis, a rhetorical term that denotes the substitution of cause for effect or effect for cause, a substitution that disturbs that relationship of early and late, or before and behind" (176).

In *Psycho*, such "(be)hindsight" functions as a way for the film to allow its viewers to "experience" the symptoms of spectatorial paranoia. In this light, it is almost unnecessary to remind ourselves that the famous final sequence of "seeing things" and "hearing voices" to which I have already alluded, in which Mrs. Bates's skull appears for a fleeting moment on Norman's face, is played *for the spectator*. It is, after all, not Norman who sees this grisly vision, but the spectator who does. It is likewise we who hear the mother's voice, and discern what is only slowly distinguishable as Marion's car being recovered from the swamp. In fact, some prints of the film do not have the superimposition of the mother's skull at all. According to Stephen Rebello, Hitchcock "just wasn't sure which version he wanted to put in the release print—with or without the subliminal cut of Mother's death skull smiling out from [Norman's] face." He said: "It's got to be on

Figure 13. Now you see it, now you don't: Norman's brief death mask in *Psycho* (1960).

and off that [snapping his fingers] quickly. I want the audience to say, 'Did I *see* that?' " (134–135). In effect, by only having only *some* prints of the film with the "subliminal cut," Hitchcock compounds the uncertainty of our vision of the dead mother; according to *Psycho*, this vision can only be a paranoid vision, and the spectator only a paranoid case.

If *Psycho* therefore turns its male viewers into paranoid cases, with the symptoms of paranoia on full display, it also teaches them how to overcome, expel, and banish these symptoms and their troublesome condition. By doing this, *Psycho* attains the status of aversion therapy, and this is why the mother's body in this picture can rightly be termed "phobic." Earlier, I suggested that the film conforms in many ways to classic Gothic tropes, and that Norman's case shares certain affinities with Freud's study of Dr. Schreber. But the film also introduces a crucial modification. Both the Freudian scenario and the Gothic tradition would lead us to expect Norman's persecuting double to be another man. According to Freud, the paranoiac's originary homosexual desire ("I, a man, love him") has to be contradicted by the assertion that "I do not love him, I hate him." As a result, Freud suggests, in a by-now famous formulation,

> the proposition "I hate him" becomes transformed by projection into another one: "He hates (persecutes) me, which will justify me in hating him." And thus the unconscious feeling, which is in fact the motive force, makes its appearance as though it were the consequences of an external perception:
> "I do not *love* him—I *hate* him, because HE PERSECUTES ME."
> Observation leaves room for no doubt that the persecutor is some one who was once loved. ("Psychoanalytic Notes" 166)

In *Psycho*, however, it is Mrs. Bates who assumes the place of this perse-cuting double, and it is this double that it is the thrust of paranoia to kill off. To put this more explicitly, *Psycho* continues the Gothic tradition of counseling a murderous homophobia as response to homosexuality, but it shifts the lesson ever so slightly to imply that this "necessary" homophobia can only be constituted by our constantly seeking to cast out the mother in ourselves. Homophobic paranoia in *Psycho* is thus not "only" directed against gay men, but also, through the figure of the mother, against women. Not quite the old Oscar Wilde thing: each man must kill the thing, the mother figure, he loves, because only then can he *be* a man.

ACKNOWLEDGMENTS

Thanks to Diana Fuss and Paul Tschudi.

NOTES

1. Hitchcock's fondness for "directing" his viewers contrasts interestingly with his just as well-documented annoyance at directing performers (or his annoyance at them, period). "Actors!" he notoriously proclaimed. "I hate the sight of them! Actors are cattle—actresses too!" Little wonder that James Stewart, during the filming of *Rope*, complained about how the "really important thing being rehearsed here is the camera, not the actors!" (qtd. in Spoto 301 and 306).

2. For a fuller account of Hitchcock's insistence in this arena, see Williams, "Discipline and Distraction" (especially 103–115), who credits *Psycho* for "transform[ing] the previously casual act of going to the movies into a much more disciplined activity of arriving on time and waiting in an orderly line" (104). Williams is therefore more interested in the general disciplinary innovations introduced by *Psycho*; although she discusses this in the context of how the film "violated spectatorial identification with a main character" (108), she doesn't fully consider the way the identification is switched, or the sexual implications of the move.

3. At least two critics have suggested that paranoia inheres in film and filmwatching in general. Jacqueline Rose has theorized, using a Lacanian definition of "paranoia" and Hitchcock's *The Birds* as her key example, that, when threatened with instability and reversal, the film system pushes its inherent paranoia to the narrative surface. Even more generally, Robert Scholes argues that "narrativity," "the process by which a perceiver actively constructs a story from the fictional data provided by any narrative medium," is a kind of "licensed and benign paranoia [since the] interpreter of a narrative process assumes a purposefulness in the activities of narration" (286, 289).

BIBLIOGRAPHY

Bellour, Raymond. "Psychosis, Neurosis, Perversion." *A Hitchcock Reader*. Ed. Marshall Deutelbaum and Leland Poague. Ames: Iowa State University Press, 1986.

Bersani, Leo. *The Culture of Redemption*. Cambridge and London: Harvard University Press, 1990.

Bieber, Irving, et al. *Homosexuality: A Psychoanalytic Study of Male Homosexuals*. New York: Vintage, 1965.

Cameron, Ian, and V. F. Perkins. "Interview with Alfred Hitchcock." *Movie* 6 (1963): 4–6.

Clover, Carol J. "Her Body, Himself: Gender in the Slasher Film." *Representations* 20 (Fall 1987): 187–228.

Cohen, Keith. "*Psycho*: The Suppression of Female Desire (and Its Return)." *Reading Narrative: Form, Ethics, Ideology*. Ed. James Phelan. Columbus: Ohio State University Press, 1989. 147–161.

Doane, Mary Ann. *The Desire to Desire: The Woman's Film of the 1940s*. Bloomington and Indianapolis: Indiana University Press, 1987.

Edelman, Lee. *Homographesis: Essays in Gay Literary and Cultural Theory*. New York and London: Routledge, 1994.

Freud, Sigmund. "Leonardo Da Vinci and a Memory of his Childhood." *The Standard Edition of the Complete Psychological Works of Sigmund Freud.* Vol. 11. Ed. James Strachey. London: Hogarth Press, 1955. 59–230.

———. "Psychoanalytic Notes Upon an Autobiographical Account of a Case of Paranoia (Dementia Paranoides)." *Three Case Histories.* Ed. Philip Rieff. New York: Collier Books, 1963.

———. "Some Neurotic Mechanisms in Jealousy, Paranoia, and Homosexuality." *The Standard Edition of the Complete Psychological Works of Sigmund Freud.* Vol. 18. Ed. James Strachey. London: Hogarth Press, 1955.

Laplanche, Jean, and J. B. Pontalis. *The Language of Psycho-Analysis.* New York: Norton, 1973.

Lo, Mun-Hou. "David Leavitt and the Etiological Maternal Body." *Modern Fiction Studies* 41.3–4 (1995): 439–465.

Michie, Elsie B. "Unveiling Maternal Desires: Hitchcock and American Domesticity." *Hitchcock's America.* Ed. Jonathan Freedman and Richard Millington. New York and Oxford: Oxford University Press, 1999. 29–53.

Miller, D. A. "Anal *Rope.*" *Inside/Out: Lesbian Theories, Gay Theories.* Ed. Diana Fuss. New York and London: Routledge, 1991. 119–141.

Modleski, Tania. *The Women Who Knew Too Much: Hitchcock and Feminist Theory.* New York and London: Methuen, 1988.

Naremore, James. *Filmguide to Psycho.* Bloomington and Indianapolis: Indiana University Press, 1973.

Powell, Paige. "Hitch Up: Interview with Movie Director Gus Van Sant." *Interview* (December 1998). 1 October 2004 <http://www.findarticles.com/p/articles/mi_m1285/is_12_28/ai_53368770>

Psycho. Dir. Alfred Hitchcock. Perf. Anthony Perkins and Janet Leigh. 1960. DVD. Universal, 1999.

Rebello, Stephen. *Alfred Hitchcock and the Making of Psycho.* New York: St. Martin's Griffin, 1990.

Scholes, Robert. "Narration and Narrativity in Film." *Quarterly Review of Film Studies* 1.3 (1976): 283–296.

Sedgwick, Eve Kosofsky. *Between Men: English Literature and Male Homosocial Desire.* New York: Columbia University Press, 1985.

———. *The Coherence of Gothic Conventions.* Rev. ed. New York and London: Methuen, 1986.

Silverman, Kaja. *Male Subjectivity at the Margins.* New York and London: Routledge, 1992.

Spoto, Donald. *The Dark Side of Genius: The Life of Alfred Hitchcock.* Boston and Toronto: Little, Brown, 1983.

Truffaut, François. *Hitchcock.* Rev. ed. New York: Simon and Schuster, 1983.

Williams, Linda. "Discipline and Distraction: Psycho, Visual Culture, and Postmodern Cinema." *"Culture" and the Problem of the Disciplines.* Ed. John Carlos Rowe. New York: Columbia University Press, 1998. 87–120.

———. "When a Woman Looks." *Re-Vision: Essays in Feminist Film Criticism.* Ed. Mary Ann Doane, Patricia Mellencamp, and Linda Williams. Frederick: University Publications of America and the American Film Institute, 1984.

————. "When Women Look: A Sequel." *Senses of Cinema* 15 (July–August 2001). 26 December 2004. <http://www.sensesofcinema.com/contents/01/15/horror_women.html>

Wood, Robin. *Hitchcock's Films Revisited.* New York: Columbia University Press, 1989.

NINE

PARANOIA, COLD SURVEILLANCE, AND THE MATERNAL GAZE

Reconsidering the "Absent Mother"
in *Ordinary People*

Mark Harper

While existing textual work has been accurate in its strident assessment of the representation of upper-middle-class WASP motherhood in Robert Redford's 1980 melodrama *Ordinary People*, such analysis fails to take into account the equally powerful and complex interplay of domestic design, panoptic vision, and the maternal gaze at work in the film. Certainly, the interdependence and conflict of the physical domestic space with the female body has been a commonplace of melodrama studies.[1] However, the deployment of these two fields in *Ordinary People*, combined with a quasi-art film narrative style, suggests an underlying tone of external paranoia and social surveillance at work in the text toward the mother in the nuclear family that bears exploration. Furthermore, this reevaluation might illuminate the complexities with which Hollywood melodrama at the end of the cold war situates motherhood as a comforting site of containment, mechanically synonymous with the protective domestic space, but ultimately incompatible with the technology of that domestic space, and wanting elimination.

To be sure, the film participates in what is now a well-accepted paradigm, one in which the narrative situates the powerful, domineering mother next to an absent or weak-willed father in the American home. In either the (male adolescent) "coming-of-age" story or melodramas of youthful (female) romance, the underlying tension in need of resolution is the risk presented by the adolescent's emotional state and his or her susceptibility to adulteration from undesirable, outside forces; at the heart of this "weakness" lies the mother's bad influence. Seen as such, this type of post–World War II domestic melodrama becomes a site for rooting out the subversive force within the family, restoring it to its proper health.[2]

Hence, popular melodramas of the late 1940s through the early 1960s (as well as political and suspense thrillers of the period) are apt to portray American domestic life as a peaceful situation on the brink of potential disaster, with well-meaning characters oblivious to the dangers threatening to overtake their lives because of the imbalance of gendered power in the household. The working out of the narrative, then, is a matter of putting the mother in her proper place through the father's (re)acquisition of power in the household or through a forceful break between mother and adolescent, brought about by a redeeming male figure.

The permutations of this paradigm extend well into the popular cinema and successful Hollywood genres of the late 1960s and 1970s, as is succinctly argued by Robin Wood and Vivian Sobchack. Wood, writing on the social destabilization brought about by the Vietnam War and the Watergate scandal, suggests that

> this generalized crisis in ideological confidence never issued in revolution. No coherent social/economic program emerged, the taboo on socialism remaining virtually unshaken. Society appeared to be in a state of advanced disintegration, yet there was no serious possibility of the emergence of a coherent and comprehensive alternative. This quandary—habitually rendered, of course, in terms of personal drama and individual interaction, and not necessarily consciously registered—can be felt to underlie most of the important American films of the late 60s and 70s. (50)

Sobchack, who confines her argument to generic transformations in melodrama, horror films, and particularly science fiction films of this period, documents the growing importance of the infant or child in these genres: an important figure, she argues, that "condenses and initiates a contemporary and pressing cultural drama" (144). Thus, through the generic transformation of the horror and science fiction, beginning in the late 1960s, popular notions of "the family" also change. At the end of this cycle, the American melodrama (which fell out of popularity in the 1960s) is revitalized by the late 1970s.[3]

With such revolutionary alterations in bourgeois attitudes toward the family, Wood and Sobchack both argue, popular genres of the 1970s become increasingly situated in the American home. "Consistent with the systemic rules of patriarchal relation and its economy, the mother in the family melodrama becomes hard, strong, and selfish. . . . The inability of patriarchy to cope with its loss of authority, to admit an equal distribution of familial power and responsibility, is inscribed in the opposition of bad mother and good father" (Sobchack 154).[4] In an era reeling from social upheavals of youth, gay, and feminist movements, and unable to come to terms with a residual anxiety and cynicism from the failures of the Vietnam War and the Nixon administration, the conflicting attitudes, once again, are played out within the traditional family structure. The "new" melodrama of the late 1970s, still decidedly positioned within the historical cold war, differs from the 1950s model previously discussed, however, in that the maternal figure must not only cede her position to the father, but must also leave the picture.[5]

Ordinary People chronicles the inabilities of the wealthy Jarrett family to stay unified in the aftermath of a fatal occurrence. The film depicts Calvin, the father and a successful Chicago tax attorney, his stylish wife Beth, and their teenaged son Conrad following the accidental drowning of an older son, Buck, in a boating accident, and the subsequent suicide attempt of Conrad, who survived the accident that killed his brother. In the autumn/winter months following Conrad's release from a mental hospital, tensions between Conrad and Beth grow, and are then transferred to Beth and Calvin. Initially frustrated by his inability to communicate with his parents and peers, Conrad, with the help of Dr. Berger, a psychiatrist, begins to take control of his life: he quits the high school swim team, which appears to have been his brother Buck's celebrated domain, and successfully pursues a relationship with Jeannine, a fellow choir student.

Meanwhile, conflict deepens between mother and father. Emotionally unequipped to deal with the loss of her older son, Beth seeks solace in domestic order and the normalcy of routine. With Conrad, she is brisk and cool to the point of indifference, rarely inquiring into his emotional state and conducting herself around him as if he is a guest in the house. Calvin, on the other hand, can do nothing but worry over his family's fate and Conrad's mental health. The divergence of these responses exacts an increasing toll throughout the narrative, marked by Beth's embarrassment over her son's continued need for psychotherapy, her inability to communicate with him, and her resentment (and jealousy) toward Calvin's solicitousness toward him. She also resists Calvin's suggestion that they all seek family therapy (Calvin himself goes to see Dr. Berger as his anxiety grows).

The film concludes after Conrad, upon hearing of the suicide of Karen, a teenaged friend of his from the mental hospital, is forced to accept, but able to process, the guilt and grief from his own past. Mentally stable once more, he attempts unsuccessfully to connect emotionally with his mother. Calvin and Beth, meanwhile, reach an impasse in their relationship when

Calvin recognizes his wife's inability to grow past the tragedies the family has experienced. The conclusion of the narrative is signaled by Beth's voluntary exit from the house early one morning after Calvin, distraught, suggests in a lengthy, twilit monologue that he no longer loves her.[6]

As mentioned earlier, that Beth would need elimination almost seems beside the point when analyzing the film through a traditional grid of Marxist/feminist criticism. Academic critics of the film note the consistency of the story line with the 1970s version of this cold war paradigm, since Beth is represented as emotionally cold and distant, preoccupied with an ideal vision of a private, ordered family life, and defiantly strident in her upholding of discipline at the expense of her child. Several feminist critics have read Beth's final departure from the domestic sphere as a conventional turn of this cold war archetype. William Luhr writes:

> Beth cannot live without her sense of control and doesn't feel that she has a problem. Her leaving comes quite "naturally" and inevitably, given the new levels of psychotherapeutically aided growth evident in the household. The film thus insulates its men from direct assaults upon Beth; it presents them instead as progressing psychotherapeutically while she rigidly refuses to change. *The men do not attack Beth; the film does.* (57, emphasis mine)

And in their comparative study of the best-selling novel on which the film is based, Victoria Szabo and Angela D. Jones form conclusions almost identical to Luhr's findings:

> Both the novel and the film present the family as an inherently unstable unit that requires the excision of women in order to function effectively, and both highlight the importance of emotional expression and connection, qualities that are linked largely to the central male characters, Calvin and Conrad. Beth, by contrast, is unable to emote; that inability, along with her desire for control and addiction to privacy, ultimately results in her banishment from the family. (45)

The use of adjectives such as "natural" and "inherent" is well in keeping with this archetypal narrative structure. By the late 1970s, the American home, good intentions aside, was still an unstable ground for the family, thanks to the bad influence of the mother. Beth is not necessarily combative or domineering so much as she is cold and unloving. Her unreasonably high expectations and emotional indifference to the needs of her maturing, endangered offspring finally force her out of the picture as incompatible with the needs of the family.

It is important to consider the position of this melodrama within the broader arc of cold war "mom-paranoia" to understand not only the tight space accorded to more traditional maternal figures in late 1970s feature cinema, but also the evolution of domestic melodrama "style."[7] Luhr's conclusion that the film *Ordinary People* itself attacks Beth is significant in this case since it suggests broader cinematic forces at work beyond the scope of a basic engagement between film text and sociopolitical *zeitgeist*. Furthermore, if critical studies of the film have tended to emphasize its implicit demonization of mothers, they just as frequently privilege analysis of the film's "art" and "high style." And both mother and style are found to be equally problematic, apparently for their excess; numerous critics have strongly (and disparagingly) noted the controlled schematics of *Ordinary People*.

Pauline Kael, for instance, complaining that the film "reeks of quality," remarked on the influence of Robert Bresson and compared *Ordinary People* to Ingmar Bergman's *Scenes from a Marriage* (1973) (184). David Denby unequivocally compared the style of Redford's film to that of Woody Allen's Bergman-inspired, 1978 film *Interiors*: "So much restraint is especially ironic in a movie calling for free play of the emotions. *Ordinary People* is Robert Redford's *Interiors*" (58).[8] He adds: "Scene after scene is carefully controlled to show how much feeling the characters are repressing, and after a while you may want to scream from all the repressed filmmaking" (58). Redford himself describes directing the film "from the gut": "That's the way it has always been with me—in sports, and in painting, when I was an artist" (11). More than one critic made mention of the fact that the overall cinematic style appeared to match the personal style of the controlling mother depicted.

But Marxist/feminist critic Robin Wood dismisses any interest in the cinematic aesthetics of *Ordinary People* as negligible and considers the film only noteworthy as a sociological artifact. He remarks:

> The film's popularity, within its social context, was presumably due to its total complacency and complicity. . . . Otherwise, nothing in the film challenges or troubles: its quite insistent play on the emotions does not correspond to any disturbance of establishment values or dominant ideological assumptions. The ignominious position of women within the patriarchal family system is never acknowledged (if the mother can't accept it, that's her problem . . .). The archetypal patriarchal resolution is offered without a hint of irony, criticism or complexity of attitude. (263)

Wood's totalizing dismissal of the film's aesthetics appears to be rash, however. For much of the film's interest and ambiguity—perhaps part of the possible cause of its sustained popularity—may be studied in its cinematography and editing, wherein, I argue, the film demonstrates a much stronger and ambivalent relationship to cold war ideologies than has previously been maintained.[9] The so-disparaged "high style" of the film and Redford's own status as "pretender to the art-film director throne" are replete with the complexities Wood mentions.

As Sobchack argues, the family melodrama of this era carries the traces of the concurrent social upheavals in America at the end of the cold war. But, if so, I argue that it holds just as strongly to some of the conventions of the political films, suspense thrillers, and disaster films of the decade, which, in conjunction with domestic policies of "national security," document the penetration of spy technology into everyday life. As Michael Rogin documents, the mid-1960s to the mid-1970s saw not only the development of an illegal domestic surveillance network in the CIA under the director-ship of Richard Helms, but also the expansion of the FBI's COINTELPRO program, which sought to disrupt dissident political groups through infiltra-tion (76). Remarkably, the success of the latter often depended on secretly pitting marital partners against one another for political advantage. Hence, it is not just the mother who is under scrutiny in Ordinary People, but the entire family, the family home, and the community.

Examples of these popular genres from the decade abound; sci-fi films and suspense thrillers combining surveillance technology, organized spy tac-tics, and loosely defined and sinister corporations/organizations affiliated with the government or big business include: A Clockwork Orange (1971), The Andromeda Strain (1971), Klute (1971), Westworld (1973), The Conversation (1974), The Towering Inferno (1974), The Parallax View (1974), Three Days of the Condor (1975), All the President's Men (1976), Demon Seed (1977), Close Encounters of the Third Kind (1977), The Fury (1978), and Eyes of Laura Mars (1978). And the narratives of each of these films, regardless of genre, bear out the recent conclusions of Paul Miller and John S. Turner II: the 1970s was the decade in which surveillance technology, previously the domain of action and adventure pictures, effectively plagued the existences of everyday characters. In all of these examples, some sort of omniscient, outside force invades the life of a private citizen, an American home, or a small, American community. The presence of this technology, they contend, whether in the hands of a stalking killer or a government agency, effectively dismantles the boundaries between public and private life, the objective and the subjective gaze.

Turning his critical attention toward architecture and production design, Fredric Jameson makes much of the underlying paranoia in these popular American films, which follow, stylistically, from the influences of European art cinema of the 1960s, notably that of Michelangelo Antonioni and Ingmar Bergman. Jameson considers All the President's Men, produced by Robert Redford, and the hollow, vacant spatial planes dwarfing the characters throughout this paranoid political suspense thriller. He refers to the façades of the buildings, which suggest a "combination of anonymity and power, of the imposing-fearful and the empty-trivial" (75), and concludes: "The point, however, is that when space itself is thus foregrounded, it is itself thereby deprived of any natural background, as which a kind of inert and conventionalized space normally serves. Reality and matter are released from their ground, and become peculiarly free-floating" (75). Elsewhere, Jameson remarks on the proliferation of close-ups in these films that, in their political contexts, overnarrate the characters beyond traditional cause-effect dynamics to a secondary level of voyeuristic/omniscient scrutiny of imperfection, surprise, and vulnerability. So while such cinematic devices, as they were deployed by prominent art film directors in the 1960s, might destabilize notions of objective truth and a perceiving, unified identity, their presence in Hollywood-produced films of the 1970s suggests a less existential, more conspiratorial omniscience on private life, identifiable to the film spectator, yet ultimately left "unidentified" as a rational force.[10]

The opening shots of Ordinary People have an effect of ambiguous "beauty" that seem designed to situate and awe simultaneously. It is as if, in drawing the spectator into the narrative, the film presumes the aesthetic savvy of its audience, one that should "understand" the exquisite formality presented. But this appeal to an aesthetic sensibility also subtly enlists the spectator's gaze into complicity with the gaze of surveillance. In Redford's film, the trajectory of the beginning sequence appears calculated to focus the spectator's look from the outside to the inside of the beautiful artifice, subtly prompting the gaze to seek out the crack in the pediment, the flaw in the surface, the problem that needs to be fixed.

Just after the opening credits—white font on black background—the opening notes of "Canon in D" by baroque composer Johann Pachelbel quietly play on a solo piano. The first shot is a slow, short tilt-pan down from a relatively clear sky over Lake Michigan, over the water, across a row of quaint moorings, to the wooded bank. Successive shots, which are static, move further inland to seasonally picturesque views of spacious roads and sprawling yards on a sunny afternoon, strewn with colorful autumn leaves, and unencumbered by people (the Jarretts, we later learn, live in Lake Forest, an affluent suburb to the north of Chicago). Finally, following a shot of a gazebo and the front of a church—a modern structure possessing elements of both Prairie style and Wrightian architecture—the sequence concludes with a perfectly framed shot of the façade of a stately home: an extremely formal domicile composed of elements of Federal, Georgian revival, and classical revival.

Like the first shot in the sequence, and unlike those in between, this conclusive shot is mobilely framed (a slow forward zoom toward the main section of the house), drawing our interest, curiosity, and appreciation. The extradiegetic, neoclassical score shifts in this moment to a related piece of music and an intradiegetic score: a high school choir singing a choral arrangement of the piece. And in one smooth dissolve, the shot of the stately home is replaced by an establishing shot of that choir, during its daily practice.

Following another smooth dissolve, still moving forward in its/our relentless search (and approval), the camera slowly tracks across the healthy, clear complexions of young, upper-middle-class men and women, all casually dressed in stylish, quality clothing, and all singing with the strength and vacancy of teenaged enthusiasm. At the last note of the choral piece, the camera stops on the drawn, haggard face of Conrad Jarrett, the mentally ill protagonist in the body of this melodrama who will need recuperation. The flaw has been found.[11]

The strength of these shots is not entirely in their "artistic-ness," so much as in the hesitancy they promote toward that beauty. The placid shot of the lake and the boat, as is revealed in the narrative, is less important for its natural charm than to situate the location of the narrative trauma—the boating accident that resulted in Buck's death and Conrad's attempted suicide. Furthermore, the shot encroaching upon the stately home is even more indefinite as an establishing of setting. Whose home is this? The slow dissolve to the choir might suggest that it is the building where they are practicing, but, logically, it is not. Later shots of the exterior of the Jarrett's home confirm, likewise, that it is not their house either. Such ambiguity of narrative perception in the opening shots of the melodrama seem as predisposed to unsettle spectators as to situate them.

That this opening sequence ends with a close-up of Conrad—eyes shadowed by lack of sleep and anxiety, hair roughly cut from the rudimentary procedures of electroshock therapy, body relatively thinner than the other students—is instructive. For if the camera has singled this young man out as a carrier of illness, represented by his face, then we must consider the investigatory camera movements just prior as motivated by similar concerns. The question "Whose home is this?" leads to "What's wrong with this boy?" and recalls the earlier shot in the question, "What's wrong with this house?"

Thus, while encouraging spectatorial pleasure in such scenic externals, this opening sequence simultaneously draws our attention, ever so subtly, to what's wrong with them, enlisting our help in interpreting them. The gradual forward penetration from the lake to the stately, domestic façade, just like the gradual cutting in from the establishing shot of the high school choir, while highlighting natural healthiness and aesthetic pleasure, is also a penetrating examination of surfaces for weakness.

If the opening sequence is filled with such knowing, panoptic omniscience, the rest of the narrative seems saturated with it. The subtlety of this approach to the subject, firmly established in the first shots, finds a natural correlation in the interdynamics of the represented characters, where quiet surveillance of family members is the norm and Beth maintains the most directed gaze, and the mightiest. The first image of Beth and Calvin occurs as they watch a play with another couple. Beth's corrective gaze catches Calvin asleep during the performance. Later, when Calvin drunkenly confides in a friend (a female contemporary of Beth's) at a dinner party, revealing that Conrad is seeing a psychiatrist, Beth watches and listens from around a corner and intervenes in the conversation. At a family gathering for Thanksgiving, Beth insists on taking the camera from Calvin (a ruse to avoid being photographed with Conrad). The tumultuous scene around the Christmas tree (where the tensions between Conrad and Beth reach the point of verbal assault) begins with Beth broodingly entering the room, unseen by Calvin, and staring at him until he notices her presence.

More than any other character, Conrad is beset by the gaze of others. Virtually every scene featuring his character in the first half of the film begins with his being "caught unawares" by another character: a teacher, a friend, Karen, Beth, the swim coach, Calvin, Dr. Berger, and so on. Conrad's first visit with his psychotherapist is a clear demonstration not only of how at odds Conrad is with his interior surroundings and the scrutinizing gaze that dogs him, but also Berger's awareness of it. Standing nervously in the office hallway, Conrad presses the buzzer to be admitted and waits in an awkwardly formal posture for this first meeting outside of what he thinks is Berger's office door. In a medium-long shot, Berger appears from a second door, behind Conrad, startling his new patient. Sensing Conrad's embarrassment, Berger says, "It's okay. They all do that."

This situation and the balance of power are thus established, indirectly, from the beginning, but are consistent throughout the film, and inform the dynamics of the characters and the drama to the very end of the film. Furthermore, if the film makes a primary point of establishing Beth, the mother, as the strongest bearer of the surveillant gaze, then a focal point of the narrative becomes a matter of demonstrating her loss of that power, as is evinced in the scene following Conrad's first visit to Dr. Berger. An establishing shot reveals the Jarrett family quietly dining in the evening around a mutely lit table (Beth to the left of the screen, Conrad to the right, and Calvin in the middle). Conrad is characteristically silent, eyes cast downward to his plate, while Beth and Calvin, unanimated, share details from the day between bites. Almost undetectably, the camera moves omnipresently forward upon the family supper, abruptly stopping when, mid-conversation, Beth, looking directly at her son all of a sudden, demands: "Is that shirt ripped?" and, without waiting for a response, "Leave it on my sewing table in the hall."

The conversational dynamics that follow are an added gloss on who possesses the most controlling gaze. Beth, on her feet now to clear away the dishes, brightly asks Conrad if he is interested in playing round robin at the country club, clearly her favorite nondomestic location. "I haven't played for over a year," he responds. His mother, optimistically and firmly directing her gaze at him asks, "Well, don't you think it's time to start?" A medium close-up profile shot of Conrad, unable to answer as he drops his gaze to his plate, is followed by a medium close-up of Calvin, mutely witnessing this exchange, his eyes moving from his son at his left to his wife at his right, above him. Not wishing to press the point, Beth drops the subject and continues her tidying up.

Undoubtedly, Conrad presents the greatest threat to Beth's controlling gaze, as demonstrated by a powerful scene early in the film, before Conrad has begun therapy. Finding herself alone in the house, Beth momentarily steps into Buck's bedroom, still kept clean and furnished with personal memorabilia intact. She sits on his bed quietly and takes in the space, point of view shots registering the legacy of his life through camera pans across the walls. Unexpectedly, Conrad appears in the doorway, innocently looking into an otherwise closed doorway, and witnessing this private moment of his mother. In a close-up reaction shot, Beth gasps at his sudden presence and her eyes fly open in fright. "Don't do that!" she orders him, with momentarily shocked outrage.

Throughout the midsection of the film, as Conrad and Calvin begin to look into their pasts, and as Beth begins to resist, actively, any personal analysis, the question of vision and authority becomes openly examined. The only scene in the film in which Beth and Conrad appear to *begin* to connect starts with a shot of Beth gazing from inside the house at her son sitting alone in the backyard. Joining him, she attempts to have a conversation that falls apart quickly when the sore subject of Buck is addressed: Conrad counters his mother's reluctance to discuss the dead family member with a violent verbal outburst that sends Beth back into the house. Minutes later, when Conrad goes indoors and penitently attempts to pick up the conversation, he is coolly rebuffed by Beth as she sets the table for dinner. Awkward in their emotionally isolated states, the two momentarily stare at each other across the dining room table in contrasting medium

Figures 14–15. Conrad (Timothy Hutton) unwittingly startles his mother with her guard (or gaze) down in *Ordinary People* (1980).

close-up shots when a close friend of Beth's telephones, finally ending the unbearable tension.

Although the sequence begins with Beth watching Conrad unawares, it ends with Conrad watching Beth as she talks with her friend, now giggling and gossiping animatedly, unaware or indifferent to his presence behind her. The narration balances Conrad's steady gaze with a flashback from his remembered past, prompted by Beth's laughter: Calvin and Buck in the backyard with Beth, presumably two to three years earlier, as Buck shares a funny story with his appreciative family audience. The final shot in the sequence, however, takes the gaze beyond Conrad's consciousness to the home's architecture and interior design itself: in a master shot like the one earlier of the Jarretts at dinner, Conrad watches his mother from the left of screen and a hallway mirror at the right of the screen reflects his watchful stance. Beth, lost in her conversation on the phone, is the object of scrutiny in the middle of the frame; she is watched and evaluated now by both son and domestic design.

The question of the ability to "see" things increases, following a shouting match around the Christmas tree. Calvin goes to Conrad's room, attempting to communicate, but Conrad lies first on his stomach, his face buried in a pillow, and then turns over onto his back, the back of his hand placed over his eyes. "Everything's jello and pudding with you dad, you just don't see things!" he bitterly declares. And when Calvin tries to explore the topic, Conrad retorts, "It doesn't change the way she looks at me!" Shortly after this exchange, Calvin begins therapy himself, summoning forth his own personal difficulties with Beth's formal management of their lives.

It makes sense then, that, following Calvin's initial analysis, which we might read as the beginnings of his reclaiming of the authoritative gaze in this context, Beth will begin to be caught unawares by the watchful gaze of others. In an upscale shopping mall, riding an escalator and surrounded by anonymous shoppers, Beth is greeted by the shouts of a friendly peer coming from behind her and must look about, disoriented, to answer back. In this brief take, Beth is uncharacteristically framed at an extreme long shot, and at a downward angle. Her addressing peer is barely shown; a voice from an adjoining crowded escalator. Later, gazing distractedly at a mannequin, she is approached and startled by a saleswoman of similar dress, personal appearance, and age. Politely declining any service, Beth exits the frame, but the camera continues to record the saleswoman, indifferently watching her departure for a moment of undetermined interest.

Conrad, meanwhile, is ultimately recuperated by the watchful eye of the sympathetic new girlfriend, Jeannine. Throughout the film, Jeannine is presented as a warm foil to Beth's coolness—she tenderly queries Conrad about his suicide attempt and in three different instances, she is associated with the image of a rainbow. In the scene just following his climactic emotional breakthrough in Dr. Berger's office, wherein he accepts his feelings of self-worth, casting off the guilt he has felt for surviving his older brother, compounded by Beth's neglect, Conrad stands pacing in the cold outside his classmate's (smaller) home. In a shot that echoes the earlier scene in which Beth watches her son through the back window, sitting outside, Jeannine is seen in medium close-up looking outward. Unlike Beth, however, who ultimately leaves Conrad outside (following his outburst) with an admonition toward appearance: "Put that [a jacket] on if you're going to stay out here," Jeannine invites Conrad into her home for breakfast, calling into the house to announce her guest enthusiastically: "Mom?!"

The scenes that follow this recuperation—and the relief it entails for the audience (through its identification with Conrad)—do nothing but document Beth's irrevocable loss of the gaze, however. For if Conrad has finally been retrieved by the accepting and affectionate gaze of "good" femininity, the next three scenes represent an arc by which this ongoing surveillance of the family finally settles upon the mother as the integral flaw, and does so within the confines of the domestic space. In this way, the film momentarily shifts the gaze of surveillance from the omniscient to the personal in that it is through the paternal gaze (Calvin's) that the maternal gaze is "seen" as a powerful failure.

This begins on the golf course in Houston, where Calvin finally verbally challenges Beth's resistance to personal engagement with Conrad, prompting her emotional public outburst and expression of frustration, and continues on the airplane trip back to Chicago, where Calvin soberly recalls his youthful courtship of Beth, and concludes in the Jarrett's living room back in Lake Forest, where Beth fails to return Conrad's affectionate embrace. As described earlier, each sequence appears to be designed to place Beth further and further under the scrutiny of the watchful gaze of others (and of the camera) as her ability to "see" degenerates, just as others, particularly Calvin, watch her more closely and with less emotional involvement.

On the golf course in Houston, Beth is surrounded (in a long shot) by her brother Ward, his wife Audrey, and Calvin as she expertly putts the ball into the hole on the green. We watch Beth's success over the shoulder of Calvin, who has his back to the camera (in medium close-up), before she joins him in what will be the longest take in the film. The initial framing of the shot, seemingly designed to capture the friendliness of good sportsmanship at the end of a game of golf, is jarring however, because of the lack of frontality of the principal characters (a complement and then an ironic contrast to the retreating backs of Jeannine and Conrad just prior). And as the tension begins to build in the conversation between mother and father, it is Calvin's gaze at Beth, not Beth's gaze, that becomes the audience's focal point. His eyes stay on her steadily, as his growing, angry inquiry of her continues. Beth, on the other hand, though equally angry, is hardly able to return his gaze, frequently dropping her eyes to the golf green, the pavement, the golf ball she carries, her glove, the golf cart, and so on.

To highlight this "searching" for the crucial flaw, the camera doggedly follows the two as they walk across the parking lot back to the golf cart, Calvin almost pursuing Beth, in a lengthy tracking shot. In the background of this shot, Audrey and Ward appear alongside the couple, keeping their distance in the socially awkward situation, but discreetly watching them nonetheless. Other anonymous golfers, particularly one much older man, unabashedly watch Beth's outburst in the extreme background.

The climax of the scene, though, when Beth indirectly declares her grief at the loss of Buck and the irreparable damage it has wrought on the family, is preceded by a cut-in of Calvin abruptly lifting his head to look with greater determination at Beth. And the following shot, with Beth speaking directly to her brother in rage, is framed with Audrey between the two, looking with equal intensity at her sister-in-law, protesting the indelicacy of Beth's rhetorical defense. The final shot, as Beth begins to cry, has her departing to the left of the frame (Calvin following) with the remaining two, dumbfounded, staring after her.

This gradual elevation of scrutiny continues into the opening of the next scene on the plane: appropriately, a shot of Beth in extreme close-up, staring directly into the camera. Assumedly, as before, she is looking outward through the window; however, there is no pane of glass, as before, to mediate the gaze. As if anticipating the discomfort the audience might feel at looking into such grief-stricken eyes, she closes them and leans back in her seat, revealing the subtle, emotionless, and studied gaze of Calvin (now wearing large framed eyeglasses) at his wife from her left, securing Beth's position at this point as the visually studied object between him and us.

The climactic scene in the living room also positions Beth between those who can finally "see" as her own vision fails. The master shot presents father and mother in a long shot, in different seats and at right angles in the living room when Conrad enters. As Conrad bids them good night, Calvin (still in eyeglasses) in medium close-up, watches his son's and wife's behavior closely. Beth, completely objectified in this point-of-view shot, is almost hidden by Conrad's head, torso, and arms as he awkwardly hugs her; her stunned eyes, staring vacantly forward, are the only visible facial features. And after Conrad silently retreats (and presumably leaves the room), Beth quietly and slowly closes her eyes, turning her face and body away from the camera and Calvin (in defeat). Tellingly, early the following morning, Conrad awakens to the sound of a car door shutting and looks out his bedroom window. A point-of-view shot registers the top of a taxicab as it leaves the Jarrett's driveway. Now fully recuperated, Conrad's gaze is the one to document his mother's departure.

Such a reading of the film as an arena of competing, controlling looks from character to character, all kept before us, the spectators, in our watchful gaze, may not seem quite so politically loaded, if not for comments made by Redford himself, indicating his awareness of these stylistic patterns. In an interview given less than ten years after the release of *Ordinary People*, he suggests a consciousness of "objective" versus "subjective" reading of characters in his cinema, and his motivation as a filmmaker for drawing audiences into the inner lives of these family figures.

> There are a lot of villains in motion picture history that audiences love, because they've gone with them. *Ordinary People* was not just about that boy. The boy was the *stalking horse* for the other characters. It was through the boy's problem that you were brought into their lives. They behaved in a way that they didn't know you were coming in, they thought you were coming in *to look at* the boy, but you were really coming in *to look at* them. So it was as much about the father, and the father and mother, and the father and son, and mother and son, and the son's friends, and the community, as it was about the boy. (10–11, emphasis mine)

Political connotations of the term "stalking horse" aside, such remarks make it abundantly clear that Redford considers the spectator/character relationship as strongly motivated by an objective look from the audience into the world of the narrative, and sees his role as director as strongly manipulative. Furthermore, Redford's (inconsistent) referencing of the "them" of Calvin and Beth suggests not only that the characters are conscious of themselves as scrutinized objects, but also implies an *acceptance* of that scrutiny.

The final shot of the film, a corollary to the opening forward tracking shot of the stately home, is thus more portentous in this panoptic context. With Calvin (and Conrad) now positioned as watchful subjects and Beth's mastery of the gaze now eliminated, the narrational mode returns to its omniscience and artful, schematic order. Father and son, seated on the back patio steps, embrace. And as the camera tracks backward from them (an extreme long shot taken from a crane), the neoclassical notes of Pachelbel occur once more on the soundtrack until the entire home is registered externally in the shot, fully restored (sans mother). Thus, as Jameson suggests about Redford's earlier film, "space is scarcely an incidental player in this particular work of art, where the relative withdrawal of the narrative actants or characters in some sense determines the enlargement and investment of hitherto incidental spatial features into protagonists in their own right" (74). The school, the doctor's office, the shopping mall, the golf course, and, to be sure, the suburban home are all participants in this melodrama since they are all under equal scrutiny.

The driving thesis of the post–World War II paradigm discussed earlier is that, in feature cinema, the maternal dynamic is laden with unspoken ideological currents. Michael Rogin argues, "Cold war cinema displays a progressive deepening of domestic anxiety, which is structured in three layers, family, state, and society; each is a response to the layer above. The first identifies Communism with secret, maternal influence. The second replaces mom's surveillance by that of the national-security state" (245). Thus, it is not simply the genetic or behavioral influence of motherhood that brings about the crisis of the teenager at risk; the complexities of the maternal gaze are also factors in the equation. Furthermore, the resolution of the narrative becomes a contest between the patriarchal gaze of the state and the watchful eye of the mother. And it is essentially in the American home that the maternal gaze proliferates.

In a similar analysis, Elaine Tyler May's *Homeward Bound* analyzes the popular discourses surrounding the acquisition and maintenance of suburban homes and lifestyles in the post–World War II era. May effectively contextualizes the desirability of conventional domestic life in the 1950s within the larger framework of cold war politics and American foreign policy toward Russia, frequently citing popular films of the decade. The acquisition of personal space through the purchase and enjoyment of a ranch-style home, according to May, not to mention the attainment of consumer goods for domestic leisure, was integral for proper family living. Again, the two forces at work are the state and the mother:

> The government, along with the National Associate of Home Builders, provided plans in the 1950s for smaller, inexpensive ranch-style homes that would allow for openness, adequate room for appliances and other consumer goods, and the easy supervision of children. Appliances were not intended to enable housewives to have more free time to pursue their own interests, but rather to achieve higher standards of cleanliness and efficiency, while allowing more time for child care. The suburban home was planned as a self-contained universe. (171)

May astutely refers to housewives' "own interests" in the negative since those interests seem to be irrelevant (to the state). The point of post–World War II architectural design, relevant in the American home, though uncomfortably, is ease of supervision.

Films such as *Ordinary People* are examples of such self-contained and easily supervised spaces, but they also pronounce the tensions between the panoptic maternal gaze and an unsituated, omniscient gaze beyond. And, all the while, such films implicate the spectatorial gaze in uncomfortable complicity. The cultural regulation of the maternal gaze, particularly when it is represented as wielding any level of power within the self-contained universe of the suburban home in cold war America, is a practice that would both value but disallow that gaze. Hollywood melodrama, by the end of the cold war, relies on the maternal gaze, but ultimately distrusts that aspect of femininity. And even if the maternal gaze is integral, almost indistinguishable from the surveillance technology that permeates American communities, it must still be eliminated as a competing force.

ACKNOWLEDGMENTS

Parts of this chapter were given as a presentation at the Twenty-Ninth Colloquium on Literature and Film at West Virginia University in September 2004. I am grateful to Heather Addison, Mary Kate Goodwin-Kelly, and Elaine Roth for their thoughtful suggestions on earlier drafts. Great thanks also to Laura Browning, Barb Klinger, and Dale Slater for their much-needed assistance with the preliminary draft.

NOTES

1. The wealth of critical work on representations of domestic space in melodrama and their relationship to sexuality is expansive. See especially Charles Affron and Mirella Jona Affron, *Sets in Motion*; Thomas Elsaesser, "Tales of Sound and Fury"; Christine Gledhill, "The Melodramatic Field: An Investigation"; and Geoffrey Nowell-Smith, "Minnelli and Melodrama."

2. The most extended analysis of this paradigm is offered by Michael Rogin, *Ronald Reagan, The Movie*. For other analyses of this paradigm not discussed here, see Jackie Byars, *All That Hollywood Allows: Re-reading Gender in 1950s Melodrama*; Nina C. Leibman "Leave Mother Out: The Fifties Family in American Film and Television"; Robert B. Ray, *A Certain Tendency of the Hollywood Cinema, 1930–1980*; and Thomas Schatz, *Hollywood Genres: Formulas, Filmmaking, and the Studio System*.

3. For further examination of genre shifts and hybrids of this period, see also: John G. Cawelti, "*Chinatown* and Generic Transformation in Recent American Films" and William Paul, *Laughing Screaming: Modern Hollywood Horror & Comedy*.

4. For an excellent, earlier study of family melodramas and comedies of this period, see Marina Heung "Why E.T. Must Go Home: The New Family in American Cinema."

5. Rogin, previously cited, offers a full elaboration on American anti-communist political policies through the Reagan era. For a broad, though accurate analysis of Hollywood responses to cold war issues through the early 1990s, see William J. Palmer, *The Films of the Eighties: A Social History*.

6. *Ordinary People* was nominated for and received numerous awards, particularly for acting (Mary Tyler Moore, Judd Hirsch, and Timothy Hutton), direction, and writing, by the Academy of Motion Picture Arts and Sciences, the British Academy of Film and Television Arts Awards, the Los Angeles Film Critics Association Awards, the New York Film Critics Circle Awards, and the Writers Guild of America. In

addition, Robert Redford received the highest award for his direction by both the Directors Guild of America and the National Board of Review. *Ordinary People* won the Oscar for Best Picture.

7. E. Ann Kaplan's comprehensive study on representations of motherhood in popular culture examines the unstable place left for maternal figures starting in the late 1970s, at work or at home, includes *Ordinary People* as an example. See E. Ann Kaplan, *Motherhood and Representation: The Mother in Popular Culture and Melodrama.*

8. Numerous critics made (and make) this same comparison, as both Hollywood films have experienced a peculiar and similar history. Like *Ordinary People*, *Interiors* received lavish and unsympathetic critical attention upon its release, was nominated for and won numerous prestigious awards, and was later deeply castigated by Marxist/feminist academic criticism for its harsh villainization of women, particularly mothers. Moreover, while both films were marketed, for the most part, as "personal, artistic achievements" by celebrated male directors (and welcomed by fans as such), to some they have become emblematic of a certain "high art" conceit, albeit at times effective, on behalf of their producers. Some critics even conclude that both films are nothing more than pretentious directorial gestures made by successful, crowd-pleasing Hollywood entertainers who yearned for the auteur status and following of European directors. Tellingly, this popular status has been couched as a "guilty pleasure" by more than one enthusiast. See John Waters, *Crackpot: The Obsessions of John Waters* and Armond White, "Armond White's Guilty Pleasures." Both Waters and White make ample note of these two maternal characters.

9. Wood, writing on the social destabilization brought about by the Vietnam War and the Watergate scandal, advocates reading Hollywood films of the late 1960s and 1970s for their tendency to register the political quandaries and social disintegration of the period in terms of personal drama and individual interaction.

10. For other readings of this evolution, see J. Dudley Andrew, "The Stature of Objects in Antonioni's Films"; Roy Armes, "Robbe-Grillet, Ricardou, and *Last Year at Marienbad*"; Dennis Turner, "The Subject of *The Conversation*"; and Peter Wuss, "Narrative Tension in Antonioni."

11. In his review of *Ordinary People* for *New Leader*, Robert Asahina notes the ponderousness of the film's opening: "Conrad is momentarily picked out, and the point of this [opening sequence of the film] travelogue is suddenly clear: This is a Goddamn Serious Big Deal movie about the horrors of affluent suburban family life" (20).

BIBLIOGRAPHY

Affron, Charles, and Mirella Jona Affron. *Sets in Motion: Art Direction and Film Narrative.* New Brunswick: Rutgers University Press, 1995.

Andrew, J. Dudley. "The Stature of Objects in Antonioni's Films." *Tri-Quarterly* 11 (1968): 40–59.

Armes, Roy. "Robbe-Grillet, Ricardou, and *Last Year at Marienbad*." *Quarterly Review of Film Studies* 5.1 (1980): 1–17.

Asahina, Robert. "Seminars and Suburbs: *Ordinary People*." *New Leader* (20 October 1980): 20.

Blake, Richard A. "Surfaces." *America* (18 October 1980): 231.

Brooks, Peter. "Melodrama, Body, Revolution." *Melodrama: Stage, Picture, Screen.* Ed. Jacky Bratton, Jim Cook, and Christine Gledhill. London: British Film Institute, 1994. 11–24.

Byars, Jackie. *All That Heaven Allows: Re-Reading Gender in 1950s Melodrama.* Chapel Hill: University of North Carolina Press, 1991.

Cawelti, John G. "*Chinatown* and Generic Transformation in Recent American Films." *Film Genre Reader.* Ed. Barry Keith Grant. Austin: University of Texas Press, 1986. 183–201.

Consandaey, Mikelle. "Combining Entertainment and Education: An Interview with Robert Redford." *Cineaste* 16 (1987–1988): 8–12.

Considine, David M. *The Cinema of Adolescence.* London: McFarland, 1985.

Denby, David. "Movies: Robert Redford's '*Interiors.*' " *New York* (29 September 1980): 54–59.

Eberwein, Robert T. "The Structure of *Ordinary People.*" *Literature/Film Quarterly* 11.1 (1983): 9–15.

Elsaesser, Thomas. "Tales of Sound and Fury: Observations on the Family Melodrama." *Home Is Where the Heart Is: Studies in Melodrama and the Woman's Film.* Ed. Christine Gledhill. London: British Film Institute, 1987. 43–69.

Forshey, Gerald E. "Struggling Toward Autonomy." *The Christian Century* (29 October 1980): 1169–1171.

Gledhill, Christine. "The Melodramatic Field: An Investigation." *Home Is Where the Heart Is: Studies in Melodrama and the Woman's Film.* Ed. Christine Gledhill. London: British Film Institute, 1987. 5–39.

Guest, Judith. *Ordinary People.* New York: Penguin, 1976.

Hajal, Fady. "Family Mythology: *Ordinary People.*" *Literature/Film Quarterly* 11 (1983): 3–8.

Heung, Marina. "Why E.T. Must Go Home: The New Family in American Cinema." *Journal of Popular Film and Television* 11.2 (1983): 79–85.

Interiors. Dir. Woody Allen, United Artists, 1978.

Jameson, Fredric. *The Geopolitical Aesthetic: Cinema and Space in the World System.* 1992. Bloomington: Indiana University Press, 1995.

Kael, Pauline. "The Current Cinema: The Man Who Made Howard Hughes Sing and The Iron-Butterfly Mom." *New Yorker* (13 October 1980): 184–190.

Kaplan, E. Ann. *Motherhood and Representation: The Mother in Popular Culture and Melodrama.* New York: Routledge, 1992.

Leibman, Nina C. "Leave Mother Out: The Fifties Family in American Film and Television." *Wide Angle* 10.4 (1988): 24–41.

Luhr, William. "*Ordinary People*: Feminism and Psychotherapy on a See-Saw." *Cultural Power/Cultural Literacy: Selected Papers from the Fourteenth Annual Florida State University Conference on Literature and Film.* Ed. Bonnie Braendlin. Tallahassee: Florida State University Press, 1991. 50–60.

May, Elaine Tyler. *Homeward Bound: American Families in the Cold War Era.* New York: Basic Books, 1988.

Miller, Stephen Paul. *The Seventies Now: Culture as Surveillance.* Durham: Duke University Press, 1999.

Nowell-Smith, Geoffrey. "Minnelli and Melodrama." *Home Is Where the Heart Is: Studies in Melodrama and the Woman's Film.* Ed. Christine Gledhill. London: British Film Institute, 1987. 70–74.

Ordinary People. Dir. Robert Redford. Paramount Pictures, 1980.

Palmer, William J. *The Films of the Eighties: A Social History.* Carbondale: Southern Illinois University Press, 1993.

Paul, William. *Laughing Screaming: Modern Hollywood Horror & Comedy.* New York: Columbia University Press, 1994.

Ray, Robert B. *A Certain Tendency of the Hollywood Cinema, 1930–1980.* Princeton: Princeton University Press, 1985.

Rogin, Michael. *Ronald Reagan, The Movie: And Other Episodes of Political Demonology.* Berkeley: University of California Press, 1987.

Schatz, Thomas. *Hollywood Genres: Formulas, Filmmaking, and the Studio System.* New York: McGraw-Hill, 1981.

Sobchack, Vivian. "Bringing It All Back Home: Family Economy and Generic Exchange." *The Dread of Difference: Gender and the Horror Film.* Ed. Barry Keith Grant. Texas Film Studies Series. Austin: University of Texas Press, 1996. 143–163.

Szabo, Victoria, and Angela D. Jones. "The Uninvited Guest: Erasure of Women in *Ordinary People*." *Vision/Re-Vision: Adapting Contemporary American Fiction by Women to Film.* Ed. Barbara Tepa Lupack. Bowling Green, OH: Bowling Green State University Popular Press, 1996. 45–63.

Turner, Dennis. "The Subject of *The Conversation*." *Cinema Journal* 24.4 (1985): 4–22.

Turner, John S. II. "Collapsing the Interior/Exterior Distinction: Surveillance, Spectacle, and Suspense in Popular Cinema." *Wide Angle* 20.4 (1998): 92–123.

Waters, John. *Crackpot: The Obsessions of John Waters.* 1983. New York: Vintage, 1987.

White, Armond. "Armond White's Guilty Pleasures." *Film Comment* 39.3 (2003): 8, 61.

Wood, Robin. *Hollywood from Vietnam to Reagan.* New York: Columbia University Press, 1986.

Wuss, Peter. "Narrative Tension in Antonioni." *Suspense: Conceptualizations, Theoretical Analyses, and Empirical Explorations.* Ed. Peter Vorderer, Hans J. Wulff, and Mike Friedrichsen. Mahwah, NJ: Erlbaum, 1996.

Yakir, Dan. "Danger: Do Not Touch." *Film Comment* 17 (1981): 49–51.

TEN

SCREAM, POPULAR CULTURE, AND FEMINISM'S THIRD WAVE

"I'm Not My Mother"

KATHLEEN ROWE KARLYN

The 1990s might well be remembered as the decade of Girl Culture and Girl Power. New phrases began sounding in the air and new images surfacing in our media, changing the face of popular culture in a decidedly more youthful and feminine direction. In 1994, Mary Pipher's *Reviving Ophelia* helped put the issue of teen girls on the national cultural agenda. Indicting our "media-saturated culture" for "poisoning" our girls, the book sold 1.6 million copies. In cinema, teen girl audiences emerged as one of the most powerful demographic factors of the late 1990s, creating surprise hits out of movies ranging from the low-budget romantic comedy *Clueless* (1995) to the slasher parody *Scream* (1996). In 1997, teen girls saved the romantic epic *Titanic* from financial disaster when groups of them flocked to theaters for repeat viewings. *Clueless*'s success was followed by a television spin-off and a wave of teenflick romances, and the cult around *Scream* led to two sequels. On television, more programming than ever began featuring teen girl protagonists in situations ranging from the everyday (*Felicity* [1998–2002] and *Dawson's Creek* [1998–2003]) to the fantastic (the highly rated *Buffy the Vampire Slayer* [1997–2003], based on a 1992 movie of the same name). In music, phrases such as "Girl Power," first articulated by the underground "riot grrls," moved into the mainstream with the international if short-lived phenomenon of the Spice Girls, adored by very young girls (if reviled by almost everyone else). "By sheer bulk," according to one studio executive, "young girls are driving cultural tastes now. They're amazing consumers" (qtd. in Weinraub E4).

Girls now control enough money to attract attention as a demographic group. This may or may not represent an advance in terms of girls' actual social power, but it does indicate that girls are being listened to by cultural producers who are taking them and their tastes very seriously. That has not necessarily been the case, however, for people with far more compelling personal and political stakes in understanding young women and what drives them: that is, their mothers, their teachers, and feminist thinkers in general. And while more academic feminists are beginning to follow British scholar Angela McRobbie's lead in examining the relation between feminism and youth cultures, these investigations (in special issues of *Hypatia* and *Signs*) have more often focused on alternative, independent, and subcultural venues, such as riot grrls, rather than mainstream popular culture. Like Mary Pipher, educated and liberal-minded adults from widely differing backgrounds have more often felt a deep unease about the connections between girls and popular culture, especially youth-oriented genre films and television.

This unease stems from real fears about the damaging effects of popular culture on young people, and from real desires to protect girls from those effects—fears that increased dramatically after a wave of school shootings in the 1990s. Worries about violence focused on boys, while worries about sex focused on girls. However, adult disapproval of films such as *Scream* stands as a poignant example of a missed opportunity for women of my generation—feminists of the Second Wave, or the "mothers" of contemporary feminism—to learn about where our daughters are today and to mend or at least better understand some of the rifts and fissures that divide us. For despite the preferences of many educated adults for more refined examples of culture, for Jane Austen's *Emma* over Amy Heckerling's *Clueless*, for Mary Shelley's *Frankenstein* over Wes Craven's *Scream* trilogy, popular culture infuses the world in which today's young women live, and the face of feminism today, for better or worse, is being written across media culture. A startling image on the cover of a 1998 issue of *Time* magazine depicted succeeding generations of U.S. feminism with the faces of Susan B. Anthony, Betty Friedan, and Gloria Steinem in black and white, followed by Calista Flockhart's in "living color." (Flockhart is the actress who played Ally McBeal, the most popular female character on television that year.) The headline on the cover, "Is Feminism Dead?," suggests that if feminism lives, it does so in the fictionalized characters of popular culture.

The tension I have observed between mothers and daughters on the issue of popular culture resonates elsewhere in the U.S. feminist movement today. The challenge of making feminism represent more than a class of privileged white women is not new, of course, and inspired productive internal conflict within feminism's Second Wave. What appears new, however, is the generational dimension to this tension. On the one hand, "Girl Power" and "Girls Kick Butt" are familiar phrases on magazine covers, bumper stickers, and T-shirts, one sign of the ways the Second Wave has changed the world in which young women are growing to adulthood. On the other hand, feminism itself seems most evident as a "structuring absence" for middle-class young women attempting to define their identity. "I'm not a feminist, but . . ." has become the most ubiquitous reference to feminism today, heard in university classrooms, the popular press, and a wave of recent books on contemporary feminism. Brought up during a period of social conservatism, young women today are reluctant to identify themselves with any social movement and instead more likely to place their faith in free-market individualism. This resistance to thinking collectively, however, has serious political consequences at a time when collective action remains necessary not only to advance feminist goals in an age of globalization but to protect its still-vulnerable achievements in the areas of abortion rights, affirmative action, education, and health care. For example, feminists have failed to protect the social safety net for poor women and the families of illegal immigrants.

Thinking collectively requires both real and imaginative models of productive relationships, which have been hard to come by for girls and women in high art as well as popular culture. While representations of sisterhood or female friendship have begun to appear with more frequency in popular culture, especially with the new presence of female sport teams after Title IX, the mother-daughter bond, a key model of female connection remains, as Adrienne Rich has argued, invisible, unexplored, or taboo. With a few important exceptions (the *Alien* films, especially *Aliens* [1986] and *Alien Resurrection* [1997], and *Species II* [1998]), movies have tended to dispatch mothers with a vengeance, relegating them to sentimentality (*Stepmom* [1998]), hysteria (*American Beauty* [1999]), monstrosity (*Titanic* [1997]), or mere invisibility (*Rushmore* [1998]). Similarly, as Lucy Fischer has argued in *Cinematernity,* film criticism itself is characterized by a kind of "amnesia" about the maternal. As a result, girls have been hard-pressed to imagine what female collectivity might look like among women of their own generation or across time. Sentimentalizing sisterhood as an ideal of false solidarity among women is not the answer, especially when that ideal obscures real differences among women and the power differentials that accompany those differences. However, without models of common goals and action, the liberal ideology of free-market individual power can and does thrive. A film such as *Scream* provides an opportunity to sort out the relation between the highly commodified "Girl Culture" (of popular magazines, television, film, music, zines and the Internet) and the real empowerment of girls.

My purpose here is not to mount an unconditional defense of popular culture, but to argue that women who care about the next generation of girls need to learn more about the popular texts they are drawn to, whether those texts are *Ally McBeal* or *Buffy*, *Y/M* magazine or MTV. If a productive conversation is going to happen among women of all ages about the future of the feminist movement, it will have to take place on the terrain of popular culture where young women today are refashioning feminism toward their own ends. As Australian feminist Catherine Lumby argues, "If feminism is to remain engaged with and relevant to the everyday lives of women, then feminists desperately need the tools to understand everyday culture. We need to engage with the debates in popular culture rather than taking an elitist and dismissive attitude toward the prime medium of communication today" (174). Catherine M. Orr similarly warns that academic feminists may find themselves "positioned uncomfortably" against the populism implicit in the Third Wave (41).

This chapter takes a step in that direction first by mapping out the connections between Third Wave feminism and popular culture, then by illustrating those connections with a reading of the *Scream* trilogy. In Third Wave feminism, popular culture is a natural site of identity-formation and empowerment, providing an abundant storehouse of images and narratives valuable less as a means of representing reality than as motifs available for contesting, rewriting, and recoding. As I will show, these films provide a rich opportunity to study the contradictions and possibilities of feminism in a postmodern age. *Scream* (1996) stands as a key text in identifying girls as a powerful audience and, as Jonathan Hook and Steven Jay Schneider have argued, it had a major impact on the Hollywood film industry. The cult following that developed around the film led to two sequels (*Scream 2* [1997] and *Scream 3* [2000]) as well as *Scary Movie* parodies (2000, 2001, 2003, and 2006, with a fifth entry planned for 2011 release) and contributed to the wave of movies and television shows targeted to teen girls in the late 1990s. Built around themes of female empowerment and narratively driven by the ambivalent but powerful connection between mother and daughter, the trilogy raises the issue of bonds among women across time, gesturing toward a way out of current feminism's "relational crisis." Unabashedly postmodern in its celebration of B movies, it provides keen insights into the tastes, desires, and issues that move young women today, as well as the cultural landscape from which Third Wave feminism, or the feminism of our daughters, is emerging.

SCREAM (1996)

If any popular text brings together the issues of power, danger, desire, and anger for girls of the 1990s, it is *Scream*. Understanding the place of these issues in girls' lives today provides a helpful context for assessing the meaning of sensational material that adults might well find disturbing. Indeed, the *Scream* films demonstrate the potential of the highly commodified popular texts of Girl Culture to yield meanings consistent with Girl Power. Like popular culture itself, the trilogy is built on familiar old narratives, but, in its effort to capture and address changing audiences, it bends those narratives in new ways.

The plot of the first *Scream* film, like many horror movies with teen protagonists, is set in an affluent, predominantly white, bucolic community being preyed on by a masked, serial killer. It begins with the stalking and violent murder of a blonde teen girl, then shifts its attention to another girl, Sidney, who becomes the killer's next target. Sidney, whose mother had been raped and murdered a year ago, has been left alone by her father for the weekend. At the same time, because of unresolved grief for her mother, she resists her boyfriend Billy's ongoing pressure for sex. Meanwhile, Gale Weathers, an ambitious television newscaster, pursues the story of the new killings. Gale's appearance on the scene rekindles Sidney's anger at her coverage of the events around the mother's death. The subplots culminate at a party during which Sidney decides to have sex with Billy and the killer lays siege to the gathered teens. After a violent battle, a wounded and battered Sidney learns that the killer is Billy, who claims to have killed her mother as well because her affair with his father caused his own mother to abandon him. With the help of an equally battered Gale, Sidney kills him.

The *Scream* trilogy raises key issues in the lives of teen girls: (1) sexuality and virginity; (2) adult femininity and its relation to agency and power; (3) identity as it is shaped by the cultural narratives expressed in popular culture; and (4) identity as it is shaped by the family romance, in particular, a daughter's relationship with her mother. The *Scream* trilogy confronts each of these issues head-on, resolving them in powerful and innovative ways that allow a teen girl to occupy center stage, defend herself, and assert her agency and identity according to her own desire. In addition, these films enable girls to reject codes of femininity familiar to them from the highly conventionalized genre of the teen slasher film in order to rewrite them in more empowering ways.

Scream zeroes in on virginity and sexuality as a source of anxiety for young women. It does not shrink from the realization that sex is dangerous, and tied to violence and power. It can cause a girl or woman to lose not only her reputation ("your mother was a slut bag," Sidney hears throughout the trilogy) but her life. The enduring cultural myths of heterosexual romance, as in the film *Pretty Woman* (1990), also highly popular among young women, perpetuate female fantasies of Prince Charming boyfriends who will rescue them. However, *Scream* radically revises that myth. Recent work on female adolescence such as Carol Gilligan's (see also Mary Pipher, and Joan Brumberg's *The Body Project*) explores how coming of age into heterosexual adulthood "kills off" young girls' confidence and strength and suggests how for girls the boyfriend (or desire for a boyfriend) is a killer. *Scream* literalizes the metaphor. Drawing on literary and cinematic traditions of the Gothic, it narrativizes a girl's sense of boys as mysterious and unknowable entities, who, like the killer, can wear masks that disguise their true identity. For a generation that gave a name to date rape and acquaintance rape, *Scream* shows the ease with which a trusted friend can become a potential rapist. The principal of the high school, cleverly cast as old teen idol Henry Winkler ("the Fonz" from the 1970s sitcom *Happy Days*) touches Sidney to reassure her but in doing so conveys a creepy sense of sexual entitlement. Heterosexuality can be deadly for growing girls, and adult masculinity not only mysterious and unknowable, but capable of manifesting itself in ways that are potentially psychotic. Sidney doesn't know who the killer is, and, as the film-savvy character Randy reminds the other teens, everyone in the film, including her absent father, comes under suspicion.

Undercurrents of danger run through Billy's efforts to seduce Sidney, who is a virgin when the film begins. In one scene, he invades her space when he climbs uninvited into her bedroom, a visual metaphor for his desire to penetrate her body first sexually, and then with a knife, reenacting the violent penetrations he inflicted on her mother to punish her. Sexual urgency and aggression are implicitly tolerated or even valued in teen males, and we do not know until the film's final moments whether Billy's "edge" merely reflects that urgency or is something more threatening. Yet the film also acknowledges the ambivalence of female desire for the sexual other, and the fine line that divides the crazed killer of *Scream* from the brooding, bodice-ripping romantic heroes of women's pulp fiction. Sidney remains in control of her own sexuality, however, and chooses when to have sex with Billy. The film does not romanticize or sensationalize this rite of passage, showing only her agency in initiating it and its unexceptional aftermath.

Scream's treatment of sexuality arises from its identity not only as a teen film but as a horror film. The horror genre has generated a tradition of scholarship in film studies by scholars fascinated by the powerful emotional effects these films produce. The genre took on new life when it began to absorb the concerns (and audiences) of the teen flick, beginning with *Halloween* (1978), *Friday the 13th* (1980), and *A Nightmare on Elm Street* (1984), and the many sequels they spawned. Barbara Creed and Carol Clover first established the importance of the horror genre for feminist criticism—a challenging task given the aversion of many women toward cinematic violence and its status outside the purview of more respectable criticism due to its association with B movies. For Clover, Creed, Linda Williams, Rhona Berenstein, Vivian Sobchack, Kate E. Sullivan, and others, the genre's graphic excesses provide opportunities to explore cultural connections between violence and sexual difference. Their scholarship both anchors *Scream* in its generic tradition as well as highlighting its departure from it. According to Clover in her influential *Men, Women and Chainsaws*, horror films, like fairy tales, provide raw and unmediated glimpses into unconscious fears and desires, especially around sexual difference. The killer is invariably male, like Billy, and his victims female—young, beautiful, and sexual (or sexually transgressive). He is eventually killed by a "Final Girl" who, like Sidney, is "boyish" in name, appearance, or behavior and uses an active, male gaze to hunt down the killer. Unlike Sidney, however, the Final Girl remains a virgin, allowed to kill the killer because she has not yet discovered the more threatening power of her adult sexuality. For Clover, the horror film is primarily a male discourse, with the Final Girl a point of identification for the male adolescent viewer. However, other critics, such as Isabel Pinedo in *Recreational Terror*, see in the genre the potential for female and feminist appropriation, a potential that *Scream* develops.

Scream depends on an easy familiarity with the generic conventions out of which the film is built, and the trilogy's most noted formal characteristic is its self-reflexivity. The films abound in references and in-jokes about popular culture, from the conventions of the teen slasher film to debates about violence in the media to references to trends in pop sociology ("Teen suicides are out this year. Homicide is healthier."). This self-reflexivity increases as the trilogy progresses and the films begin to build a dense layering of narratives-within-narratives and intertextual references. In the first film, the killer repeatedly quizzes his victims on their knowledge of the horror films. "Do you like scary movies?" he taunts. The young couple describes the degree of their sexual intimacy in terms of movie ratings (Sidney struggles to keep their relationship "PG-13"), and when they have sex, the scene is intercut with shots of their friends watching movies downstairs. The trilogy finally highlights the place of popular culture in teen lives by making knowledge of it the defining characteristic of those who live and those who die. Indeed, in a world infused with media culture, it is hard to dispute the implications that knowledge of how media work is a crucial survival skill.

One of the most troubling aspects of the *Scream* trilogy for many adult women is its apparent approval of violence, especially in the hands of its teen girl protagonist. This violence cannot be understood, however, apart from the narrative and generic conventions that give it meaning and which the films challenge in important ways. Young fans are also likely to bring an auteurist's understanding to these films and interpret them in the context of Wes Craven's body of work, which has consistently challenged dominant ideologies of gender and bourgeois family life (*The Hills Have Eyes* [1977]) as well as those of race (*The People Under the Stairs* [1991]). (See Heba, Lehman and Luhr, and Markovitz.) *Scream* is structured around two very different kinds of female protagonists, whose differences lead to radically different narratives. The female protagonist in most narratives plays a familiar and unchanging role: she is the passive object of the active male hero's quest or the prize at the end of his journey. Action, agency, movement, and change belong to the male hero, and action, even violent action, is not only sanctioned for him but serves as a means of proving his courage and strength. The slasher film exaggerates this opposition according to its own highly stylized generic requirements: blonde female victims ("some big-breasted girl" as one character in *Scream* observes) and male psychopaths. Male fear of female sexuality becomes encoded in the slasher convention that only female virgins can survive—a convention that *Scream* notably rejects.

Scream begins with a graphic and exaggerated display of those conventions in order to undermine and rewrite them for the remainder of the film. Its first joke on viewers' expectations is its witty casting of Drew Barrymore, the film's biggest teen star attraction, to draw on her personal history of exploitation and victimization, and then kill her within the first fifteen minutes. In the film's most sustained sequence of suspense and gory violence, Casey Becker, the character she plays, is ruthlessly trapped by the killer's threatening gaze and taunting vocal address, as well as by the camera's complicitous, voyeuristic gaze. Most importantly, the film hinges her death on her ignorance of popular culture: when the killer quizzes her about knowledge of slasher films, she falters, and her ignorance of the rules—where the killer is hiding, how to elude him, and so on—takes her right to his knife. By killing off this character so decisively, the film also kills off a certain model of femininity—dumb, passive, dependent, victimized—in order to replace it with another that is more knowing, less glamorous, and far more capable. Sidney, played by Neve Campbell, then a lesser-known model and star from television, knows the rules, but resists her assigned part and in the end succeeds in unmasking and killing the murderer herself. In effect, she usurps the male role in the narrative for herself. She resists the passivity of the traditional female protagonist and the model of femininity on which it is based.

The film constructs Sidney's character with quiet visual references to icons of Girl Power, such as the poster of the Indigo Girls in her bedroom, and shows her techno-confidence when she uses her computer to signal for help. Like Buffy the Vampire Slayer and Xena Warrior Princess, Sidney is physically active, strong, resourceful, and capable of taking care of herself. (Campbell, in fact, is an athlete who performed some of her own stunts.)

She has sex according to her timetable, not her boyfriend's, and the loss of her virginity does not mean the "end of the story" for her, as it does in the traditional slasher film as well as an enduring tradition of romantic comedies and melodramas that conclude the woman's story when she reaches the altar. Instead, it marks the beginning of her real power as an adult woman. She does not depend on male authorities to rescue her, whether the school principal, the cop, her father, or her boyfriend.

One of the most telling moments of the film occurs in a brief moment of calm when the battle to kill Billy has apparently ended. One of the surviving teens—Randy, the film buff, who has given a metacommentary on the action throughout the film—warns Sidney that the killer always rises once again from apparent death, and Billy lurches up to attack one last time. "Not in my movie," Sidney responds, before killing him for good. With that remark, she claims her place not only as a new kind of female protagonist, but as the "auteur" or author of her own movie, or in fact her own life, in an age where the movies and life are indistinguishable. As the killer says, "It's all a movie, just pick your genre." The happy ending of this script does not require the union of a heterosexual couple, the staple of Hollywood films and most traditional narratives. Following the lead of *Heathers* (1989), another important teen girl film that refuses the romantic ending, *Scream* concludes with the teen girl heroine independent and unattached.

According to the logic of realism, *Scream* might well be considered an endorsement of violence in the hands of a teen girl. But when viewed in its cultural and formal context, the film, like the slasher genre in general, provides an opportunity to examine cultural and individual fantasies as they relate to gender and power. The film's particular revision of the genre invites female viewers imaginatively to "try on" a new model of femininity more suited to young women of the Third Wave. Moreover, its generic license for excess and exaggeration enables it to make its points with bold strokes: the boyfriend can be a killer quite literally, and the girl can defend herself boldly and take on power formerly off limits to girls. Interestingly, our culture has yet to create such exercises in female imagination in the genres of realism, which continue to consign girls and women to traditional roles. "Supergirls" like Buffy, Xena, Sabrina the Teenage Witch, and Sidney remain thinkable only in the realms of fantasy.

Teen films from *Rebel Without a Cause* (1955) to *Clueless* have traditionally addressed issues of generational tension, but this tension takes on a new dimension in the 1990s when it is played out against the social backdrop of divorce, single-parent homes, and houses empty after school. Indeed, the empty house signifies more than an opportunity for a wild party but the occasion for terror, and parents no longer stand as towering figures of authority against which to rebel, or even neutral absences, but haunting specters of impotence and loss. The film's title is taken from Edvard Munch's famous Expressionist painting of 1893, evoking the inarticulate anguish of an alienated age, and the killer always wears a mask bearing the image of Munch's *Scream*. However, the *Scream* trilogy uses this image to evoke the angst of its own historical times, where it manifests itself in deep-rooted fears about changes in the family and the desire to blame women for the consequences of these changes, especially as they relate to boys and men.

These themes are set up during opening sequence, when Casey is home alone. Her parents return but too late, as she is near death. In a horrific image of botched communication and the limits of technology to substitute for real contact, parents and child are within close proximity, screaming to each other into cordless phones, but cannot "connect." Similarly, Sidney's father has left her alone and so put her at risk. He has also rendered himself a suspect, tapping on recent cultural awareness of violence and sexual abuse in the home and fathers as figures of potential risk to their daughters. He returns during the siege, but is unable to help his daughter. In an exaggerated image of paternal weakness, the killer ties him up with duct tape, rendering him even more powerless until Sidney rescues him. Indeed, the film's critique of idealized figures of masculinity is as telling as its reconstruction of femininity: from father to principal to boyfriend to cop, male authorities are suspicious, silly, or weak. As the trilogy progresses, the cop develops stature as a new and gentler model of masculinity, but, in the first film, the only male who is both trustworthy and able to approach the killer on his own turf is Randy, the teen cinema buff who draws on his vast knowledge of pulp film to provide a metacommentary on the unfolding events both for characters within the film and for viewers without.

Despite the presence of failed father figures, however, it is absent mothers who provide the underlying narrative enigma in the *Scream* trilogy. The first segment of *Scream* concludes with Casey gasping "Mom" as she dies, and the remainder of the trilogy becomes an investigation of the mystery of Sidney's mother and the events of her life and death. This mystery is only heightened when the killer discloses his motives and we learn that Billy lost his mind when he lost his mother, all because of Sidney's mother, whose affair with his father drove her away. The film highlights the depth of Billy's obsession with his mother by having him refute current conventional wisdom about what creates violence and all other contemporary social ills: It is not "movies," he insists, but mothers. Movies only make killers "more creative." Quoting pop psychology, he informs Sidney that "maternal abandonment creates psychopathology." This loss sends him on a rampage to punish all mothers and potential mothers for the loss of his own.

"Maternal abandonment" triggered by maternal sex lies at the core of the films, and both evoke powerful cultural taboos. Our culture likes its mothers "immaculate" and maternal sexuality unacknowledged and unrepresented, so Sidney's mother has ensured her own violent punishment and death by having sex outside marriage. (The same rules, of course, do not apply to fathers, and Billy's father doesn't warrant a mention for his role in the affair.) Throughout cinema history, a mother shown as sexual, especially outside marriage, is certain to suffer and probably die by the end of the film. The 1990s have been particularly fixated on the missing mother, who, like feminism itself, becomes a scapegoat for the malaise of a generation brought up with divorce, low economic expectations, and empty houses. However, a more careful look at the trope of maternal abandonment exposes it as a stunning ideological inversion of the social reality of teen lives, where in most cases of divorce and blended families, it is not the mother but the father who is missing from the home.

Initially, the films provide very little information about Sidney's mother. Billy accuses Sidney of being a "slut" who is "just like her mother," and Sidney acknowledges her confusion about who her mother was and her fear of turning out like her, suggesting her own vulnerability to the power of the double standard, especially as it applies to mothers. Her struggle, like that of all girls, is to know her mother not only as her mother but as a person in her own right, and as the trilogy advances, the focus intensifies around Sidney's quest for her own identity as it relates to her mother's.

The trilogy takes its first step toward that understanding with the relationship between Sidney and Gale Weathers, played by another popular television star, Courtney Cox. The character of Gale brings together stereotypes of the ambitious career woman and bloodthirsty tabloid television, both targets of derision in our culture, but revises them in interesting ways that redeem this culturally unpopular figure without domesticating her. Gale is allowed the film's only successful romance when she falls in love with Dewey, the dim but endearing cop. She, not Sidney, was right in her suspicions about the trial of Casey's killer, which left the real killer at large and an innocent man in prison. And by the end of the film, it is Gale—not any of the film's well-intentioned but helpless boys and men—who comes to Sidney's aid.

An accomplished woman a decade or so older than Sidney, Gale stands as a displaced maternal figure, a locus of the conflicted feelings teen girls often feel toward their mothers. This is clear when Sidney punches her the first time the two face each other early in the film, and again when they meet in *Scream 2*. Sidney's relationship with Gale, however, not only paves the way for the renegotiation of her more complex relationship with her mother but also models a kind of solidarity among women who, despite their differences, can unite toward common goals. In the first two films of the trilogy, Sidney and Gale never come to like each other. But they develop an uneasy alliance as they recognize the common goal of survival, and in that way they suggest a kind of coalition politics for the Third Wave.

SCREAM 2 (1997)

Scream 2 takes place a year later, in a college town where Sidney is studying drama and attempting to put her past behind her. She has a new boyfriend and a close girlfriend who is encouraging her to join a sorority. She is also preparing for her role as Cassandra in the college production of *Agamemnon*, the blood-soaked Greek tragedy that, like the *Scream* films, hinges on issues of maternal rebellion and adultery, the primacy of mother-daughter bonds, and the struggle between patriarchal and matriarchal orders.

The film begins in a movie theater with the opening of *Stab*, a film based on Gale Weathers's book about the Hillsboro slayings. The film triggers a series of copycat killings that end when Sidney kills the killer, after learning that it is Mrs. Loomis, Billy the boyfriend's avenging mother (an allusion to *Friday the 13th*, in which the killer is also the mother of a dead son).

Scream 2 is moodier and darker than the first film, with Sidney and other returning characters bearing the emotional scars of the events of the first film. It is also more ambitious in scope, making bold claims for popular cinema as a serious means of enacting a culture's most profound anxieties and myths. Most dramatically, in its use of Greek mythology and drama, it links the teen horror film of today with a long tradition of respected dramatic and narrative antecedents. As literary critics such as Northrop Frye and others have shown, popular audiences have always been drawn to sensationalistic treatments of highly charged subject matter on stage, page, and screen, from the tragedies and comedies of antiquity to the violent dramas of the Jacobean stage, the melodramatic fiction of Dickens, and the action-packed, emotionally charged cinema of Spielberg.

Following the rule of sequels—spelled out in an early scene set in a university cinema studies class—not only are the stakes raised in *Scream 2*, but the self-reflexivity is even more layered and complex. The film includes overt visual allusions to such classics of the genre as *Nosferatu* (1922) and *Psycho* (1960). The first characters introduced by the film are a young black couple who argue over Hollywood's racial politics on their way to see *Stab*. The woman, a cinema studies student, criticizes the horror genre for its exclusion of blacks and its violence against women. As if to underscore her point, the couple becomes the new killer's first victims, violently reasserting the genre's, and Hollywood's, narrative privileging of white characters, while at the same time exposing these cinematic mechanisms of racism to a teen audience already familiar with Craven's earlier treatments of race.

With the use of Billy's mother, Mrs. Loomis, as the new killer, the trilogy deepens its investigation into the place of motherhood in the cultural myths and narratives of the 1990s, suggesting once again that even before the movies could be blamed for kids gone wrong, there were mothers. Hovering over the trilogy is Clytemnestra, the tragic queen of *Agamemnon* who is remembered for her many transgressions: her rebellion against her husband for killing her daughter, her eventual adultery, her death at the hands of her son, and the curse he must bear for killing her. "I'm sick of everyone saying it's all the parents' fault," Mrs. Loomis rages, and acknowledges that the weight of that blame falls more heavily on mothers than fathers. "I was a good mother," she says, adding, "You don't know what it's like to be a mother." To be a mother is not an easy task in a culture where mothers are liable to be blamed for loving too much or not enough, for being too present or not present enough, for leaving their homes to work if they are middle class or for staying home to care for their children if they receive public assistance. Played by Laurie Metcalf with the kind of controlled hysteria she brought to her role in the sitcom *Roseanne,* Mrs. Loomis does not fold in despair over her losses, however, but rears up as a demonic fury who becomes readable and even sympathetic within the horror genre. A crazed Clytemnestra seeking revenge for the loss of her child, she is neither pitiable nor weak but a figure of superhuman strength who refuses to be a victim. Muscling herself to the center of the narrative, she usurps the place of the villainous male serial killer and stands face to face with the new Girl Power hero.

In *Scream 2,* Sidney also develops into a more mature and complex hero for the Third Wave. By casting her as Cassandra in the production of *Agamemnon,* the film identifies her with a figure of mythic stature, described by Sidney's drama teacher as one of the "great visionaries of literature" who was fated to see the truth but not to be believed. Sidney offers a powerful image of a new girl hero who not only has the wits and physical courage to defend herself but a growing capacity to understand herself and the cultural scripts that would write who she is. This time when she defeats the killer, Sidney puts an extra bullet in her head for good measure, and walks away with a cool self-assurance.

SCREAM 3 (2000)

The ghost of Sidney's mother, a structuring absence in the first two films, becomes the focus of the final film, which zeroes in on the mystery of Maureen Prescott's life and its meaning for Sidney. *Scream 3* finds Sidney isolated once again in a bucolic setting where she takes calls for a women's Crisis Center. Meanwhile, *Stab 3,* based on the Windsor College killings, is in production in Hollywood. On the studio set, the masked killer strikes again, leaving photographs of a young Maureen Prescott, Sidney's mother, with each victim. When the killer starts calling Sidney, she travels to Hollywood where she begins to learn about a missing chapter in her mother's life: when her mother was her age, she had appeared in several horror films under the name of Rena Reynolds. In her final showdown with the killer,

Figure 16. The missing chapter: In *Scream 3* (2000), Sidney must discover the truth about her mother's past in order to come to terms with her own identity.

Sidney learns that he is Roman Bridges, the director of *Stab 3*, who also turns out to be her half-brother. He tells her that their mother ended her career and began a new life after she had been raped and left pregnant by studio executives. Roman tracked her down four years ago, only to have her reject him as the child of someone who no longer existed. In a rage, he turned on her and Sidney, the daughter she acknowledged, and masterminded the murders to follow. Sidney puts an end to the horror by killing him, then returns to the mountains to take up her new life in the company of Dewey and Gale, who decide to get married.

As the mother's story moves into the foreground in *Scream 3*, so does the story of Hollywood with which it is so closely intertwined. As if to signal the scope of its critique, the film begins with a helicopter roaring over the "Hollywood" letters in L.A. and the film's self-reflexivity deepens to include practices within the film industry itself. Like the earlier films, *Scream 3* abounds in references to other films and most of its action takes place on a Hollywood studio set that recreates the settings of the earlier films. Randy, the video buff who died in *Scream 2*, addresses the characters on a videotape to let them know that the final chapter of a trilogy differs from a sequel in its inevitable return to the beginning. Like Freud's return of the repressed ("The past will come back to bite you," Randy warns) and the trilogies of classic Greece, film trilogies uncover past secrets and "unexpected backstories."

Stab 3 is more a ghost story than a horror film, haunted as it is by Sidney's dead mother. Maureen Prescott appears as a narrative device in the photographic images, as a ghostly hallucination in Sidney's mind, and as a key to Sidney's identity finally to be faced. Throughout the film she appears as a monstrous ghost, expressing the daughter's ongoing struggle to reconcile her conflicting ideas about who her mother was. On one hand, Sidney experienced her as "the perfect mother" at the heart of a "perfect family." On the other, she has learned about her extramarital affairs, heard her judged a "slut," and discovered that she had a secret life in her past. This monstrous mother is the mother as seen by the social world and the woman Sidney fears she will become herself. However, the film eventually provides a "backstory" to that judgment that redeems the mother and points an accusing finger where it belongs.

Sidney's final discoveries about her mother occur in a sequence that imagistically returns the viewer to the maternal body. Her struggle with the killer in the paternal mansion takes her down secret passageways suggesting the birth canal, and she and Roman confront each other in a dark, womblike room. The real villain, however, is not Roman, but John Milton, the powerful studio mogul and emblem of the patriarchal power Roman both exposes and aspires to possess. As a legendary director of horror films, Milton made millions of dollars on young women like Maureen, only to destroy them. Sidney learns that he was renowned for hosting wild parties for powerful men and young women seeking careers in the movies. At one of the parties that Rena attended, "things got out of hand," and Rena ended up leaving Hollywood for good.

By unmasking Milton as the real killer, Roman emerges at this point not so much as a monster but as the male victim of a cruel and exploitative gender system, an Orestes figure driven by the patriarchal order to commit the sin of matricide. The film portrays Sidney's killing of her brother as yet another dimension of a fate that deepens her character, and the two clasp hands as he nears death. By linking his mother's subsequent sexual behavior to the sins inflicted on her by a paternal figure who "gave away" her innocence, Roman demystifies the term "slut." "She never got over it," he says of her Hollywood experience. As Milton said in trying to defend himself, Hollywood is "not the city for innocence." While focused on Hollywood, however, the *Scream* trilogy points to the very essence of a culture in which women, from Monica Lewinsky to the sorority girls of *Scream 2*, see sexually servicing men as their most immediate access to power or even survival. When Sidney learns about her mother's past, she also learns that they are connected not only biologically but through shared experiences of betrayal or violence against women.

Rena Rowlands, however, is not only the victim Roman describes, but a fighter like her daughter. "The bottom line is, Rena Reynolds wouldn't play by the rules," Milton says. Just as Sidney refused to follow the script of the classical horror film in *Scream*, her mother resisted the script for success in Hollywood. Moreover, Rena succeeded in rewriting her identity in order to create a new life for herself—one that represented success for a woman of her generation. By the end of the film—and the trilogy itself—Sidney has completed a horrific journey into her own past and put the ghost of her mother to rest. The knowledge she has gained of her mother's history enables her to redeem her mother's life and expose the systemic injustices that had brutalized her. As such, she moves from protagonist or film star to auteur or director of a new movie with a new script.

CONCLUSIONS

The trilogy concludes in the pastoral setting of Sidney's mountain retreat, where shots of Sidney walking alone in a setting bathed in golden light return the film to an Edenic beginning. Dewey and Gale are present, along with the golden retriever who was Sidney's only companion at the beginning of the film. When Gale accepts an engagement ring from Dewey, the film reconstitutes the lost nuclear family, replacing the family of origin—with the repressed secrets and horrors implicit in the very structure of the nuclear family—with one that has battled openly and hard for its rewards. Sidney has conquered her demons of isolation, and leaves the door ajar, signaling her openness to a new life. For director Craven, according to Kate E. Sullivan, the moral center of contemporary culture lies with girls, and in this trilogy Sidney has been assaulted on all sides not only by physical violence but by corruption and compromise. By locating Sidney's most dangerous threat within her family and requiring her to commit fratricide to survive, the film dramatizes a devastating vision of female isolation and vulnerability. The trilogy suggests that female adolescence is a lonely place to be, especially for young women such as Sidney who are willing to confront the sexual politics of their world. The trilogy's success in capturing that loneliness suggests one reason for its appeal to young female audiences. Sidney is a "Final Girl" who stands as a figure of identification for girls, not boys, and in that way the trilogy stands firmly outside the tradition of horror Carol Clover documented.

Feminism is never mentioned in the *Scream* trilogy, but the films address head-on the issues of representation, power, and sexuality that speak to Third Wave audiences. Like the Girl Power phenomenon, they operate in the realm of myth rather than rationality, acting out scenarios of female desire, pleasure, and anger. The films abound in female characters who refuse to play by rules that would diminish them, from Maureen Prescott to Gale Weathers to Sidney. In Sidney, the trilogy provides a new model of femininity for Third Wave audiences: a girl who is active, who can protect herself through physical resources, who can claim power over her own sexuality, and express rather than repress her rage. This new girl hero knows her culture, from the legends underpinning its institutions to the popular culture and technology of her own generation, using the tools it offers as a means of rewriting old narratives that no longer serve her.

Most importantly, the film's model of a daughter's struggle to come to terms with her mother is a suggestive one for contemporary feminism. In Hollywood, collective histories are always retold as personal stories, and the story of the missing mother might well be seen as the repressed history of the women's movement itself and the injustices that brought it about. Sidney's journey forces her to face the historical realities of her mother's life when they erupt as horrors in her own. The trilogy suggests the necessity of facing history because the failure to do so threatens the security of the present, and the subtle erasure of historical consciousness is the surest way to take the teeth out of any liberation movement Without knowing and remembering the world of their mothers and grandmothers, young women remain vulnerable to having to fight old battles once again. The *Scream* trilogy teaches Sidney about the bonds that connect generations of women, but without sentimentalizing her acceptance of her mother and Gale. Instead it shows her growing in her own strength through her experiences with these figures of motherhood or displaced motherhood.

At the same time, the films remind women of the Second Wave of the need to remain conversant with the culture of today's young women. The *Scream* films are not unambiguous treatises on feminism and sexual politics. Like all popular culture texts, they are riddled with contradictions that account for their emotional power and appeal. These contradictions, however, also beg careful analysis based on an informed understanding of media culture and representation, of history, and of the issues that matter to young women today.

ACKNOWLEDGMENTS

Thanks to Julia Lesage, Chuck Kleinhans, Karen Ford, Louise Bishop, and James Earl for helpful comments; to Catherine Earl for introducing me to *Scream*; to Kate E. Sullivan for crucial help with the horror genre; and to Carol Siegel for her work on feminism and youth culture and her editorial advice.

NOTE

A longer version of this chapter was originally published by *Genders* (38) in 2003. Reprinted with permission.

BIBLIOGRAPHY

Beck, Debra Baker. "The 'F' Word: How the Media Frame Feminism." *National Women's Studies Association Journal* 10.1 (1998): 139–149.
Bellafante, Ginia. "Feminism: It's all about ME!" *Time* (29 June 1998): 54–62.

Berenstein, Rhonda. *Attack of the Leading Ladies: Gender, Sexuality, and Spectatorship in Classic Horror Cinema*. New York: Columbia University Press, 1995.

Bhavnani, Kum-Kum, Kathryn R. Kent, and France Winddance Twine, eds. *Feminisms and Youth Cultures*. Special issue of *Signs* 23.3 (1998): 585–841.

Brumberg, Joan Jacobs. *The Body Project: An Intimate History of American Girls*. New York: Random House, 1997.

Carlip, Hillary. *Girl Power: Young Women Speak Out: Personal Writings from Teenage Girls*. New York: Warner Books, 1995.

Clover, Carol. *Men, Women, and Chain Saws: Gender in the Modern Horror Film*. Princeton: Princeton University Press, 1992.

Clueless. Dir. Amy Heckerling. Paramount Pictures, 1995.

Cole, Alyson. " 'There Are No Victims in This Class.' " *National Women's Studies Association Journal* 10.1 (1988): 72–85.

Creed, Barbara. "Horror and the Monstrous-Feminine: An Imaginary Abjection." *Screen* 27.1 (1986): 44–70.

Douglas, Susan J. *Where the Girls Are: Growing Up Female with the Mass Media*. New York: Times Books, 1994.

———. "Girls 'n' Spice: All Things Nice?" *The Nation* (25 August/1 September 1997): 21+.

Faludi, Susan. *Backlash: The Undeclared War Against American Women*. New York: Crown, 1991.

Fischer, Lucy. *Cinematernity: Film, Motherhood, Genre*. Princeton: Princeton University Press, 1996.

Fox-Genovese, Elizabeth. *"Feminism Is Not the Story of My Life": How Today's Feminist Elite Has Lost Touch with the Real Concerns of Women*. New York: Nan Talese, 1996.

Friday the 13th. Dir. Sean S. Cunningham. Paramount Pictures, 1980.

Garrison, Ednie Kaeh. "U.S. Feminism—Grrrl Style! Youth (Sub)Cultures and the Technologies of the Third Wave." *Feminist Studies* 26.1 (2000): 141–170.

Gateward, Frances, and Murray Pomerance, eds. *Sugar, Spice and Everything Nice: Cinemas of Girlhood*. Detroit: Wayne State University Press, 2002.

Gilligan, Carol. "Getting Civilized." *Who's Afraid of Feminism? Seeing Through the Backlash*. Eds. Ann Oakley and Juliet Mitchell. New York: New Press, 1997. 13–28.

Green, Karen, and Tristan Taormino, eds. *A Girls' Guide to Taking Over the World: Writing from the Girl Zine Revolution*. New York: St. Martin's Griffin, 1997.

Halloween. Dir. John Carpenter. Compass International Pictures, 1978.

Heathers. Dir. Michael Lehman. New World Pictures, 1989.

Heba, Gary. "Everyday Nightmares." *Journal of Popular Film and Television* 23.3 (1995): 107–115.

Heyes, Cressida J. "Anti-Essentialism in Practice: Carol Gilligan and Feminist Philosophy." *Hypatia* 12.3 (1997): 142–163.

Heywood, Leslie, and Jennifer Drake, eds. *Third Wave Agenda: Being Feminist, Doing Feminism*. Minneapolis: University of Minnesota Press, 1997.

The Hills Have Eyes. Dir. Wes Craven. Vanguard, 1977.

Hoff-Sommers, Christina. *Who Stole Feminism? How Women Have Betrayed Women*. New York: Simon Schuster, 1994.

Hook, Jonathan. "*Scream's* Impact on Hollywood and Horror." Unpublished paper. Evanston, Ill: Northwestern University, 2001.

Jenkins, Henry. "Empowering Children in the Digital Age." *Radical Teacher* 50 (1997): 30–35.

Kamen, Paula. *Her Way: Young Women Remake the Sexual Revolution*. New York: New York University Press, 2000.

Kearney, Mary Celeste. "Producing Girls: Rethinking the Study of Female Youth Culture." *Delinquents and Debutantes: Twentieth Century American Girls' Cultures*. Ed. Sherrie A. Inness. New York: New York University Press, 1998. 285–310.

Lehman, Peter, and William Luhr. *Thinking About Movies: Watching, Questioning, Enjoying*. Forth Worth: Harcourt, 1999.

Lotz, Amanda D. "Postfeminist Television Criticism: Rehabilitating Critical Terms and Identifying Postfeminist Attributes." *Feminist Media Studies* 1.1 (2001): 105–121.

Lumby, Catherine. *Bad Girls: The Media, Sex and Feminism in the 90s*. St. Leonards, New South Wales: Allen & Unwin, 1997.

Maglin, Nan Bauer, and Donna Perry, eds. *"Bad Girls"/"Good Girls": Women, Sex and Power in the Nineties*. New Brunswick: Rutgers University Press, 1996.

Markovitz, Jonathan. "Female Paranoia as Survival Skill: Reason or Pathology in *A Nightmare on Elm Street*." *Quarterly Review of Film and Video* 17.3 (October 2000): 211–221.

McRobbie, Angela. *Feminism and Youth Culture: From "Jackie" to "Just Seventeen."* Houndsmills: Macmillan, 1991.

McRobbie, Angela, and Jenny Garber. "Girls and Subcultures: An Exploration." *Resistance Through Rituals: Youth Subcultures in Post-War Britain*. Eds. Stuart Hall and Tony Jefferson. London: Centre for Contemporary Cultural Studies, 1976. 209–222.

Neisel, Jeff. "Hip-Hop Matters: Rewriting the Sexual Politics of Rap Music." *Third Wave Agenda*. Eds. Leslie Heywood and Jennifer Drake. Minneapolis: University of Minnesota Press, 1997. 239–254.

Nightmare on Elm Street. Dir. Wes Craven. New Line Cinema, 1984.

Oakley, Ann and Juliet Mitchell, eds. *Who's Afraid of Feminism? Seeing Through the Backlash*. New York: New Press, 1997.

Orr, Catherine M. "Charting the Currents of the Third Wave." *Hypatia* 12.3 (1997): 29–45.

The People Under the Stairs. Dir. Wes Craven. Universal Pictures, 1991.

Pinedo, Isabel Cristina. *Recreational Terror: Women and the Pleasures of Horror Film Viewing*. Albany: SUNY Press, 1997.

Pipher, Mary. *Reviving Ophelia: Saving the Selves of Adolescent Girls*. New York: Putnam, 1994.

Powers, Ann. "Everything and the Girl." *Spin* (November 1997): 74–80.

Rich, Adrienne. *Of Woman Born: Motherhood as Experience and Institution*. New York: W. W. Norton, 1986.

Scary Movie. Dir. Keenan Ivory Wayans. Dimension Films, 2000.

Scary Movie 2. Dir. Keenan Ivory Wayans. Dimension Films, 2001.

Scary Movie 3. Dir. David Zucker. Dimension Films, 2003.

Scary Movie 4. Dir. David Zucker. Dimension Films, 2006.

Schneider, Steven Jay. "*Scream.*" *Understanding Film Genres*. Ed. Tom Pendergast, Sara Pendergast, and Steven Jay Schneider. New York: McGraw-Hill, 2003.

Scream. Dir. Wes Craven. Miramax, 1996.

Scream 2. Dir. Wes Craven. Dimension Films, 1997.

Scream 3. Dir. Wes Craven. Dimension Films, 2000.

Sidler, Michelle. "Living in McJobdom: Third Wave Feminism and Class Inequity." *Third Wave Agenda*. Eds. Leslie Heywood and Jennifer Drake. Minneapolis: University of Minnesota Press, 1997. 25–39.

Siegel, Carol. *New Millennial Sexstyles*. Bloomington: Indiana University Press, 2000.

Sobchack, Vivian. "Bringing It All Back Home: Family Economy and Generic Exchange." *The Dread of Difference: Gender and the Horror Film*. Ed. Barry Keith Grant. Austin: University of Texas Press, 1996. 143–163.

Sullivan, Kate E. Conversation with author. Eugene, Oregon. 29 July 2002.

———. "Stephen King's Bookish Boys: (Re)Imagining the Masculine." *Michigan Feminist Studies* 14 (1999–2000): 29–57.

Titanic. Dir. James Cameron. Paramount Pictures, 1997.

Turow, Joseph. *Breaking Up America: Advertising and the New Media World*. Chicago: University of Chicago Press, 1997.

Walker, Rebecca. "Becoming the Third Wave." *Ms.* 39 (January/February 1992): 41.

———, ed. *To Be Real: Telling the Truth and Changing the Face of Feminism*. New York, Anchor, 1995.

Weinraub, Bernard. "Who's Lining up at the Box Office? Lots of Girls." *New York Times* (23 February 1998): E1+.

Williams, Linda. "When the Woman Looks." *Dread of Difference: Gender and the Horror Film*. Ed. Barry Keith Grant. Austin: University of Texas Press, 1996. 15–35.

Zita, Jacqueline N., ed. *Third Wave Feminism*. Special issue of *Hypatia* 12.3 (1997).

IV

MATERNAL ANXIETIES OF CLASS,

RACE, AND GENDER

ELEVEN

GREAT LADIES AND GUTTERSNIPES

Class and the Representation of
Southern Mothers in Hollywood Films

AIMEE BERGER

This chapter examines *Gone with the Wind* (1939) as both product and producer of nostalgic versions of the South, and *Bastard Out of Carolina* (2000) as an example of an equally familiar stereotype of the South as the site of white poverty, a stereotype that dominates Hollywood films of the late 1990s and early twenty-first century. Significantly, despite the differences in these films' visions of the South, they share a strikingly similar vision of the poor white Southern mother, a figure that brings together in her representation stereotypes of three separately but similarly denigrated groups: the poor, Southerners, and mothers. In both films, and the versions of the South they represent, these stereotypes combine to demonize the poor white Southern mother.

Significantly, films of the middle to late 1990s and early twenty-first century that feature poor or working-class whites are often set in the South, and even films that do not focus on the South or on Southerners may nonetheless carelessly participate in the conflation of "Southerner" with "white trash,"[1] the pejorative term that circulates widely, tellingly, and without comment in place of more neutral terms such as "poor white working class" or "poor white." Peter Applebome, among others, has observed that views of the South as a "hellhole of poverty, torment and depravity" have alternated

in public discourse with views of the region as "an American Eden of tradition, strength and grace," and contends that Hollywood participates directly
in the construction of these monolithic and "embarrassingly stereotypical"
portrayals, moving between these two limited views, Edenic or hellish (10–11).
These competing constructs are not always available simultaneously in the
cultural imaginary and its repositories; instead, one monolith can be seen,
through the proliferation of images that represent it, to gain ascendancy in
a given period over the other(s).

Accordingly, over the course of the twentieth and early twenty-first
centuries, Hollywood representations of the South have moved along a predictable trajectory to reshape the discursive object of the South in a variety
of ways, all of which nonetheless reduce its complexity, limit its dimensional-
ity, and "work together to oversimplify the South into one of two or three
monoliths" (Polk ix): the moonlight and magnolia Old South populated
by great ladies, chivalrous gentlemen and happy slaves; the dangerous rural
backwater populated by rednecks and "white trash";[2] and the quaint small
town populated by eccentrics and "simple folk." *Gone with the Wind* (1939),
following closely on the heels of the popular *Jezebel* (1938), is representative
of the first. But in the 1960s and 1970s, the pendulum swung the other
way, and films like *In the Heat of the Night* (1967), *Easy Rider* (1969), and
Deliverance (1972) brought viewers to focus on the second monolith. And
then, in the 1980s and 1990s, nostalgia for the mythic South returned and
what Tara McPherson has called "the New Old South," the third monolith
of the Hollywood South, was born in the popular imagination with television
shows like *Evening Shade* and *Designing Women*, and films like *Crimes of the
Heart* (1986), *Steel Magnolias* (1989), and *Forrest Gump* (1994).[3]

Contemporary Hollywood privileges a version of the South that recalls
the second monolith that held sway in the 1960s and 1970s; recent Hollywood films increasingly portray Southerners as backwards inhabitants of
ugly little towns or semirural spaces. Whether comedies or dramas, such
films often focus on poor whites rather than on the middle- or upper-class
subjects of the Old South and New Old South films,[4] though the redneck
or "white trash" figure is still visible as a stock character across the whole
spectrum of films about the South.

The conflation of "redneck" and "white trash" with "Southerner" works
conveniently to situate white poverty in the South, making it a Southern
rather than a national problem. To envision the South as a space that
contains white poverty underscores a connection between the South and
white poverty in the collective imagination, or even further suggests that
white poverty occurs exclusively in the South. In turn, this enables a fantasy
of poverty as something removed from the American "norm." Representations of the poor as innately lazy, willfully destructive, and dangerous work
to objectify, homogenize, and demonize, and ultimately to obscure the mate-

rial reality of poverty. Confinement of the white poor to the South serves to obscure the character and reach of poverty in America, "allow[ing] a national disavowal of the broad extent of social injustice, [by] locating it all conveniently 'down there' in the South" (McPherson 201).

Cinematic scapegoating of the mother operates in similar ways and from similar principles. It has been well documented, argues Maggie Humm, that "film . . . often and anxiously envisions women stereotypically as 'good' mothers or 'bad' " (3). Representations of the mother provide insight not only into gender problematics, but also other ideologies, such as those of class and region. On screen, poor white mothers raise flawed or frightening children; they are implicated in their children's abuse; their sexuality is often problematized and they are, in short, to blame for many a cinematic tragedy. Rarely is the audience brought to speculate on the mother's own victimization or to relate to her subjectively. E. Ann Kaplan observes that both literary and filmic discourses of abusive/neglectful mothers are "predominantly representations about, and addressed to, the poor [and] usually speak from an implicit, judgmental, middle-class position. These discourses inevitably lean toward mother-blaming" (192). Underlying most representations of the mother in discourses of white poverty is the assumption that, being "low class," she is naturally inclined to be abusive or neglectful.

The paradigmatic film about the South, *Gone with the Wind* (1939), showcases stereotypes of the "good" mother, while simultaneously constructing "that poor white trash Emmie Slattery," as she is repeatedly referred to in both the novel and the film, as both an unfit mother and a danger to the "good" people whose charity sustains her. (Emmie is a secondary character who has a child by a Yankee and is later indirectly blamed for the death of Scarlett O'Hara's mother.) Importantly, the film does not develop the character of Scarlett O'Hara as a "bad" mother, though the novel on which the film is based clearly does. To that end, the film leaves out two of Scarlett's three children (the two she despises), and all of Scarlett's unwholesome feelings about motherhood and children, highlighting instead her grief over a miscarriage and the death of her only child. In order for Scarlett to fulfill her role as Southern lady, she must be seen to embrace motherhood; it is simply part of the package, like the hoop skirt and the loving Mammy. *Gone with the Wind* serves up a vision of the South as "American Eden," and the Southern lady as wholesome and virtuous is essential to this vision. For similar reasons, the novel's many references to the Ku Klux Klan were also eliminated in the film. The monolith of the Old South as American Eden has no room for ladies who would eschew motherhood, or for heroes in hoods murdering their former slaves.

While the novel delves into the complexity of Scarlett's maternal feelings, the Hollywood version streamlines things quite a bit. Thus, the "good" mother/"bad" mother split plays out wholly along class lines in the film, in keeping with other films of the period, such as *Stella Dallas* (1937). The trend toward filmic figuration of "good" mothers/"bad" mothers as divided along class lines reemerges quite clearly in Hollywood films of the mid-1980s to mid-1990s.[5] These nostalgic representations, produced during a period of backlash against feminism and cultural liberalism, work to reinstate, among other things, "traditional family values." In this way, nostalgic figurations of the South can be seen to serve overarching cultural needs, as the South comes to stand in for America in important ways even as it is held at a distance. As historian Howard Zinn famously remarked in *Southern Mystique*, the South is the mirror of a nation that does not want to admit the truth about itself, and it functions in a number of ways.[6] One function of the South is to provide the nation with a model of "an imagined perfect past" (Applebome 344) that is conveniently resurrected at times of social change or upheaval as if to enable escape into fantasies of the good old days when strict divisions of race, class, and gender were cultural norms, without having to acknowledge the gross inequities of such ideology.

Gone with the Wind, in both its literary and filmic incarnations, is predominantly concerned with depicting the caste systems of the Old South and the ways in which their destruction during the periods of the Civil War and Reconstruction brings about profound negative change. Written in 1936 and produced in 1939, the text(s) came into being during a time of economic unease, which was in some ways more pronounced in the South than in other regions, given the relative paucity of resources and jobs to begin with, and served to exacerbate racial tensions. Because of its investment in upholding the happy slave mythology of Southern apologists, the novel is overtly nostalgic for the "peculiar institution" of slavery while also serving to enforce the Jim Crow ideology of the author's own period. More subtly, it advances an essentialist notion of class and portrays classist ideology as normative. The film, made by Hollywood moguls and not by Southern apologists, distances itself from the novel's overt racism and focuses instead on the safer realm of class as the primary area in which clear distinctions and hierarchies must be maintained.

Strategically, it is Scarlett's Mammy even more so than her mother, Ellen, who functions to uphold class privilege and reinforce two fundamental propositions of the narrative: first, that the master-slave relationship is essentially familial, and, second, that lower-class status is an essential property of individuals that manifests in laziness, slovenliness, and "bad" mothering such that regardless of the position from which one views them (privileged class or slave), poor whites are clearly marked as inferior. Not coincidentally, it is Mammy, whose primary purpose is to safeguard and advance Scarlett's claim on white femininity, who most vilifies poor whites, and, in particular, poor white women.

Both the film and the novel construct white femininity and maternity as connected, and represent them according to the norms of the privileged class. However, the film undercuts or erases the novel's focus on showing the masquerade each involves. For example, the novel makes clear that Scarlett's femininity is a façade, and the reader is constantly aware, largely through narrative forays into Scarlett's thoughts and perceptions, that Scarlett's performance of femininity is almost always in the service of distinctly "unfeminine" desires. Similarly, the novel also includes numerous scenes of Scarlett's bad mothering. The reader is repeatedly confronted with Scarlett's tyranny over her frightened young son, Wade, and references to her daughter Ella as ugly, simple, and resembling a monkey. Scarlett likes Bonnie only because she sees Bonnie's beauty and charm as reflections of her own. She frequently expresses a desire not to have any more children, and considers abortion when she finds herself pregnant with her fourth. While the film depicts her decision to request that she and Rhett have separate bedrooms as stemming solely from her feelings for Ashley, the novel has her thinking brightly of a future with "no more babies" (Mitchell 894).

Thus, no reader of the novel could be led to conclude that Scarlett ever assumes her mother Ellen's "good" mother mantle. Likewise, the novel, unlike the film, clearly shows that proper femininity is not a matter of breeding or an essential trait of high-born women but rather a masquerade *available* to them, largely because of the presence of black women (Mammy) who lace their corsets, police their behavior, safeguard their reputations, and later raise their children, all the while acting as the dark backdrop against which the delicate whiteness of their charges is more pronounced.[7]

Because of the film's focus on class distinctions, and the close ties between good mothering and true Southern womanhood, the film is invested in reconstructing Scarlett as a "good" mother and so leaves out the many troubling scenes that complicated Mitchell's heroine and the text's overall representation of motherhood. To this end, Scarlett's homecoming and her mother's death are significantly altered in the film to include scenes that indicate Scarlett's transformation into a lady. In the novel, Ellen has already been buried by the time Scarlett arrives, but the film depicts Scarlett's collapse at the sight of her mother's body. She falls to the floor, hysterical and weeping, a child, but she emerges from the room, dry-eyed and controlled, clearly, at last, her mother's daughter, an impression heightened by the scenes that follow.

Scarlett mothers her childlike father and takes over management of the household in a scene that is clearly meant to create a parallel to an earlier scene featuring Ellen. Ascending the staircase and looking down at her three bickering slaves over the banister, Scarlett visually recalls for the viewer Ellen O'Hara on the same staircase, in the same position, looking down at her three bickering daughters on the eve of the Twelve Oaks barbeque in the film's opening scenes. Redrawing Scarlett to parallel Ellen while leaving out evidence of Scarlett's "bad mothering" maintains class distinctions between the film's women that are clearly related to the idea that "good" mothering is the province of women who were literally "to the manor born."[8]

The Slatterys are never once referred to in either the novel or the film without their surname being preceded by the phrase "poor white trash." Moreover, the only two members of the family referred to individually are Emmie and her mother, both of whom are referenced specifically *as mothers*, though their claim on the role is seen as illegitimate and their mothering clearly inadequate. Emmie is referred to only a few times in the novel or the film, but her power as a symbol and destructive force is disproportionate to her marginal presence.

Emmie is introduced as a discursive object long before she appears in person. Early in the film, a poised Ellen O'Hara, close-up and in profile to highlight the lifted chin and turned up nose, says to Jonas Wilkerson, who is situated behind and below Ellen in the frame, "I've just come from Emmie Slattery's bedside. Your child has been born. Been born, and mercifully has died." Sympathy for mother and child are withheld, and the film's next scene serves to further distance viewers from Emmie and her child, as we are drawn into Gerald O'Hara's evident amusement over "the white trash Slattery girl['s]" sexual transgression with "the Yankee Wilkerson." The scene presents Emmie's sexuality as titillating, obscuring the sad fact of her child's death and reducing both to a single item of salacious gossip to be chuckled over.

Ellen's death is blamed on Emmie Slattery in both the film and the novel, though the novel also blames Emmie's mother for not taking better care of Emmie herself (417). Each text also makes clear that Ellen's death, while tragic, was an act of maternal sacrifice and thus not unusual or even undesirable for a true Southern lady. Ellen nurses Emmie, then her own two daughters, predictably sacrificing her own life in her efforts to provide nurturance and care to others. Melanie Wilkes, the texts' other "great lady," will enact the same paradigm of maternal sacrifice. Again, the connection between the Southern lady and the good mother, in this case united under the ideal of self-sacrifice, is highlighted.

A reading of the texts as focused primarily on showcasing the construction and power of white femininity and, simultaneously, the conflation of the white Southern woman with the South itself, explains why Emmie Slattery is demonized and shown as not only a "nightmare image underscoring the effect on the social order of not maintaining clear distinctions" (McPherson 57) but as a lethal and destructive force on par with Yankee invaders. To this end, the film connects Gerald's death with Emmie Slattery as well, and also establishes visual and rhetorical connections between Yankees and poor "white trash."

Through the union of Jonas Wilkerson and Emmie Slattery, Yankees and poor "white trash" are collapsed into one force bent on the destruction of the old ways so treasured by the film's main characters, both black and white. In the only scene in which Emmie appears, the film's longing to uphold traditional class hierarchies is clearly manifested in the positioning of Scarlett on the porch with Jonas and Emmie below her, the latter almost out of the frame. Camera angles in this scene are such that when Scarlett is the subject, the camera is angled up as if the scene were being shot from Emmie's perspective and the converse is also true so that the audience is literally looking down on Emmie Slattery. The visual logic here implies that although signifiers of class (Emmie's fine clothes and carriage compared to Scarlett's raggedy dress and handful of dirt) have been reversed, Scarlett is still "above" the likes of Emmie Slattery. This reinforces the film's view of class as a matter of birth and breeding rather than mere material wealth, and so underscores Emmie's "natural" inferiority.

The film's move to render Gerald's death a result of Emmie's "hankering" to live in Tara, coupled with Scarlett's derisive question (the only comment directed at Emmie in this or any other scene), "Who baptized your other brats after you killed my mother?" bring into focus *Gone with the Wind's* case against the poor white mother. First, the scene illustrates that the line between classes is a very thin one: they desire the same thing, and, with the collapse of the social order brought about by the fall of the privileged class, could potentially occupy the same space. This idea, too terrible to be borne, drives Gerald O'Hara to his death. Second, Scarlett's comment reminds viewers that Emmie is dangerous on two fronts: as a breeder of low-class brats (the novel repeatedly refers to Emmie as "rabbity," which seems a clear reference to her status as a consummate breeder of small and useless things) and a threat to proper femininity and values, which Ellen, whom she destroyed, clearly represented. In any case, the film's poor "white trash" Emmie Slattery visits more destruction upon the O'Hara clan than the entire Yankee army.

The treatment of Emmie Slattery in both the novel and the film are indicative of the view of poor white Southerners *as trash* and nothing more: the death of a "white trash" bastard is nothing to cry over; it is a blessing or even a joke. But as cause of both Ellen's and Gerald's death, Emmie, and by extension her "class" of uppity "white trash," impudent Yankee carpetbaggers, and other social detritus of the old order, are made to take the blame for the destruction of what Ellen and Gerald, the lady and the kindly master, represented: the Eden that was the Old South.

While much has been made of the portrayals of slaves in this film, the demonization of the poor white mother in the form of Emmie Slattery has gone largely unnoticed by critics and scholars—but not by Bone Boatwright, the young narrator of Dorothy Allison's mostly autobiographical novel, *Bastard Out of Carolina*, which was made into a film by Anjelica Houston in 2000. Watching *Gone with the Wind* on television, the film's Bone, who has just endured another abusive episode with her stepfather, Daddy Glen, astutely recognizes herself in the depiction of Emmie Slattery, realizing that Emmie, not Scarlett, is "who we were." While in the film version of *Bastard*, this is a throwaway line and seems directly tied to Bone's feelings of worthlessness stemming from the abuse, in the novel, Bone's epiphany in this scene is profound and connected to her feelings of shame over being seen as "white trash." Importantly, the scene also highlights Bone's increasing internalization of stereotypes of poor whites as trash. In the novel, the scene begins not with Glen's abuse, but with Bone's memory of her friend Shannon Pearl, who had broken their friendship by calling Bone, her mother, and her grandmother "dirty trash" (Allison 171). Throughout this chapter, Bone struggles with the knowledge that this is how her family is seen, and how she will always be seen. Reading an edition of *Gone with the Wind* containing "tinted pictures from the movie," Bone loves the story until one evening she

> looked up from Vivien Leigh's pink cheeks to see Mama coming in from work with her hair darkened from sweat and her uniform stained. A sharp flash went through me. Emma Slattery, I thought. That's who I'd be, that's who we were ... I was part of the trash down in the mud-stained cabins, fighting with the darkies and stealing ungratefully from our betters, stupid, coarse, born to shame and death. (206)

The novel addresses on multiple levels the dangers inherent in the unexamined circulation of deleterious stereotypes. Bone's behavior begins to mimic her understanding of who she is as defined by the dominant discourse, just as her mother's behavior is consistently shown to be a reaction to the label of "white trash" as well.

In the cultural discourse of contemporary America, "poor whites are increasingly constructed as obsolescent, the throw-aways of modern society" (Jarosz and Lawson 19). Pop culture discourses construct the poor, regardless of racial identity, as a monolithic group characterized by laziness, intolerance, deviance, and a proclivity for violence. As the poor white character is increasingly identified in national discourse as Southern, the stereotypes of the South combine with stereotypes of the poor to produce the characters we encounter in the film version of *Bastard Out of Carolina*. In one of the film's early scenes, the camera captures an ugly little house with a dirt-scrabble yard. Assorted chairs litter the crooked porch where the Boatwright women stand looking down at a rickety playpen perched unsteadily in the dusty yard, crowded with babies. The staging of this scene initially allows the reader to interpret the ugliness of their lives as a result of material circumstances—until a skinny, unkempt dog wanders over and lifts his leg to urinate near the playpen. The women on the porch look on, but make no move to stop the dog, move their children, or clean up the urine. This is one of the few scenes in the movie that has no connection with any scene in the book. It indicates a deeply different view of the poor than is held by the novel's author, and further, the scene clearly suggests that poor white Southern women are naturally neglectful, lazy mothers. Allison's autobiographical novel offers a complex portrayal of the Boatwrights and of rural poverty in the South in general, and is by turn as funny and as tender as it is shocking and horrific. The film strips away this complexity to trot out the usual stereotypes and ultimately leaves the viewer with the clear message that the tragedies that ensue in the lives of the poor are their own damn fault—or, more likely, their mothers'.

For Allison, the focus of the story is not only Daddy Glen's sadistic abuse of his stepdaughter, Bone, but also, as she writes in "A Question of Class," the "complicated, painful story of how my mama had, and had not, saved me as a girl" (34). The film ultimately constructs a story that is in

Figure 17. A dog urinates near neglected Boatwright children in *Bastard Out of Carolina* (2000).

keeping with the novel in terms of what happens to Bone, but sponsors a vastly different perception as to why. Bone herself is radically changed as well. As Allison told *Curve* magazine in a 2002 interview, "they left out all the parts where Bone has agency, where she's not a victim. I complained about that with the script, but they didn't get it." Still, Allison felt that director Anjelica Houston had done a "damn fine job . . . considering who she is and where she came from" (qtd. in Wilkinson). Clearly, Allison didn't feel that Houston had managed to capture the complexity of the situation or of the characters. Instead, the film repackages familiar stereotypes of the "white trash" Southerner and, in particular, ignores the clear ambivalence with which the young narrator renders her loved and hated mother. The filmic representation of Bone's mother, Anney Boatwright, recalls Emmie Slattery in no uncertain terms. Like Slattery, Anney is a wholly destructive force on whose shoulders must be laid the blame for the novel's terrible events.

The reduction of Anney to a stereotypical "white-trash"-so-by-definition-bad mother is at the heart of the primary differences between the novel and filmic texts. Allison's first-person narrator loves her mother, and Anney's character, then, is rendered through the ambivalent filter of a twelve-year-old girl's fierce love, confusion, and rage. The reader's response to Anney, like the narrator's, is shifting, contradictory, and complex. The book's narrator recognizes, at many key junctures, that Anney's own victimization is in large part the reason she is unable (not unwilling) to save Bone. For example, while listening to her mother's apologies for having deserted her to stay with her abuser, Glen, Bone's "heart broke all over again" and she thinks, "The child I had been was gone with the child she had been" (307). Though the film reproduces many of Bone's thoughts about her mother and the way Anney's life "had folded into" Bone's (309), the voiceover narration by Laura Dern robs the words of the power they had when voiced by the child narrator. The disembodied adult voice cannot capture the immediacy and poignancy of this moment, in which a young girl stands on the porch in the wake of her mother's sad departure with a full understanding of their *shared* tragedy.

Further, these lines feel tacked on, and come too late to undercut the impression created throughout the film of Anney as willfully complicit in her daughter's abuse. It is also important to note that the novel clearly positions Anney's love for Glen as distinctly maternal, and it is maternal, not sexual, love that keeps her from leaving him. When seen by Anney or in relation to Anney, Glen is most often depicted as a little boy. Anney tells Raylene that during their courtship, he would look at her daughters asleep in the car "with his face so open I could see right into his soul. You could see the kind of man he wanted to be so plain. It was like looking at a little boy, a desperate hurt little boy. That's when I knew I loved him" (133). In the novel's climax, Glen has raped Bone and Anney has found them; Glen "sobbed like a child" and "whined like a little boy" (288). In the terrible scene that follows, in which Anney has to choose between Bone and Glen, the novel's narration clearly positions Anney and Glen as mother and child, while underscoring the physical distance between Anney and Bone. Glen has taken Bone's place as the broken child seeking comfort in its mother's lap, as if he had become the little son Anney lost early in their marriage. "Her cry was low, sibilant, painful. She was holding him, his head pressed to her belly. His bloody hairline was visible past the angle of her hip. . . . 'Help me, God,' she pleaded in a raw voice. 'Help me' " (291).

The film, on the other hand, inscribes Anney's feelings for Glen as being strictly (and in their context, disturbingly) sexual. It leaves out scenes of Anney's maternal tenderness toward him and depicts Glen as anything but a "desperate hurt little boy." His anger is much more in evidence around and even toward Anney, whereas the novel shows the lengths he goes to in order to hide this side of himself from her and to act the part of a child. In the novel, Anney even calls him Baby, which is also what she calls her daughters. In the film, then, Anney has to recognize that this is one angry, violent man. The novel's insistence that she sees him as a hurt child and truly believes that he loves her daughters is nowhere in evidence.

Figure 18. Anney (Jennifer Jason Leigh) and Daddy Glen (Ron Eldard) embrace after he beats Bone (*Bastard Out of Carolina*, 2000).

But the most damning piece of evidence against Anney in the film comes in the bedroom scene that follows Glen's beating of Bone in the bathroom. Anney and Glen are in bed, and he is recounting the event, saying that Bone called him a bastard. He relives his anger, the beating, becoming more excited as he talks about it. Anney is on her side, looking into the camera, her face blank. Behind her, Glen is breathing hard, whispering. He embraces her, bringing his lips to her neck. The viewer expects that he will be rebuffed (after all, he's clearly getting off on recalling his abuse of her daughter) but instead the camera moves in and shows her arm coming up to encircle his neck, pulling him closer. Thus, not only is she now seen as complicit in Bone's abuse through her acceptance of Glen's behavior and rationale for it, but she is also implicated in his sexualized response to the violent abuse of her daughter, and so can be seen for the remainder of the film to have sacrificed her daughter to her own deviant sexuality.

Reduced to a stereotype, Anney is a different animal entirely, a "bad," "white trash" mother of extreme proportions. The spaces opened up by Allison's novel for recognition of Anney's victimization and of Bone's identification with her have been closed, and the filmic narrative underscores the deviant, dangerous essence of poor "white trash." While the novel ends with Bone thinking, "I was who I was going to be, someone like her, like Mama, a Boatwright woman" (309), the film adds, "a bastard, a bastard out of Carolina." So instead of highlighting Bone's feelings of connection to her mother and her family as the novel intends, the film ends with an assertion of her status as a bastard, a status conferred on her by her "white trash" mother's uncontrolled sexuality.

Or it may simply be a status conferred on her by a social order that does not seek to interrogate stereotypes of white poverty or of "bad" mothers, but instead circulates them widely and without scrutiny. The poor mother, represented consistently in film and the national discourse as neglectful, incapable, or downright dangerous, comes in for special vilification as her transgressions are often specifically sexual and her class status is seen to define her automatically as a "bad" mother. In linking her representation to the South, race, gender, and class, national anxieties coalesce and find easy outlet. By demonizing poor white Southern mothers, Hollywood not only extends a dangerous legacy of mother-blaming, but also creates a scapegoat that conveniently forecloses on other arenas of inquiry into national poverty.

NOTES

1. For example, Michael Moore's *Fahrenheit 9/11* (2004), which focuses primarily on people in Flint, Michigan, nonetheless ventures South to small-town Virginia to obtain footage of tattooed garage mechanics saying, "Well, you just can't trust outsiders" and dotty old women wondering whether terrorists might want to

target (pun intended) their Wal-Mart, as if the only people likely to utter such sentiments are Southerners. I mention this as an example of what Noel Polk in *Outside the Southern Myth* refers to as "the imbalance in the visual representation of the South in the national media, even when there's nothing . . . to be gained" (xi), and of the casual acceptance of Southern stereotypes this belies. It is unlikely that Moore or any other filmmaker under discussion here had a malicious purpose in representing such stereotypical images. Unexamined, these long-standing stereotypes pass into discourse and imagination as simple truths, obscuring the fact that these "types" exist outside as well as within the region.

2. In *A Question of Class*, Duane Carr defines "poor white" as "a term used in the past to describe disadvantaged and dispossessed Southern white citizens . . . [which] has evolved into a largely derogatory term" and rednecks as poor whites and their descendants who may be working class, but maintain their identity as part of the original group (vii). I maintain this distinction, but would add the following observations. First, "redneck" is a clearly gendered term and, second, it has come unmoored from geographic or socioeconomic particularities. Having been conflated with another Southern stereotype, the Good Ole' Boy, which J. Wayne Flynt defined as "part redneck, part practical genius . . . he belonged to a world of moonshining, modified cars, country music and Saturday night wrestling" (115), today's redneck is an embodiment of acceptable American values and attributes, whereas white trash is figured as an aberration of those values.

3. Other popular films that could be classed as New Old South films include: *The Big Easy* (1987), *Everybody's All American* (1988), *Blaze* (1989), *Driving Miss Daisy* (1989), *Fried Green Tomatoes* (1991), *The Man in the Moon* (1991), and *Ramblin' Rose* (1991). This period also saw a number of Civil War films such as *Glory* (1989) and *Sommersby* (1993), the miniseries *North and South* (1985) and frequent television airings of *Gone with the Wind*, as well as its nationwide rerelease in theaters in 1998 and numerous VHS and DVD collector's editions. I would be remiss if I failed to mention *The Coal Miner's Daughter* (1980), a film that demonstrates great sensitivity in its depiction of white Southern poverty and stands as a clear exception to the arguments advanced here about Hollywood's treatment of the South's working poor.

4. These films include *Sling Blade* (1999), *Bastard Out of Carolina* (2000), *Waking Up in Reno* (2001), *Monster's Ball* (2001), and *Sweet Home Alabama* (2002).

5. A good example is the "new classic" *Steel Magnolias* (1989). In this film, maternal sacrifice as well as affluence are seen as keys to not only good mothering but being a good (Southern) woman; the motherhood of the two lower-class characters, Truvy and Annelle, is problematized in the case of the former and a source of comic relief in the case of the latter. Their claims to femininity and to True Southern Womanhood are also consistently brought into question by the film's narrative and visual logic.

6. See especially pages 217–263.

7. Tara McPherson offers a fuller treatment of this subject.

8. The deletion of Dilsey serves a similar function relative to race. Dilsey is depicted in the novel as strongly maternal and a "good" mother, certainly a more nuturing and caring mother to her child, Prissy, than Scarlett is to any of her

children. In the economy of the film, though, only white upper-class mothers can be "good" mothers.

BIBLIOGRAPHY

Allison, Dorothy. *Bastard Out of Carolina*. New York: Penguin Books, 1992.

———. "A Question of Class." *Skin: Talking about Sex, Class and Literature*. Ithaca, NY: Firebrand, 1994. 13–36.

Applebome, Peter. *Dixie Rising: How the South Is Shaping American Values, Politics, and Culture*. New York: Random House: 1996.

Bastard Out of Carolina. Dir. Anjelica Huston. Showtime, 2000.

Carr, Duane. *A Question of Class: The Redneck Stereotype in Southern Fiction*. Bowling Green: Bowling Green State University Popular Press, 1996.

Fahrenheit 9/11. Dir. Michael Moore. Columbia, 2004.

Gone with the Wind. Dir. Victor Fleming. MGM, 1939.

Humm, Maggie. *Feminism and Film*. Edinburgh, UK: Edinburgh University Press, 1997.

Jarosz, Lucy, and Victoria Lawson. "Sophisticated People Versus Rednecks: Economic Restructuring and Class Difference in America's West." *Antipode* 34.1 (2002): 8–27.

McPherson, Tara. *Reconstructing Dixie: Race, Gender and Nostalgia in the Imagined South*. Durham, NC: Duke University Press, 2003.

Mitchell, Margaret. *Gone with the Wind*. New York: Macmillan, 1936.

Polk, Noel. *Outside the Southern Myth*. Jackson: University of Mississippi Press, 1997.

Wilkinson, Kathleen. "Dorothy Allison: The Value of Redemption." *Curve: The Best Selling Lesbian Magazine* 8.3 (1998). 31 January 2005 <http://www.curvemag. com/Detailed/5.html>.

Zinn, Howard. *The Southern Mystique*. New York: South End Press, 1964.

TWELVE

"DON'T SAY MAMMY"

Camille Billops's Meditations on Black Motherhood

JANET K. CUTLER

Since the 1940s, African American filmmakers have produced independent documentaries that challenge the often uninformed and distorted images of black life projected in mainstream media, especially Hollywood films. Their works offer counter-narratives; they chronicle the multiplicity of black experience and defy cultural stereotypes in order to redress a history of exclusion and misrepresentation.

This chapter focuses on cinematic representations of black maternity in two works by African American documentarian Camille Billops (with her husband James Hatch)—*Suzanne, Suzanne* (1982) and *Finding Christa* (1991)—viewed against the backdrop of two classic Hollywood melodramas, John Stahl's heartfelt *Imitation of Life* (1934) and Douglas Sirk's ironic remake (1959). Considered together, these works shed light on the film industry's depictions of black motherhood during the 1930s–1950s studio era and the black documentary movement's more recent attempts to revise those images.

At first glance, these works seem to have little in common. The film adaptations of Fanny Hurst's 1933 novel, *Imitation of Life*, are elaborate products of the commercial cinema, designed to engage mass audiences in convention-bound narratives, while Billops/Hatch's intensely personal documentaries are modestly produced, yet intellectually ambitious "chapters" of an autobiographical saga planned to chronicle the history and explore the "secrets" of Billops's African American family. Yet, the Stahl/Sirk films and the Billops/Hatch films—made a half-century apart under radically different production circumstances—are linked by an overarching, often painful attempt to articulate the challenges of black maternity; they feature deeply troubled mother-daughter relationships and various forms of struggle to "make things right" against all odds, including abusive or absent fathers and oppressive social conditions. In their own ways, all these films enact traumas of black family and identity.

Nonetheless, Billops/Hatch's work can be viewed as a "corrective" to the Stahl/Sirk films, which celebrate the Christian stoicism of dark-skinned, self-sacrificing "Mammy"[1] figures spurned by their light-skinned, mulatto daughters. Billops/Hatch's nuanced and at times unflattering views of black maternal figures constitute radical departures from *Imitation of Life*'s saintly black mothers who lavish attention and affection on their children and those of their employer, and who die of broken hearts when abandoned by their rebellious offspring. The black women depicted in both versions of *Imitation of Life* are struggling single mothers, who, while given tragic dimensions, exhibit the most basic traits of the Mammy: they are devoutly religious, unfailingly loyal to white families, skilled at housekeeping and nurturing children, and determined to sustain their own families without men.[2] As Sybil DelGaudio points out, the Mammy figure intersects two myths associated with black motherhood: "The Mammy's image is inexorably linked to either the slave-society image of surrogate maternalism and domestic service (in the rearing and socialization of white children), or to the pernicious myth of black matriarchy (in the sole parenting of the fractured, father-absent black family)" (23).

Billops/Hatch's autobiographical documentaries subvert the myths of black motherhood underlying Hollywood melodramas, especially the idea of the black mother as martyr. Their unsentimental representations of black motherhood depart from the traditions of domestic melodramas, instead depicting flesh-and-blood African American mothers who struggle to reconcile the "nobility" of suffering with the "selfishness" of self-actualization. In this way, Billops/Hatch introduce complexity and ambivalence to the more one-dimensional views of Stahl and Sirk.[3] Their works advocate a life that values self-realization, the inverse of the self-sacrificing life of the Hollywood Mammy; and they call attention to the maternal desires that, while apparently absent, simmer below the surface in *Imitation of Life*. In recuperating black motherhood, Billops/Hatch do not simply substitute positive images for negative ones; in fact, the view of black maternal figures they present is deeply troubling, raising questions about women's responsibilities for child-rearing, the societal limitations on women's choices, and the condemnation that single mothers routinely receive.[4] Yet Billops/Hatch's provocative works disturb in productive ways; they argue passionately for an unflinching reconsideration of black motherhood.

Formally, Billops/Hatch also reject the codes and conventions of Hollywood narrative cinema—straightforward in Stahl's film and stylized in Sirk's—and instead employ experimental modes to convey the multifaceted and open-ended lives of black mothers. Freely interweaving interviews, home movies, dramatic reconstructions, and fantasy sequences, Billops/Hatch's innovative documentaries incorporate disparate materials to convey the varying and at times contradictory "realities" of their protagonists.

Finally, while the Hollywood melodramas offer audiences cathartic experiences, Billops/Hatch's works fulfill a therapeutic function: they expose rifts in the family in order to promote healing.[5] The filmmaking process, itself a means of self-actualization, brings the family together and provides opportunities for reconciliation. Billops/Hatch's filmmaking redefines the family in part by instating the value and authority of memory, especially women's memories. Though profoundly personal, Billops/Hatch's works also engage larger social issues, presenting unconventional, transgressive images of motherhood that provoke and inform.

IMITATION OF LIFE: MARTYRED MOTHERHOOD

During the height of the Hollywood studio era, the figure of the Mammy who single-handedly nurtures white adults and children[6] dominated mainstream films, yet representations of black mothers caring for their own children were virtually absent from the screen. The two film versions of Imitation of Life are exceptions in that their Mammy insists on raising her own daughter, while serving as a live-in housekeeper-nanny for a widowed white woman and her daughter.[7] In both films, the Mammy is also a key player in a "rags to riches" fantasy: the single white mother rises to the top of her profession while the single black mother cares for the home and children. Both films blur the nature of the financial relationship between the black and white women: they are less employer-employee than a "team."

In the 1934 Stahl version of Imitation of Life, Delilah comes into the lives of Bea Pullman and her daughter Jessie by accident, with her own daughter Peola in tow, having misread the address on a want ad for a maid. Rather than continuing her search for employment, Delilah offers to care for Bea's harried household in exchange for room and board because "I just can't be separated from Peola." After excusing herself to prepare her daughter for day school, Bea is surprised to find that Delilah has magically produced a lavish family breakfast.[8] Delilah continues to sell her skills, noting her abilities as a nurturer: "I'm right handy with housework and takin' care of children that just comes natural to me." Persuaded, Bea acknowledges, "That's 200 pounds of mother fighting to keep her baby." Over the course of the film, Delilah rubs Bea's feet when she's tired, produces a recipe that Bea parlays into a successful boxed pancake mix business, poses as the company's "Aunt Delilah" trademark, and encourages Bea to make room for a man in her busy life: "You need some lovin', honey chile." Donald Bogle places this iconic Mammy in historical context: "she was the perfect foil . . . for Depression heroines, women forced by the times to be on their own, yet needing someone in their corner to cheer them up when things looked too rough, to advise them when personal problems overwhelmed them" (62).

While Delilah contributes to Bea's success, her relationship with her own daughter disintegrates. When Delilah arrives at the elementary school to bring her daughter rain gear during a downpour, she inadvertently exposes Peola as black in front of the students with whom she's been "passing" as white. Peola runs from Delilah, saying, "I hate you, I hate you, I hate you. Go away and leave me alone." Later, when Peola has dropped out of a Negro college and disappeared, Delilah's search for her takes her to an all-white restaurant where Peola is again "passing" and working as a cashier; Peola vehemently claims not to know her mother, asking the manager, "Do I look like her daughter?" Increasingly, Peola blames her mother for ruining her life and begs to be left alone. Delilah only redoubles her efforts; holding her adult daughter in her arms, she argues, "I borned you, I nourished you. I love you. I'm your Mammy." "Don't say Mammy," Peola pleads.

In the 1959 Sirk version,[9] the black mother Annie and her mulatto daughter Sarah Jane bond with white mother Lora and her daughter Susie during a chance meeting at Coney Island after Annie finds and feeds the lost Susie. Like Delilah, Annie insists that "my baby goes where I goes" when she implores "just let me come and do for you." Accompanying Lora home, Annie ingratiates herself by cooking, doing the laundry, and addressing Lora's "piecework" envelopes; it doesn't take long for Lora to acknowledge that it "seems like you intend to stay." Annie is physically slimmer and lighter-skinned than Delilah,[10] and she has no direct role in Lora's rise to fame as an actress, but she makes Lora's career possible by taking on the Mammy's roles: domestic service and surrogate mothering. Made five years after the Supreme Court's school desegregation decision, Sirk's film depicts Annie as someone "without much she could call her own" (Halliday 129) in order to focus attention more specifically on racial issues.[11]

The Mammy's suffering is also intensified in the Sirk version of the film, as is the humiliation suffered by her daughter, who is not only exposed as black before classmates and employers by her mother, but also viciously beaten by a white boyfriend when he learns that her mother is a "nigger." In a perverse parody of Lora's stage acting career, Sarah Jane then becomes a performer in vaudeville and later in a cheap nightclub. Annie travels to see Sarah Jane in both workplaces and is heartbroken that her daughter's degrading attempts to pass for white make her a sex object for leering white customers.

Both versions of *Imitation of Life* valorize the Mammy figure, especially her unflagging commitment to her daughter's well-being. In that way, the black mother serves as a rebuke to her counterpart, the white mother who pursues romance or a career at the expense of maternal devotion. In the 1934 film, Delilah makes this comparison explicit when she argues with Peola: "I'm your mammy, chile. I ain't no white mother. . . . You can't ask me to unborn my own chile." In the 1959 version, Susie upbraids the much-absent Lora, saying, "Let's face it, Mama! Annie's always been more like a real mother. You never had time for me."

Several parallel scenes indicate that the critique of white motherhood is stronger in the later film, in which the world is more out of control, more false, and more an "imitation of life."[12] At the start of the 1934 film, Bea is distracted and Jessie tumbles into a bathtub, but in the beginning of the 1959 remake, Lora completely loses track of Susie at a crowded beach. At the end of the 1934 film, following Delilah's death and funeral, Bea decides to send her boyfriend away, having learned that motherhood is more important than romantic love. In the 1959 version, Lora tells her daughter that she will give up her boyfriend, to which Susie sarcastically responds, "Oh, Mama, stop acting. Please don't play the martyr." Unlike Stahl, who ends the 1934 film with Bea and Jessie bonding (and Peola having decided to return to the Negro college), Sirk leaves open-ended whether his characters' lives will change. The 1959 film concludes with Annie's grand funeral—including a performance by Mahalia Jackson and an image of the family in a limousine on the way to the graveyard—but it is unclear that the problems revealed have been resolved. As Sirk explains,

> In *Imitation of Life*, you don't believe the happy end, and you're not really supposed to. What remains in your memory is the funeral. . . . You sense it's hopeless, even though in a very bare and brief little scene afterwards the happy turn is being indicated. Everything seems to be OK, but you well know it isn't. (132)[13]

While Hollywood's black mothers underscore the importance of maternal devotion over personal ambitions, they also assert the futility of challenging a racially polarized world. They repeatedly urge their daughters to accept reality, to acknowledge that they are black despite their light skin, and to trust in religion. Their only wish is for a transcendent funeral, rather than material rewards in their lifetime, and they invoke religious faith to counter their daughters' deep discontent. Delilah tells Peola, "Open up and say, 'Lord, I bows my head.' He made you black, honey. Don't be telling Him His business. Accept it, honey." Annie tells Sarah Jane, "It's a sin to be ashamed of what you are."[14]

At the same time, the films present Peola/Sarah Jane as agents of social criticism: they don't just want to be white; they demand the opportunities that whites enjoy. As Rainer Werner Fassbinder's *Imitation of Life* piece notes, "life is better when you're white" (244). Unlike their mothers, Peola and Sarah Jane rebel against inequities in their world. In fact, Peola's rejection of her mother and black identity stand in sharp contrast to her mother's dedication to her employer. When Delilah is offered a twenty percent share of Bea's thriving pancake business and the resulting economic freedom to buy a home of her own, she is shocked: "My own house? You gonna send me away, Miss Bea? I can't live with you? Oh, honey chile, please don't send me away. How I gonna take care of you and Jessie if I ain't here? I'se your cook and I wantta stay your cook." Like Peola, Sarah Jane rejects black identity from the beginning: as a child she tosses away a black doll and rankles at "living in the back." Later, in the scene in which she provocatively imitates a plantation servant serving crawdads to Lora's dinner guests, she counters a compliment by drawling, "I learned it from my mammy and she learned it from massah before she belonged to you." Her performance is intended to undercut the fantasy of a true bond of friendship and equality between the white and black mothers.

Figure 19. Sarah Jane (Susan Kohner) apologizes to her mother (Juanita Moore) after mocking Lora's guests with a "plantation servant" performance (*Imitation of Life*, 1959).

As Jeremy Butler suggests, social critique in these two films is expressed primarily as the rage of daughters against their black mothers, rather than against white society; thus, the mother-daughter conflict that is the stuff of maternal melodrama becomes a conflict over racial identity (26). Much depends on the problem of identification. Peola and Sarah Jane reject mothers who look nothing like them but define their place in the world. Peola points to a mirror and says to her mother, "I want to be white like I look." Sarah Jane says of being white, "I look it, and that's all that matters." In contrast, the white daughters emulate and compete with their mothers, even developing crushes on their mother's boyfriend (named Steve in both versions).[15]

Though it is abandonment by their daughters that kills them, both Delilah and Annie are depicted as victims of a racist society that they inadvertently defend. Delilah is exploited—her image as "Aunt Delilah" used to sell pancakes, her pancake recipe the source of Bea's wealth. Though ostensibly a member of the family, Annie is a mystery to Lora, who remarks toward the end of the film, "It never occurred to me that you had friends." Annie replies, "You never asked." Their exchange signals yet another area of Lora's self-centered blindness (like her ignorance of her daughter's life); it also momentarily throws into sharp relief Annie's off-screen life as part of a thriving black community that is invisible to Lora and to the film viewer as well.

The mulatto daughters themselves are concrete evidence of white exploitation, especially the history of sexual violation of black women by their masters during slavery. In his study of "mulatto divas," Hiram Perez points out convincingly that, although the Mammy is a desexualized figure, and although perfunctory references are made to the light-skinned fathers of Peola and Sarah Jane, the presence of these mulatto daughters serves to recall the deeply troubled past of black/white sexual relations.[16]

Thus, although the Mammy figures in *Imitation of Life* are used to buttress a racially divided patriarchy, there is an implied critique of the society that discriminates and that makes the mulatto's life tragic: Annie says, "How do you explain to your child she was born to be hurt?" Their daughter's pain means that for Delilah and Annie motherhood is necessarily painful. In both films, black maternity is "natural," but Delilah and Annie cannot protect their daughters despite their self-abnegation and suffering.

SUZANNE, SUZANNE AND *FINDING CHRISTA*: MISCAST MOTHERHOOD

Imitation of Life (1934, 1959) is atypical of the Hollywood maternal melodrama not only because it addresses the issue of race, but also because its selfless black domestic is a mother, deeply invested in raising her own, problematic daughter. Similarly, Billops/Hatch's *Suzanne, Suzanne* (1982) and *Finding Christa* (1991) are unconventional black autobiographical documentaries in their insistence on revealing painful and forbidden truths that lurk just below the surface of seemingly placid middle-class mother-daughter relationships. In *Suzanne, Suzanne,* a mother/daughter "confess" their fear and shame at a lifetime of secret beatings by their husband/father, an outwardly benevolent patriarch of an apparently enviable clan, throwing into question the ability of the mother to protect her daughter and the lengths she would go to preserve the nuclear family. In *Finding Christa*, the filmmaker shows herself to have been a free spirit who, in her youth, turned her four-year-old daughter Christa over for adoption in order to escape the suffocating demands of single motherhood, then traveled to North Africa to pursue romance and an artistic career. In fact, the martyred mother/selfish daughter paradigm of the mammy/tragic mulatto relationships in *Imitation of Life* is virtually reversed in Billops's representations of herself and Christa. In telling personal stories, and especially in presenting iconoclastic images of black maternity, Billops/Hatch challenge gender roles, critique the limits placed on women by motherhood, and make even the most ardent feminists uncomfortable.[17]

Motherhood is an abiding concern of Billops/Hatch's works, which grew out of decades of interviewing and filming Billops's African American family, especially its women. Assuming the role of family chroniclers,[18] they initiated a series of films intended to document apparently solid, yet actually damaged lives.[19] In a sense, their films are "like family reunions with all the joy, pressure, and tension that such events entail" (Guillory 88). Thus, they are not simply celebrations: they are unblinking examinations of "domestic entrapment . . . revealing the secret lives of women and their emotional entanglements" (Lekatsas 408). It cannot be overstated that Billops/Hatch's work on motherhood is deeply transgressive: it breaks "one of the most salient rules of propriety for the Black family, the business of airing dirty laundry in public . . . [thereby yielding] powerful rewards in apparent emotional catharsis for the subjects and a valuable reconsideration of such proscribed cultural tenets for the audience" (Guillory 68).[20]

In *Suzanne, Suzanne,* Billops/Hatch use the filmmaking process to explore the root causes of their niece's struggle with drug addiction. On-screen Billops interviews her mother Alma, sister Billie, and Billie's daughter Suzanne and son Michael. Midway through the film, Suzanne offers an explanation for her addiction that unalterably shifts the film's topic: her substance abuse was a desperate attempt to mask self-loathing resulting from frequent beatings by her late father, "Brownie." "Brownie," it is revealed, terrorized both Suzanne and her mother Billie. Billie speaks about hiding in the shower on hearing Brownie come home drunk, while Suzanne recounts waiting on

"Death Row" for her father's brutal visits. Michael is interviewed about his memories of his father's rages and his own attempts to be the man of the family now that his father is gone.

Yet Suzanne asserts that it was "Brownie" who "kept the family together." And she identifies with him, convinced that her features and coloring look more like his than like her mother's. A participant in the 1979 Mrs. America contest, Billie is depicted as beautiful and glamorous; she is shown putting on makeup and dressing up for local fashion shows, in which three generations of women participate—grandmother Alma, mother Billie, and daughter Suzanne—despite Suzanne's discomfort and sense of inadequacy. Ultimately, Suzanne's revelation that "I thought I was really ugly, really stupid" serves to condemn a family that the mother struggled to maintain, while failing to address and contributing to its fundamental problems.

"Brownie" himself is seen only in photographs and home movies that convey the impression of a stable, happy home. As Valerie Smith points out,

> ...pictures of Brownie smiling, embracing his children, footage of the family off to church in their Sunday best...all establish the family in familiar middle class respectability. These pieces of documentary evidence thus memorialize a picture-perfect family, one whose history might be reconstructed out of the photographic record of public events: holidays, celebrations...weddings, and so on. ("Telling Family Secrets" 383)

At the same time, the testimony of family members exposes the mental and physical dangers faced by the women in that setting. In her analysis of *Suzanne, Suzanne*, Smith tellingly notes that the reality of family life is often far different from the evidence offered in its "official" documentation: "However much one might wish to read photographic images as denotative—signs of what really existed—they too are fictive constructs; like the techniques of cinematic or literary realism, they represent a body of conventions that privileges particular ideological positions" ("Discourses of Family" 254–255). Thus, *Suzanne, Suzanne* undercuts the myth of the happy nuclear family, while calling into question photographic evidence often associated with celebrations of family life.

The high point of *Suzanne, Suzanne* is an extended scene, filmed on a darkened set, in which Suzanne and her mother express their feelings about "Brownie" and confront disturbing truths.[21] Suzanne asks Billie a set of painful questions (prepared by Hatch, although she adds some of her own as the scene goes on) that produce revelations about her mother's experience: "Do you love me? Mom, why didn't you stop Dad from beating me? Did Daddy beat you from the beginning? Do you remember Death Row? Was it the same as your being on Death Row? Would you like to hear what it was like for me?" Although Suzanne and Billie do not initially look at each other (both face the camera, with Billie standing behind Suzanne), Suzanne eventually turns and they embrace. Thus, the process of filming facilitates a kind of family therapy, allowing mother and daughter to confront their past and acknowledge their shared pain.

The role played by Billops/Hatch is multifold: in the process of making *Suzanne, Suzanne*, they discover hidden truths, provoke a revelatory experience, and set the stage for reconciliation. Further, the film allows Billops/Hatch to revise the history of the family and recast the narratives surrounding its members. Here the adult Suzanne, known to have been arrested thirteen times, including in front of her children, vividly summons up a young Suzanne whose father regularly beat her with his belt, once lodging the buckle in her bloody thigh. The act of filmmaking redefines the family, asserting the importance and validity of the mother's and daughter's memories.

Suzanne, Suzanne, made during the production of *Finding Christa*, presages the later film in that Billie's experience of motherhood is exactly what Billops rejects: "I didn't admire motherhood . . . Billie had 'family' and what you did with family was endure" (hooks 144). *Finding Christa*, Billops/Hatch's most celebrated work, is more nuanced than *Suzanne, Suzanne*, and also much closer to home: it is an extended meditation by Billops on her decision to put her four-year-old daughter Christa up for adoption and their complicated reunion decades later. Billops's autobiographical story is generously supplemented by interviews with friends and family members that at times contradict Billops and condemn her decision to "abandon" Christa.

Finding Christa is the most provocative of Billops' works—a documentary she says elicited the strongest negative reactions from "nursing fathers" who found her treatment of Christa morally reprehensible.[22] Antithetical to idealizations of motherhood, *Finding Christa* challenges the idea that women should be more responsible than men for child-rearing—even if it means raising a child alone or largely delegating childcare to extended family members. In the film, Billops notes, "When women want to change their lives, it is absolutely unacceptable." In contrast, she tells bell hooks, "[when men leave] it's no problem. . . . And if you want to critique their failure to be responsible, everybody says, 'Don't be so hard on the brother' " (151).

Nor is the film sentimental about reunions between children and their biological parents: *Finding Christa* does not include a dramatic mother-daughter reunion scene—beyond the insertion of grainy black-and-white footage and stills shot from a distance in Newark Airport. It also shuns bonding moments like the one that anchors *Suzanne, Suzanne*. Rather, it is the making of the film that constitutes the shared experience: in documenting the family saga, Billops/Hatch stage scenes of Christa introduced to friends and family members featured in earlier interviews, incorporating her cinematically into her "lost" family.

Finding Christa begins with the adult Christa speaking in a childish voice over photographs and home movie footage of herself from around the time she was given up for adoption: "My last memory of you is when you drove off and left me at the Children's Home Society. I didn't understand why you left me and I felt so alone. Why did you leave me?" The intertitle "Why did you leave me?" signals the first section of the film in which various explanations are made for Billops's decision. She initially hoped Christa's father would decide to marry her (she half-jokes, "I was holding Christa as hostage"), but when that did not happen, Billops realized, "What I wanted was the nuclear family—I'd wanted a little Hollywood thing . . . and then when the third party wasn't there, then I didn't want to do it. I was trying to give her something else because I felt she needed a mother and a father."[23]

Figure 20. Christa Victoria at age four, just before she was given up for adoption by filmmaker Camille Billops (publicity still for Finding Christa, 1991, courtesy of the Hatch-Billops Collection).

In the absence of black family life on the screen, Billops clearly means a "Hollywood thing" featuring white families. As Monique Guillory notes, Billops is deeply influenced by and in dialogue with mainstream movies, as is apparent in Billops's introduction to the PBS screening of *Finding Christa*: "Women are not always nestkeepers. Some men want to be nestkeepers and some women, they want to be on the highways, or on the road finding the news. What was that movie with Marlon Brando? . . . He took off over those hills. We were sitting in Rotterdam with a friend in the movies and I said, 'See, that's the adventure they want to deny us'" (77).

In the documentary, Billops invites family members to talk about how they felt two decades earlier when she relinquished Christa. All claim to have objected vehemently at the time and to have personally pledged assistance. In the face of their continuing dismay at her decision, the filmmaker remains unrepentant, explaining, "I had obviously done something that's absolutely unacceptable to the tribe." An extraordinary moment during Billops's interviewing of family members occurs when she asks cousin Bertha her standard question, "Why do you think I gave up Christa?" Bertha, turning her face from the camera, says softly, "You don't want me to talk about that, do you?" and, after a pause, "Because you had met your husband." Billops contradicts

Figure 21: Camille Billops and husband James Hatch during their courtship (publicity still for *Finding Christa*, courtesy of the Hatch-Billops Collection).

her family's monolithic position that they were poised to take on child-rearing responsibilities; her reality is that only Billie and "Brownie" stepped forward at the time. Still, Billops does not challenge the claim that she left Christa in part in order to build a new life with fellow artist James Hatch. In fact, Billops/Hatch include footage of their travels in Egypt (where she had her first gallery show) just after Christa's adoption, as well as testimony from a friend about their courtship, affair, and subsequent marriage.

The second section, entitled "Where were you Christa?," focuses on the period of Christa's decades-long separation from Billops. It includes footage of Christa, laughing and being teased by her adoptive brothers and sister, starring in home movies of her wedding, and performing songs she composed. This section, however, centers on Margaret Liebig, Christa's adoptive mother, who describes at some length her passionate desire to adopt, her first meeting with Christa, and her recollections of Christa growing up. Clearly, it is Margaret who "found Christa." She and her husband raised Christa alongside their own children while Margaret pursued a jazz singing career. Margaret notes that she suggested Christa seek out her birth mother to ease Christa's chronic unhappiness, and she expresses dismay that Christa excluded her from the reunion, recalling Christa's saying, "She [Billops] gave me up alone and I want to find her alone."

The third section of the film, "OK, Christa, now what?," includes home movies and stills of the adult Christa's reunion with Billops, scenes in which Christa tells Margaret on the phone that "Bootsie's [Billops's family nickname] a hippie!" and footage of Billops showing Christa family photographs. In this part of the film, Christa is introduced to members of her biological family. *Finding Christa* ends with a coda, "Almost Home," in which Hatch reads journal entries to Christa that document Billops's sadness when giving her daughter up; the sequence concludes with ghostly images of Hatch and Billops holding sparklers in the dark and chanting "Welcome home, Christa."

Finding Christa is not a confessional work in which the filmmaker confronts her demons or exposes her pain (in fact, Billops steadfastly claims to have no wounds). Billops's questions ("Did I have a good reason for giving her up?" or "Was I justified?") draw out her interviewees rather than signal her unresolved guilt. In fact, she clearly states, "I'm sorry about the pain it caused Christa as a young child, but I'm not sorry about the act." She makes clear that she wasn't a good mother, finding single motherhood intolerable: without their separation, "I would have died, and if I would have died, she would have died." In this way, Billops clearly marks her refusal of the maternal martyrdom embraced by Delilah and Annie; she is unwilling to suffer and die for her child, choosing both a career and romantic love over maternal devotion. Billops also cedes the emotional voice in the film to

Christa. Christa is shown to initiate the reunion; she is presented as needing to understand her birth mother and meet her biological family. Christa is filmed reacting emotionally to evidence of her childhood, especially photographs of her earliest years, which time and the adoption have blurred.

Yet the film makes clear that there are strong similarities between Billops and Christa: mother and daughter are both artists, and they are both strong-willed and determined. As Lucy Fischer writes, "We sense the excitement she [Christa] feels at discovering her own artistry presaged, doubled, and validated in her mother's talent. Thus while Suzanne had suffered from underidentification with her mother, Christa experiences the pleasures of maternal mirroring" (*Cinematernity* 227). The biological link is central to Christa's search for Billops. It is important to Christa that she looks like Billops, an experience that is radically different from that of Peola and Sarah Jane, who do not see themselves in their mothers. But Billops is not moved by her biological connection to Christa. "Look like me, sing like me. That don't mean I necessarily want to be involved. Twenty years. I ain't known her in twenty years."

While Christa feels she needs the reunion, Billops fears she will be swallowed up by it. Billops films herself expressing reluctance to open up that part of her past: "I don't want to come up from under the water." She is encouraged to meet her daughter by George C. Wolfe who, in a performance piece, plays master of ceremonies at "auditions" for a mother/daughter recital: "Bootsie" appears in a child's frilly white dress, dancing and attempting to lip-synch yodeling, while Christa, dressed as a man in a bowler hat, accompanies her on the piano. Other staged, theatrical pieces follow: Christa and Billops read tarot cards and discuss Christa's connections to various relatives; Christa furiously mops the floor wearing her bridal dress, kicks over the bucket, and puts on boxing gloves. These set pieces stand in sharp contrast to the film's documents—home movies and photographs—and interview material. Such fantasy sequences, like Sarah Jane's surreal stage performances in Sirk's film, allow the participants to act out their emotions and ironically call attention to the "acting" and posturing in more naturalistic scenes of daily life. Most importantly, they allow Billops and Christa semi-comic, theatrical opportunities to "co-star" in a mother-daughter film.

Aside from these performances, Billops's autobiographical tone is matter-of-fact: she talks about the most harrowing moments in her life in an uninflected way. In Barbara Lekatsas's words, "In *Finding Christa*, the filmmaker . . . refuses to reveal herself in the way that her sister Billie did [in *Suzanne, Suzanne*], refuses to lose control. The few times we are given testimony of how it felt to give up Christa is [sic] through others" (395). Billops does not allow Christa to express her anger and resentment directly, nor does she feature the melodramatic "you ruined my life" mother-daughter scenes crucial to *Imitation of Life*. She does, however, include footage of family members whose answers to her interview questions are unsparingly critical of her.

In every way, Billops makes clear that giving up Christa for adoption was her choice alone; she even films James Hatch holding up a picture of himself at an earlier age and saying, "I told Camille, 'Don't give up Christa for me.'" Billops also acknowledges that her daughter was damaged by her decision: Christa is filmed practicing martial arts, while her voice-over asserts, "I think of myself as very strong, but inside I'll always be a frightened four year old girl." And Billops undercuts the sentimentality of a "happy ending": she shows Christa drawing portraits of herself as a grasping and needy octopus and Billops as a spiked and withholding cactus; she makes clear that she'll continue to resist being overwhelmed by motherhood because "I was afraid to get caught again." She even refuses to give Christa a childhood photo during a show-and-tell session, countering her daughter's plea with a self-consciously childish, "It's mine." Assessing the film, she tells bell hooks "I appear cold, very cold" (147).

In contrast, Billops depicts Christa's adoptive mother, Margaret, as warm and patient with the headstrong Christa. bell hooks tells Billops that her depiction of Margaret avoids the persistent Mammy stereotype:

> We rarely see the heavyset, dark black woman imaged in any kind of film, by black filmmakers or anybody else, as tender, as loving, as open-hearted, but not in the traditional mammy way. We see her [Margaret] as an existentially self-reflective person, and we see her as a person who clearly is enormously philosophical in the way that she has thought about her relationship to you, her relationship to Christa, and her past. That was a real incredible thing you did as a filmmaker being able to draw out those elements in Margaret, who adopts Christa, a person you both have a charged personal connection to but that you are also shooting as a filmmaker. (149)

Billops is not only on-screen asking questions; she is clearly the guiding presence behind the film, determining the tone throughout. She organizes the material—Margaret is cast as the "good mother," Christa is shown radiantly performing her heartfelt "life songs," and Billops is presented as a bohemian unwilling and unable to raise children—but retains its ambiguity. Resisting simplistic equations of documentary film and "real life," Billops says, "people who see the film, who see Christa and Margaret as saints . . . think I'm a total bitch. I say, 'I am not a bitch and they are not saints. I *cut* the film.' . . . Film is constructed." (149)

If the film is brutally frank toward its subject, it is remarkably silent about the nature of its production. For example, there is no mention that filming began eight years after Billops and Christa's reunion (they met in

Figures 22–23. In *Finding Christa*, filmmaker Camille Billops (left) constructs herself as a "bohemian" and Margaret, the woman who adopted Christa, as a "good mother" (publicity stills courtesy of the Hatch-Billops Collection).

1981, a decade before the film was completed). And there is little way of determining with authority which sequences are restagings of events from the past and which are shot in the "present."[24] For example, early in the film, Billops reveals to a friend, Coreen Rogers, who is photographing Billops's artwork in her loft, that she is unsure of how to react to having received a tape from Christa asking to meet her, which she plays. Coreen expresses surprise that Billops has a daughter and then tells a story of her own: she was a foster child, and she was rejected when she called her birth mother to request a meeting. The interaction takes us back to the time when Billops first heard from Christa and allows us to hear the perspective of someone who shares Christa's point of view. But whether or not the conversation was documented at the time, reenacted, or contrived for the purposes of the film, it provides an occasion for psychological revelations in a naturalistic mode.

When Christa sits on a bed with Billops, engrossed in reviewing precious childhood photos, she is distracted by a call from Margaret, yet Billops loudly continues to "narrate" the family album; this scene serves to dramatize the competition between the two mothers for Christa's attention. Similarly, the sad, brief moment at the end of the film in which Hatch reads to Christa from his journal is staged to reveal Billops's "past" heartbreak at the time she gave up Christa, as opposed to the "present" in which Billops reveals very little emotion.

In certain ways (and perhaps because of funding problems that necessarily prolonged completion of the film), *Finding Christa* exists eerily outside of time and space—more provocation than exegesis. Unsentimental and defiant, it invites its audience to share the fragmentary perspectives of Christa and her two mothers, their individual lives as artists, and their entangled familial relationships.

One mystery that remains, however, is what happened between the time of the Newark Airport reunion and the time the film was finished a decade later. Christa tells us that she moved to New York to pursue her singing career, that she was invited into Billops's family, and that she continues to feel confused about who she is and where she belongs, since she is torn between two strong mothers. We know little else about the family dynamic except that the extended family made this film together (including Dion, one of Hatch's sons from a previous marriage, who worked behind the camera). Thus, the film raises a number of questions about motherhood, adoption, and family, and various kinds of documentary evidence. More than that, it speaks to the ways a filmmaking project can serve to unite otherwise alienated family members, and how the filmic object can depict and also create a familial cohesiveness, a virtual family that exists on the screen. A collaborative process, filmmaking is what Billops/Hatch (and now Christa) pursue together.

For Billops/Hatch, filmmaking is more than an artistic endeavor or social critique: it is a way to investigate and overcome rifts in a family. It also establishes a powerful position for those engaged in the process. Although Billops may have been miscast for motherhood, she is ideally suited to document the family's odyssey, the role she defines for herself in a later film, *A String of Pearls* (2002). Thus, a family that has serious questions about the unconventional life and choices of its eccentric artist "Bootsie" (who still makes up her eyes as if she were Elizabeth Taylor playing Cleopatra) fully cooperates with Billops's attempts to use film to solidify her family's ephemeral existence. Her painstaking and thoughtful work as a documentarian provides a venue for addressing her own problematic motherhood, as well as her extended family's problems; filmmaking is an occasion for bringing the family together, affording family members opportunities for self-expression and self-definition.

If mainstream filmmaking reinforces misconceptions about black motherhood, like the martyred Mammy figures in *Imitation of Life*, Billops/Hatch's experimental documentaries play a different role. They tell stories of black mothers from inside the culture, dispelling myths and challenging assumptions. And they do more: they fulfill a therapeutic function; healing wounds, they allow families to confront and overcome personal traumas.

Thus, the act of filmmaking becomes a means for historical revision, social remediation, and personal growth.

ACKNOWLEDGMENTS

My thanks to Sam McElfresh for his invaluable contributions to this chapter and to Hiram Perez for his insightful comments.

NOTES

1. Mammies have been characterized by their appearance (overweight, dark-skinned, desexualized), their personality traits (kind, loyal, hard-working), and their roles (domestics and caretakers). Many critics (e.g., Sybil DelGaudio and Jeremy Butler) note that the black mothers in *Imitation of Life* exemplify the Aunt Jemima version of the Mammy, as defined by Donald Bogle in his seminal study of black character types in American film: *Toms, Coons, Mulattoes, Mammies, and Bucks* (1973). Tracing the evolution of the Mammy, Bogle notes that the Aunt Jemima figures who emerge in the 1930s are different from the comical, cantankerous servants who preceded them: they are "sweet, jolly, and good-tempered . . . blessed with religion" and prone to "wedge themselves into the dominant white culture. . . . [Mammies] had become respectable domestics" (9, 35).

2. Bogle cites the beginning of the "stereotyping of Negroes in American movies" in the title character of Edwin S. Porter's 1903 *Uncle Tom's Cabin*, but adds that such codified characters did not originate in motion pictures; they were "merely filmic representations of black stereotypes that had existed since the days of slavery and were already popularized in American art and life." Bogle documents their presence in white-produced mainstream films, as well as all-black cast "race films" made for black audiences, and in more recent black independent narrative productions. While these stock characters were necessarily "modernized" over the past hundred years of the cinema, in recent editions of his book Bogle insists that, despite social change, "the familiar types have most always been present" (3–4).

3. As Hiram Perez observes, the transparency assumed by Stahl and Sirk is evident in the visual imagery: the Mammy is framed by the window in both versions of *Imitation of Life*, while the white mother is framed by the mirror in Sirk's film.

4. In *Finding Christa*, Billops recalls the stigma of single black motherhood: "If you were a single parent, you were an unwed mother, and that was close to being a whore."

5. These documentaries are variations on what Paul Arthur calls "therapy films" in which "the rigors of movie production are embraced as a therapy intended to help their makers clarify, and ultimately begin to resolve, psychosocial problems often involving familial tension or trauma" (47–48).

6. Although the Mammy is often highly regarded for her caretaker role, especially her close relationships with white families, this "positive" image blurs the historical and sociological conditions of slavery: the breakup of black families and separation of black women from their own children, the role of black women on the plantation as domestics, and the rape of black women by white masters.

7. Traces of the Mammy figure can be found in the film version of *A Raisin in the Sun* (1961). It is not until the 1970s that filmic representations of black mothers in mainstream cinema depart significantly from the Mammy stereotype, as in *Sounder* (1972) and *Claudine* (1974); nonetheless, the mother in *Sounder* is forced to keep her family together while the father is away and Claudine is a welfare mother. Certainly, both independent and commercial black narrative filmmakers—Charles Burnett (*Killer of Sheep*, 1977), Julie Dash (*Daughters of the Dust*, 1991), James Singleton (*Boyz in the Hood*, 1991), and Spike Lee (*Crooklyn*, 1994)—provide complex images of black motherhood. Black documentary filmmakers like Marco Williams (*In Search of Our Fathers*, 1992) and Thomas Allen Harris (*Vintage: Families of Value*, 1995) depict multifaceted black matriarchs in the context of their autobiographical works; Williams especially achieves a deeper understanding and appreciation of his mother—and of the matriarchs in his family—in the course of his search for his absent father. Billops/Hatch's work provides the most radical departure from conventional cinematic views of motherhood, giving voice and visibility to unconventional black mothers.

8. In this way, Lucy Fischer points out, the Mammy is a "wish-fulfillment, fantasy" figure, providing support for the single white mother preoccupied with a career while raising a child (*Imitation of Life* 17).

9. *Imitation of Life* was a great success; according to Sirk, it was Universal's highest grossing film to date (Halliday 133).

10. Sybil DelGaudio writes: "the Mammy image gets altered in a sign of the film's general fade to white. Here, the blacks are whiter and the whites are blonder, as the slim, barely Southern Juanita Moore plays the Mammy. . . . Aunt Delilah becomes Annie Johnson and Peola becomes Sara Jane. With platinum-haired Lana Turner as Lora Meredith, altered here from pancake queen to aspiring actress" (24).

11. Sirk explains, "The only interesting thing is the Negro angle: the Negro girl trying to escape her condition, sacrificing to her status in society her bonds of friendship, family, etc. . . . The picture is a piece of social criticism—of both white and black. You can't escape what you are. . . . *Imitation of Life* is a picture about the situation of blacks before the time of the slogan 'Black is Beautiful'" (Halliday 130).

12. Sirk's view of a world both false and inauthentic (although visually stunning) is underscored by his style, including ever-present two-dimensional surfaces (like mirrors) that flatten the image, garish colors that stress artifice, objects that displace the characters' emotions, and so on. For a thorough discussion of the formal elements of Sirk's films, see Fred Camper's "The Films of Douglas Sirk."

13. Sirk explains that he could go on to finish the story, emphasizing its hopelessness, but that the studio would not have accepted it: "Lana [Lora] will forget about her daughter again, and go back to the theatre and continue as the kind of actress she has been before. Gavin [Steve] will go off with some other woman. Susan Kohner [Sarah Jane] will go back to the escape world of vaudeville. Sandra Dee [Susie] will marry a decent guy . . . you would get a picture that the studio would have abhorred" (Halliday 131).

14. Bogle argues that "this Christian stoicism . . . 'elevated' [Delilah] by endowing her with Christian goodness far exceeding that of any other character" (59).

15. In the Stahl film, there is a scene in which Bea and Jessie sit together on the stairway, mirror images of one another: each carries a fur stole, tilts her hat at the same angle, and wears her hair in the same style. Sirk also employs doubling

strategies to stress the similarities between Lora and Susie, but he refracts the image even further, showing simultaneous reflections in mirrors.

16. "The figures of the black mother, mulatto child, and absent father immediately raise for American audiences not only the specter of miscegenation but also the stereotype of black and mulatto concubines engaged in adulterous relations with white 'benefactors.' All this also suggests . . . the sanctioned rape of black women and the resulting bastard mulatto populations. These two narratives . . . merge ambivalently in black cultural memory as the black mother becomes simultaneously rape victim and complicit concubine" (127).

17. In an interview with Marie-France Alderman, bell hooks describes *Finding Christa* as "disturbing on a number of levels. It's interesting that we can read about men who have turned their back on parenting to cultivate their creativity and their projects and no one ever thinks it's horrific, but a lot of us, including myself, were troubled by what we saw in Camille Billops's film. This woman went to such measures to ensure that she had the space to continue being who she wanted to be, and at the same time it felt very violent and very violating of the daughter" (117).

18. Billops says, "[Making documentaries first] became important to me, at least sub-consciously, observing my parents shooting home movies from the late forties into the seventies. When I began making documentaries, it was in the same context. I didn't know then that those projects would go on to be more than the home movies that my parents had produced" (hooks 141).

19. Monique Guillory points out, "In her attention to the dynamics of the family . . . Billops constantly blurs the divides between private life and public domain . . . winning the confidence of her family members as they entrust her with intimate facts of their private lives" (68). Billops tells bell hooks, "They believe that I am their personal filmmaker. They come to me and say, 'Well, I didn't get my film.' They want me to get the grants for them" (142).

20. As Billops says, "Our films have a tendency toward dirty laundry. The films say it like it is, rather than how people want it to be. Maybe it is my character that tends to want to do that, because I think the visual artist in me wants to say the same kind of thing. . . . I think it is just my open spirit" (hooks 142).

21. Valerie Smith notes that this sound stage provides an alternative to the domestic spaces in which the rest of the film takes place—sites that enshrine the past history of family relations. In this alternative location, the relationship between mother and daughter is altered dramatically ("Reconstituting the Image" 713).

22. Unpublished interview with Phyllis Klotman and Janet Cutler, summer 1993. Billops is referring to new fathers who have enthusiastically embraced child-rearing. The fact that audiences object more vehemently to Billops in *Finding Christa* than to "Brownie" in *Suzanne, Suzanne* is for Barbara Lekatsas evidence that "a mother who gives up her child is considered even lower on the scale of civilization than a brutal father" (398).

23. Billops unapologetically explains to hooks: "you don't always want to be a mother. I did not want to be a mother. I know that is amazing to people. I think I did in the beginning, when I got pregnant with this romantic, gorgeous black male who was a lieutenant in the air force in California. . . . I was twenty-three, I got pregnant accidentally. I loved him, because he was fine. He was everything I wanted

that thing to be. We were going to get married . . . and then I called that base and he was gone. Gone. . . . Now I see I wasn't supposed to have him. I wasn't supposed to have any of that, and I am eternally grateful. I am not a victim. I don't feel like I missed him. I just wasn't supposed to have that" (hooks 150–151).

24. Scholarship on *Finding Christa* is full of speculation about the timing of the production of each film's episodes. In an extremely useful analysis of the film, Julia Lesage cites the opening, wondering whether it is part of a tape made to assist the Children's Home Society in contacting Billops. In addressing the way that the film "masks its time line" and purposefully causes confusion about what is recreated and what is not, Lesage suggests that there may be ethical implications to some of these strategies: were the first phone call to Christa and the reunion at the airport staged or were they simply recorded at the time without Christa's knowledge?

BIBLIOGRAPHY

Arthur, Paul. "Feel the Pain." *Film Comment* 40.5 (2004): 47–50.

Billops, Camille. Personal interview with Phyllis Klotman and Janet Cutler. Summer 1993.

Bogle, Donald. *Toms, Coons, Mulattoes, Mammies, and Bucks.* Rev. ed. New York: Continuum, 1997.

Butler, Jeremy. "*Imitation of Life*: Style and the Domestic Melodrama. *Jump Cut* 32 (1986): 25–28.

Camper, Fred. "The Films of Douglas Sirk." *Screen* 12.2 (1971): 44–62.

Deans, Jill R. "Performing the Search in Adoption Autobiography: *Finding Christa* and *Reno Finds Her Mom.*" *Biography* 24.1 (2001): 85–98.

DelGaudio, Sybil. "The Mammy in Hollywood Film: I'd Walk a Million Miles for One of Her Smiles." *Jump Cut* 28 (1983): 23–25.

Fassbinder, Rainer Werner. "Six Films by Douglas Sirk." *Imitation of Life.* Ed. Lucy Fischer. New Brunswick: Rutgers University Press, 1991. 244–250.

Finding Christa. Dir. James Hatch and Camille Billops. Hatch-Billops, 1991.

Fischer, Lucy. *Cinematernity: Film, Motherhood, Genre.* Princeton: Princeton University Press, 1996.

———. "Three-Way Mirror: *Imitation of Life.*" *Imitation of Life.* Ed. Lucy Fischer. New Brunswick: Rutgers University Press, 1991. 3–28.

Guillory, Monique. "The Functional Family of Camille Billops." *Black Women Film & Video Artists.* Ed. Jacqueline Bobo. New York and London: Routledge, 1998. 67–92.

Halliday, Jon. *Sirk on Sirk.* New York: Viking, 1972.

hooks, bell. *Reel to Real: Race, Sex and Class at the Movies.* New York: Routledge, 1996.

Imitation of Life. Dir. John M. Stahl. Universal, 1934.

Imitation of Life. Dir. Douglas Sirk. Universal, 1959.

Lane, Jim. *The Autobiographical Documentary in America.* Madison: University of Wisconsin, 2002.

Lekatsas, Barbara. "Encounters: The Film Odyssey of Camille Billops" *Black American Literature Forum* 25.2 (1991): 395–408.

Lesage, Julia. "Contested Territory in *Finding Christa*." *Documenting the Documentary*. Ed. Barry Grant. Detroit: Wayne State University Press, 1998. 446–462.

Perez, Hiram. "Two or Three Spectacular Mulatas and the Queer Pleasures of Overidentification," *Camera Obscura* 67 (2008): 113–142.

Smith, Valerie. "Discourses of Family in Black Documentary." *Struggles for Representation: African American Documentary Film and Video*. Ed. Phyllis Klotman and Janet Cutler. Bloomington: Indiana University Press, 1999. 250–267.

———. "Reconstituting the Image." *Callaloo* 37 (1988): 709–719.

———. "Telling Family Secrets: Narrative and Ideology in *Suzanne, Suzanne* by Camille Billops and James V. Hatch." *Multiple Voices in Feminist Film Criticism*. Ed. Diane Carson, Linda Dittmar, and Janice R. Welsch. Minneapolis and London: Minnesota University Press, 1994. 380–390.

Suzanne, Suzanne. Dir. James Hatch and Camille Billops. Hatch-Billops, 1982.

THIRTEEN

FROM DAD TO MOM

Transgendered Motherhood in *Transamerica*

Mary M. Dalton

Everybody's family is a little dysfunctional if you scratch the surface. I think everybody has at some point in their lives felt uncomfortable in their skin, misunderstood, not perfectly loved and held by the universe, and that's what Bree's journey is. Bree is just some misfit, outsider kid we've all felt ourselves to be at some point in our lives, but the volume is turned up to ten because of who she is.

—Duncan Tucker, writer and director

He wrote a great script, which is about becoming who you really are, and it's a woman's journey. She thinks the biggest thing she can do is become a woman, and she realizes the biggest thing she can do is become a parent. And I think the internal story is something that everyone can relate to because we all want to become who we really are. We all want to come home to ourselves and be seen by our family, by our community, by our lovers as our true selves.

—Felicity Huffman, actor playing Bree Osbourne

What drew me to the story was just that I felt like it wasn't a documentary about transsexuality or about a street hustler. You meet these people, and they're in the middle of their journey.

—Kevin Zegers, actor playing Bree's son Toby

SETTING OUT

In *Transamerica*, Bree, a conservative, preoperative transsexual, learns she is the parent of a long-lost seventeen-year-old son. Bree and her son then embark on a cross-country adventure that changes both of their lives. The film is thus a road picture, but also much more. The identity and empowerment themes—not to mention the landscape—evoke *Thelma and Louise* (1991), and *Transamerica* may eventually claim a similar place as a cultural marker. *Thelma and Louise* arrived on screens in 1991 as Susan Faludi's influential book *Backlash: The Undeclared War Against American Women* hit the shelves to counter conservative discourses suggesting that Second Wave feminism was the root of all social ills; *Transamerica* was released in 2005 amid rightwing political efforts to reinforce boundaries affirming heterosexist privilege in marriage, parental rights, adoption, employment benefits, and health care decision-making. Bree Osbourne's story expands the image many people have of transgendered people or transsexuals by portraying a character who is conservative and a bit of a prude, a character described by the actor playing her as one recalling an "uptight spinster aunt."[1] Bree defies conventional expectations and, by extension, encourages a more comprehensive understanding of what it might mean to be a transgendered person.

It is clear that Bree is on a journey of self-discovery as she drives an atrocious, chartreuse station wagon across the country with her son Toby, but she is also taking the audience along for the ride. What is particularly engaging about her journey, and the journey Toby is beginning with her, is the exquisite way the film discards conventional boundaries both narratively and visually. There are not any signs designating state lines and relatively few geographic references as the two travel westward; after all, state lines are just another artificial construct placed on the landscape by humans eager to organize and neatly categorize everything in sight. Of the other boundaries that Bree crosses on her journey, first a socially constructed boundary between male and female and later a biologically constructed boundary between man and woman, the most defining part of her journey in *Transamerica* is the trip from potential father to loving mother. However, as with other social constructions, Bree suggests that labels often complicate situations by establishing a reductive paradigm that forces a normative way of being and punishes people who don't fit neatly inside established categories. This chapter explicates Bree's progress from unsuspecting dad to unprepared mom to caring parent by examining scenes in the film that specifically mark those identities along this journey, an odyssey through which she becomes the person she is meant to be.

"I'M NOT HIS MOTHER"

One week away from her sex change surgery in Los Angeles, Bree learns that a short-lived fling in college resulted in a son when the boy calls from a New York City lock-up trying to reach his father, Stanley. Bree does not acknowledge to him that for most of her life she was Stanley, and that would be the end of the story if her therapist, Margaret, did not withhold permission for the surgery until Bree handles the situation with her son. As Margaret tells her, "I don't want you to go through this metamorphosis only to find out you are incomplete." Reluctantly, Bree travels to New York and discovers that her son is surviving by working as a prostitute on the streets. At their first meeting, the boy assumes she is from the local church, Jesus the Reformer, and she counters that she is "from the church of the potential father." She bails Toby out and is prepared to leave him with a hundred bucks until he shows her a picture of his parents: his mother and Stanley. Toby has declared his intent to leave for California to find his father and become an actor, and Bree decides that leaving Toby in the squalid apartment he shares with other street kids would be irresponsible. She buys a battered station wagon from one of Toby's cronies, in hopes of selling it for a profit back in L.A., and she prepares to take the boy back to Kentucky where his stepfather lives.

They are a striking pair: Bree, in her flowing clothes of pastel pinks and lavenders with dangling earrings, tinted hose, and modest heels, is a study in buttoned-up retro femininity while Toby looks like a very scruffy child on the cusp of manhood in worn jeans and T-shirts. She is almost homely, and he is undeniably pretty. She is careful and guarded, and he is open and vulnerable. She is a prude and wears her matronly mantle to keep potential partners away, and he uses sex freely to gain leverage and get what he needs to survive. She strives for a transition toward what she perceives as culturally normative, and—for a child of the streets—he is remarkably transparent and naive simultaneously; it is doubtful from the way his character is constructed that Toby has much of a framework for assessing what constitutes the normative. If Bree is "becoming undone" in the sense of knowingly undoing a normative conception of gender, we sense that Toby is not bound by the same sense of boundaries but also that his choices have not been made with a sense of knowing and choice (Butler 1).[2] What they share beyond biology is a long history of pain. As David Morris observes, "Pain, whatever else philosophy or biomedical science can tell us about it, is almost always the occasion for an encounter with meaning" (44). From the moment their journey begins, this trip marks a dynamic unfolding of identity for both of them.

As they hit the open road, Bree tells Toby to fasten his seatbelt, corrects his grammar, makes him remove his feet from the dashboard, announces that he cannot smoke cigarettes, and turns off his music, all in a carefully modulated, maternal tone. Toby's guileless attempts to please her include folding his hands to pray before meals and, later, buying her a tacky baseball cap with "Proud to be a Christian" written across the bill. All along Bree has planned to return Toby to his stepfather in Kentucky, and just as steadfastly the boy has maintained that he does not want to go to Kentucky. When Bree finally meets his stepfather and learns that his mother committed suicide, the picture becomes much clearer: Toby has been sexually abused by the stepfather and ended up on the streets of New York after running away from his abuser. We can see the sexual and physical abuse Toby has endured and easily infer the abuse his biological mother must have endured as long as she could. As Shari Thurer has noted over and over in her work on motherhood, neglected and abused children are often the offspring of the subset of women who have likewise been neglected and abused (181). Bree tries to protect him when Toby reveals the abuse, and his stepfather starts beating the boy. The handheld camera, not easily discernible in the film, is more obvious in this scene. That this scene has more movement and a faster pace of editing ratchets up the drama and intensity visually.

Transamerica shares many similarities with *Thelma and Louise*, including the suddenness, brutality, and sexual violence of this scene, which recalls Thelma and Louise's encounter with the rapist Harlan in a bar parking lot as they begin the first leg of their journey. Bree feels acute remorse at causing additional pain for her child, and when she leaves Kentucky the next day, Toby is with her. Both films feature a pair of characters undergoing personal transitions and evolutions, both feature a cross-country race against time by car, both make extensive use of the exteriors of the Southwest so common in western films, and both feature characters who reject a narrow social construction of gender but then find that rejecting boundaries of any sort is dangerous business that can incur the loss of family and other support systems. Once they become aware of how these gender roles have been foisted upon them and their sense of their own identities is expanded, there is no turning back for Thelma, Louise, or for Bree.

Although Bree feels regret about her insistence on returning to Kentucky, she continues to resist the maternal role. In a scene that takes place after they flee Kentucky, Bree and Toby sit silently across from one another in the booth of a diner. A young waitress approaches them and says, "One chocolate milkshake for you, and coffee for your mother." The camera favors Toby's perspective, but he is still out of it, inattentive to what the waitress has said. Bree is startled, however. After a beat, she responds, "I'm not his mother." The waitress has taken the relationship for granted, but she barely registers Bree's correction. Toby, still oblivious or uninterested in the exchange, belches loudly. Bree delicately moves to the next booth and sits with her back to her son; the camera now favors both characters, but looks down on them from an uncharacteristically high angle as they sit separately and silently, unable to connect to one another yet and ease the pain they have both experienced thus far on this journey.

As the day ends, though, an important transition occurs. They sit by the fire before camping out, and Toby continues to blunt his pain, this time with alcohol. Bree gives the boy a childhood toy, a stuffed monkey that she has liberated from his stepfather's garage. As Toby accepts her gently proffered gift, the drinking catches up with him, and the boy vomits. When the sickness passes, he leans over and rests his head in Bree's lap. Finally, her scolding and corrections are replaced with tender, maternal comfort as Bree cradles her son. The scene is shown in a wide shot, with the campfire between the camera and the actors setting a tableau not entirely dissimilar to various representations of the Madonna cradling the body of her grown child. Bree has declared herself "not his mother," but it is surely a loving parent's touch that she administers by the glowing light of the fire, and the feelings that arise as a result are confusing to her.

Except for the occasional establishing shot or transitional shot of the station wagon on the open highway, *Transamerica* uses relatively few wide shots. The visual style complements the intimate narrative of the film. While one tradition of the journey film is the epic, and writer-director Duncan Tucker himself likens *Transamerica* to *The Lord of the Rings* (with Bree as Frodo and Toby as the ring), this film is smaller and more personal than traditional examples in the mold of Joseph Campbell's hero's journey, and the look of the film reinforces the theme of personal growth through connection. Tucker noted on the commentary track of the film that he chose to shoot on Super 16 for budgetary and aesthetic reasons. Super 16 produces a grittier, more realistic look than 35 mm but also maintains a greater contrast range than a digital format. Most of the film is shot hand-held, but the camera movement is very slight, which again produces a realistic look. There is very little emphasis on camera angles throughout the film. Inside the car, Bree and Toby are seldom shown within the same frame, especially early in the road trip. While they are talking, the general pattern is to cut back and forth between the two characters, which preserves their separation even within an enclosed space. The understated visual style of the film, including production design as well as cinematography and editing, enhances the power of the narrative and the performances.

"I REALLY DON'T THINK I'M CUT OUT TO BE A MOTHER"

Ready or not, Bree has assumed responsibility for her son by bailing him out of jail, returning him to Kentucky, and driving him to California. Those are the broad strokes, but she has also begun a delicate balancing act of trying to respect his individuality and autonomy while simultaneously trying to help him stay safe and envision a better life for himself than he's been able to imagine so far. The tension she feels about becoming a parent—an identity she has not chosen—is a marked contrast to the lack of ambivalence she feels about surgically becoming a woman. There is an irony here that Bree can have her "outy" turned into an "inny" but she can only mold her body so much. Judith Halberstam notes that while the transgendered body is "a symbol par excellence for flexibility, transgenderism also represents a form of rigidity" (76–77). We are reminded as we watch Bree alter her form that she can reconstruct her body from male to female, which illustrates the flexibility of her form, but she cannot physically give birth to a child, which imposes a limitation on that flexibility. There is a complexity to this formulation of Stanley/Bree as biological father/social mother that makes traditional boundaries collapse under the weight of her emerging identity. In a discussion of *The Crying Game* (1992) and *Boys Don't Cry* (1999), Halberstam notes that "gender metamorphosis in these films is also used as a metaphor for other kinds of mobility or immobility" (77). Clearly, Bree is mobile and on the move in several realms at once.

One of the most effective elements of *Transamerica* is how Tucker, as writer and director of the film, has managed to make Bree's cross-country journey parallel her path toward becoming a woman and a parent, and to make her personal story carry larger cultural and political implications for viewers. Judith Butler makes some of these same connections in her discussion of bodies: "As a consequence of being in the mode of becoming, and in always living with the constitutive possibility of becoming otherwise, the body is that which can occupy the norm in myriad ways, exceed the norm, rework the norm, and expose realities to which we thought we were confined as open to transformation" (217). As Bree learns in an Arkansas restaurant, the process of transformation may be open, but it is also uneven.

Bree confronts the perils faced by bodies that rework the norm in a scene in which she sits in a restaurant booth, alone, reading a menu for the Ozark Mountain House. The decor and attached shop suggest a cross between a Cracker Barrel and a Denny's. A little girl with round, inquisitive eyes looks at Bree intently from an adjoining booth. First in a wide shot, then with alternating shots, Bree registers the look but tries to focus on the menu. The little girl is photographed in a close-up to reveal a guilelessness in her inspection of Bree, but Bree is photographed in a medium shot, peering over her menu, which serves as a protective armor against close inspection. Finally, the little girl asks, "Are you a boy or a girl?" The little girl's mother rebukes her without turning around—she's actually off-camera as the line is delivered—"Turn around and stop bothering people." Bree glances around and visibly draws into herself as her body contracts. The film cuts from a full shot of Bree seated in the booth to a closeup of her in a telephone booth, crying.

> BREE: Margaret . . . thank god. I am in the middle of Arkansas, and an eight-year-old child just read me. I can't handle this. I had to camp out last night . . . on the ground . . . with bugs. (Pause.) Because he is impossible. I can't . . .

At this point the camera cuts to a medium shot of Toby playing a shooting game as a teenage girl watches him.

> BREE: . . . throw away my savings like this. My surgery is only five days away . . .

The girl removes a lollipop from Toby's mouth, pulls him into her arms, and starts kissing him passionately.

> BREE: Dallas . . . I don't know . . . four or five hours, why?

The camera is back on Bree, who looks over at Toby. The rest of the scene cuts back and forth from the young couple to Bree, still tightly framed by the phone booth. They are moving easily in the open space of the gift and game area adjacent to the restaurant while Bree remains tightly framed by the phone booth that encases her. Toby moves fluidly from shooting the gun to kissing the girl (Tucker refers to his body as "unpoliced" on the commentary track of the film), in contrast to Bree, who moves as little as possible and, when she does, in a way that seems both calculated and cautious.

> BREE: Hold . . . hold on . . . (she assumes a calm, carefully modulated voice). . . . Toby, Toby would you mind introducing me to your new friend?

Toby has no idea who she is, of course.

> GIRL: Taylor.
>
> TOBY: Yeah, this is Taylor.

His face erupts in a shy smile.

> BREE: It's nice to meet you, Taylor.

Taylor's father comes into the background behind the young couple.

FATHER: What's going on here? C'mon. Your mother's waiting for you in the car. (They start to walk away.) You better watch out he doesn't get some poor, innocent girl in trouble.

BREE: (Her voice rising) You better watch out she doesn't ruin some poor, innocent boy's life.

Toby looks at her, pleased she has taken his side.

BREE: (To Toby) You, go wait for me at the table.

As Toby walks away, the camera returns to the tight shot of Bree beginning to cry again in the phone booth. It is really more of a phone box, one that resembles a wardrobe or small closet, an apt visual representation because Bree has not yet revealed herself to Toby. The shot of Bree, a medium close-up, changes very little thoughout the scene whether she is inside the phone booth or leaning out from the door.

BREE: Margaret, I really don't think I'm cut out to be a mother.

What is obvious to viewers, though not yet to Bree, is that she has been mothering Toby almost from the moment they met. As Shari Thurer points out, "Motherhood—the way we perform mothering—is culturally derived" (xv), and Bree has the emotional tools for this job whether she feels ready or not. Back at the table, Toby is awkwardly squeezing a lemon wedge into his water as he has seen her do before, and he puts his hands up to pray when she sits down. Toby has finally noticed her motherly attentions, and when the two leave the restaurant, he presents her with a gift, the "Proud to be a Christian" baseball cap, which suggests that he accepts her as the person she has presented herself to be without judgment.

"SHE IS NOT MY MOTHER"

All journeys, especially those told in a classically Aristotelian narrative structure replete with complications and reversals, have setbacks and detours. *Transamerica* is no exception. When Bree and Toby stay overnight in Dallas, Texas, with someone recommended by Margaret, Bree is uncomfortable with the house party under way while Toby accepts assorted members of the trans community uncritically. At this point, the boy still sees Bree as a Christian do-gooder, who is a prude, but nice to him. In yet another reference to *Thelma and Louise*, Toby inquires specifically about going to Texas (and Bree allows that it was a hard state to miss) in opposition to Louise's insistence that she and Thelma not go there because of a trauma—presumably an unpunished sexual assault—she suffered in the state years before.

Bree's own discomfort in Dallas, which may have been evident even without Toby along because of her reserve and conservatism, is compounded by her fear that Toby will learn the truth about her. The next night he does. The diuretic effect of Bree's medication forces a roadside stop to relieve her bladder, and her fear of desert snakes causes her to stand rather than squat by the side of the car. When Toby catches sight of Bree's penis in the rearview mirror, the boy is shocked because he has been open with Bree about his circumstances, and he cannot relate to how difficult it is for her to make herself vulnerable to others.

In the hotel that night, Toby smokes against Bree's wishes and gives her the silent treatment. Sensing that something is wrong, she backs off. The next day, she tries to tell him engaging stories, but, failing to get a response, says, "You know, social ostracism doesn't work in a community of two." At this point in their journey, Toby spots a hitchhiker along the side of the road. The prominence given to the character and the way Toby registers him indicates to viewers that he is going to make another appearance and, recalling how hitchhiker J. D. pops up after Louise registers his presence only to derail Thelma and Louise on their journey, it seems clear that this long-haired youth with a big-brimmed hat is nothing but trouble. Setting the convergence of events in place, Toby speaks to Bree as a sign for a roadside stand appears and says, "I want to go to Sammy's Wigwam."

Figure 24. Toby (Kevin Zegers) gives Bree (Felicity Huffman) the silent treatment after he realizes she is transgendered (*Transamerica*, 2005).

A similar scene in *Thelma and Louise* marks a change of identity for the two women. The two women start their trip with fair skin, "fixed" hair, makeup, and feminine clothes. By the time they stop at a desert stand, each aware of the changes in their consciousness, they are tanned and beautiful without cosmetics or frills. In this desert stand scene, Bree still sports her fussy, feminine yet matronly look, but her sense of herself in relation to Toby is about to change dramatically.

The first half of the scene, at Sammy's Wigwam, is a conventional master shot with medium shot cutaways of Bree, Toby, and the proprietor—presumably Sammy. Encouraged by the fact that Toby is once again talking to her, Bree explores the stand with forced cheer, "Here's some arrowheads . . . they're only a dollar each." Toby ignores her, and Sammy looks over at them from his upholstered chair under the awning where he casually reads a newspaper. Bree is embarrassed and tries a motherly excuse to brush over Toby's coldness while at the same time attempting to hide behind oversized sunglasses. She says to Sammy, "He's been acting like that all day." Toby punctuates her statement by banging a tomahawk on the display table loudly. Bree tries again with maternal authority.

> BREE: Young man, if you don't start behaving in a civilized fashion, you and I are going to have a very serious problem.
>
> TOBY: Fuck you.

Sammy rises up in his chair.

> SAMMY: Now, you watch your mouth around your mother.

Bree doesn't respond this time to being identified as the boy's mother, but Toby is indignant.

> TOBY: She's not my mother. She's not anyone's mother. She's not even a real woman. She has a dick. (To Bree) Don't you?

Bree stands there by the side of the road in her pink jacket, purple dress, airy scarf, and dangly earrings in near shock. Her Jackie O. style sunglasses may shade her eyes, but the slack-jaw is telling; Bree looks as if she is folding in on herself, just as she did in the Arkansas restaurant when the young child read her. For his part, Toby is reacting from his own hurt at being left out of the secret. He pounds away at her verbally.

> TOBY: Don't you? Go on, tell him.

Sammy puts sunglasses over his eyes to shield himself from the scene, settles back into his chair, and picks up his paper. Bree begins to walk toward the car with all the dignity she can muster. She clutches her purse as if it can give her some much-needed support. Toby calls out to her, "You're a fuckin' lyin' freak." But he does follow her. Bree's head is high, and Toby's hurtful words reveal his own sense of betrayal. He asks Bree what she wants from him and why she didn't just tell him the truth. "You knew all about me," Toby says, and that seems true. Parents, to a point, always know more about their children than children can know about parents, and Toby's openness is matched, in this case, by Bree's need to protect herself from pain and the possibility of rejection as she comes to terms overnight with what it means to become a parent.

At this point, the hitchhiker, who has caught up to them, climbs into the car with Toby, and they move on because Bree is too overwhelmed to think clearly or to protest. When the charming hitchhiker steals their car, their money, and all their possessions (including Toby's money and Bree's hormone pills), the two have little choice but to make amends and try to get to Arizona to ask Bree's family for help—the family she has declared dead because that's been easier for her than dealing with her parents' rejection of her as a woman.

"I AM HIS FATHER"

Along the way to Arizona, Toby turns a trick at a truck stop (without Bree's knowledge) to get some quick cash while Bree meets a kind Native American man, Calvin, who takes the two in for the night and then drives them to her parents' house the next day. This is a delightful interlude in which it becomes clear the man is smitten with Bree, and Toby watches the exchange with a combination of fascination and discomfort. Bree opens up a bit as Calvin serenades her and flirts with her, and Toby doesn't out Bree to Calvin. When they part ways, Calvin gives Bree his phone number and Toby a black cowboy hat.[3] The desert interlude with Calvin, as sweet as it is, offers a number of comedic moments. Along with its placement in the film, the narrative suggests a parallel to a desert sequence in *Thelma and Louise* when Thelma and Louise take a highway patrol officer hostage and a bicyclist comes along later and blows marijuana smoke through bullet holes in the trunk of the car. It would be nice to think that Bree could go back to Calvin's desert home and live happily with him under the stars as Toby learns a thing or two about the (comparatively) uncomplicated life of teenagers. That's not an option for Bree, however, until she is able to become on the outside the woman she has embraced on the inside. Meeting her parents gives the viewer ample evidence why that road has been such a difficult one for Bree to travel.

Several important events that illustrate the difficulties of being trans-gendered occur during the visit to Bree's parents' house (which actually belongs to director Duncan Tucker's mother). It is evident right away that her parents, especially her mother, Elizabeth, still see Bree as their son, Stanley, and are not supportive of her decision to live as a woman and to undergo sex change surgery. Butler thinks of gender identity as a justice issue, and it is clear in this sequence that Elizabeth is unjust in her interactions with Bree. Butler writes:

> Justice is not only or exclusively a matter of how persons are treated or how societies are constituted. It also concerns consequential decisions about what a person is, and what social norms must be honored and expressed for "personhood" to become allocated, how we do or do not recognize animate others as persons depending on whether or not we recognize animate others as manifested in and by the body of that other. (58)

When Bree goes into her parents' home and explains Toby's presence (he has remained outside on the front lawn) by saying, "He's your grandson," it reflects a conscious choice not to call herself either his father or his mother. Elizabeth asks, "Stanley, what are you planning to do with that poor boy?" Bree's answer speaks volumes about her own experiences with her parents and reflects that she has given careful consideration as to how Toby should be parented: "Well, first of all, I'm going to make sure that he knows he is encouraged and supported. And that he's respected . . . maybe even . . . well, at least that he's respected." Elizabeth just stares at Bree.

By the end of the day, Elizabeth and her husband, Murray, have started trying to convince Toby to move in with them. They tout the charms of the country club nearby and the pool out back, but Toby is unsure. He goes to Bree's room where she is looking at a scrapbook and resorts to the only behavior he knows to get what he wants or what he needs for survival: he comes on to her. It's a painful moment that goes far beyond awkwardness and pushes Bree to show Toby the photograph she has been looking at: the same photograph Toby had of his parents in New York, but the boy doesn't immediately make the connection. Bree says, "It's your mom and me," and Toby's response is anger. Once again he has been kept in the dark about something, and even though Bree is apologizing and trying to calm her son, he punches her. Soon Toby is gone, but the remarkable thing about this moment in the film is that Elizabeth reaches out to Bree and comforts her, as one parent to another.

The next day Bree is leaving Arizona to get to Los Angeles in time for her surgery. The police have been called about Toby's disappearance, and it is clearly liberating for Bree to tell the young, woman officer, "I am his father." As she delivers the line, the camera photographs her from a slightly lower angle than usual. She looks haggard from worry over Toby and stress over getting to California for her surgery, but she is also proud of being able to acknowledge her son, and the lower angle emphasizes her empowerment. The officer doesn't bat an eye, and the moment reveals a double acceptance of fluidity, in that uptight Bree can finally claim Stanley, who is Toby's father after all, and can also complete her journey to becoming more fully Bree. She will remain Toby's biological father, and, if they reconcile, she will have the opportunity to parent her child without the necessity of reductive labels.

CONCLUSION: COMING HOME

Margaret visits Bree after her surgery and is surprised to find that the patient is sad. Bree sits holding the "Proud to be a Christian" baseball cap Toby gave her and begins to cry, "It hurts." We know she isn't talking about her surgical wounds, and so does Margaret, who replies, "That's what hearts do." This scene is a key one for writer-director Duncan Tucker:

> It's an old-fashioned coming of age, family movie. It's not about transsexuality; it's about growing up. It's about finding yourself and learning to love yourself and accepting yourself and, through that, being able to love others. She had to learn to love herself and accept herself and be not just an invisible woman, be a transsexual woman, and [be] okay with that and to feel again . . . to break down and cry, and it hurts, but it was a victory. It was a victory that the walls around her heart came cracking open and then she could become the parent that Toby needed. (Interview on the IFC Films DVD release).

In the end, Bree comes home to herself and to prepare a place for her son. There is a lovely short scene in which she bathes, surrounded by candles, and explores her new woman's body. She's also going back to school and planning to become a teacher. At the Mexican restaurant, she has been promoted from dishwasher to waitress, and her clothing and movements are more casual and open than before the surgery. For Toby, the transition is less a departure from his old life than a change of address; he starts out on the street and ends up in front of the camera in a gay porn film. Still, this is conveyed visually as a rebirth for him linked to water, a parallel to Bree's bathing scene. While he is not immersed in the water, the ocean is his backdrop. Bree's surgical transformation is also mildly echoed in Toby's transition from brunette to blonde with a bad bleach job.

When her son does turn up at Bree's door sometime later, long gone are the prim suits and constricting scarves, although it still appears that Bree buys makeup online instead of at the counter because the colors on her face are a little "off" and harsh. At first, a screen door comes between them as Bree opens the front door, and Toby asserts that he has not forgiven her but has just come to see if she had the surgery. Cutting back and forth in medium shots, she invites him in, saying she has a gift for him. This time Bree is relaxed with her arms loosely at her sides, while Toby backs away when she opens the screen door and wraps his arms tightly around himself in a self-conscious hug. He hesitates but comes inside, arms still clutching himself. Eventually, he sits and they talk casually. Just like the beginning of the road trip, they are not together within the frame, but photographed separately in medium and full shots for the first part of the scene. This time, the distance is imposed more by Toby than by Bree.

As they talk and get used to one another again, she goes into another room and gets the black cowboy hat Calvin had given him in the desert. At this point, Toby is seated and Bree is standing, and her stature is enhanced by a low angle shot that gives her maternal authority. Bree withholds judgment about his acting job in a porn film and about his smoking and beer drinking in her house, but she can't resist imposing one motherly rule as she walks to the kitchen to get his beer: "Young man, if you think you can put your dirty tennis shoes on my brand new coffee table, you're going to have to think again." Toby hesitates only an instant before removing his feet. The film ends with a shot through sheer curtains showing Bree and Toby, in a two-shot, sharing the frame, on the sofa inside her pink and green living room. Visually, it recalls the shot that ends the scene by the campfire: both are wide shots filtered by light or an object to give the viewer a sense of being a voyeur observing a tender moment between mother and child. He can't open his own beer, so she hands him her bottle and takes his to open and keep for herself. The labels don't matter; whether Bree is a father who mothers her child or a mother who started out as a father becomes irrelevant. She is Toby's loving parent, they are home together, and both of their lives will be enriched by the connection.

It is clear from looking closely at *Transamerica* that proscribed boundaries may serve the many, but in failing to serve others and by foreclosing on options that ought not be foreclosed upon, there is a larger disservice to all. Butler asks, "Why can't the framework for sexual difference itself move beyond binarity into multiplicity?" (197) In Bree's experience, the enforcement of socially constructed categories of difference provided a framework for the administration of oppressive practices, and it is only by first becoming undone that she can begin to, finally, feel done. For Thelma and Louise, the oppressive practices of patriarchy leave no room for women who "crossed over" to see beyond the categories, but Bree has the opportunity to live beyond the boundaries with her son, who seems never to have internalized them.

NOTES

1. All quotes attributed to Duncan Tucker, Felicity Huffman, and Kevin Zegers (including the epigraphs) can be found in the supplemental interviews included on the IFC Films DVD release of *Transamerica*.

2. Judith Butler frames an important discussion of the injustice of performing coercive surgery on intersex children in chapter 3 of *Undoing Gender*, "Doing Justice to Someone." On the other hand, Butler cites intersex activist Cheryl Chase as supporting hormonal or surgical interventions as justified because those decisions are "based on knowing choice" (63).

3. One note seems appropriate here regarding another film. There is a scene inside Calvin's truck in which he tells Toby how you can tell a lot about a man's character by how he wears a cowboy hat that recalls a similar scene in the 1985 film *Murphy's Romance*, which is another story about crossing perceived boundaries: a divorced mother of a son falls in love with a much older man who resists the attraction at first because of the age difference.

BIBLIOGRAPHY

Butler, Judith. *Undoing Gender*. New York: Routledge, 2004.

Campbell, Joseph, with Stuart L. Brown and Phil Cousineau. *The Hero's Journey: The World of Joseph Campbell: Joseph Campbell on His Life and Work*. San Francisco: Harper & Row, 1990.

Faludi, Susan. *Backlash: The Undeclared War Against American Woman*. New York: Doubleday, 1991.

Halberstam, Judith. *In a Queer Time and Place: Transgender Bodies, Subcultural Lives*. New York: New York University Press, 2005.

Huffman, Felicity, Duncan Tucker, and Kevin Zegers. Interviews. *Transamerica*. Dir. Duncan Tucker. Supplemental Material. DVD. IFC Films, 2005.

Morris, David. "The Meanings of Pain." In *Social Construction: A Reader*, edited by Mary Gergen and Kenneth J. Gergen. London: SAGE, 2003.

Murphy's Romance. Dir. Martin Ritt. Columbia Pictures, 1985.

Thelma and Louise. Dir. Ridley Scott. MGM, 1991.

Thurer, Shari L. *The Myths of Motherhood: How Culture Reinvents the Good Mother*. Boston: Houghton Mifflin, 1994.

Transamerica. Dir. Duncan Tucker. IFC Films, 2005.

CONTRIBUTORS

Heather Addison is an associate professor of Film Studies at Western Michigan University. Her books include *Hollywood and the Rise of Physical Culture* and *After the Film Is Before the Film: The Cinema of Tom Tykwer*, a work-in-progress that she is co-authoring with Elaine Roth.

Aimee Berger is a lecturer in English at Texas Christian University in Fort Worth, Texas, and an associated faculty member of the University of North Texas Women's Studies Program. She is a former chair of the National Women's Studies Feminist Mothering Caucus and is currently focusing her research on the ways in which representations of mothering in Appalachia are utilized to garner public support for social policies that contest women's right to mother and in many cases effect their displacement from homes and communities.

Mike Chopra-Gant is Reader in Media, Culture and Communications at London Metropolitan University. He is the author of *Hollywood Genres: Masculinity, Family and Nation in Popular Movies and Film Noir Cinema and History: The Telling of Stories*, and *The Waltons: Nostalgia, Myth and Seventies America*.

Janet K. Cutler is a professor of English and coordinator of the Film Studies program at Montclair State University. She co-edited and contributed essays to *Struggles for Representation: African American Documentary Film and Video* (with Phyllis R. Klotman); her publications on film and video include the chapter "Su Friedrich: Breaking the Rules" in *Women's Experimental Cinema* (Robin Blaetz, ed.) and articles in such journals as *Black Film Review, Cineaste, Film Quarterly*, and *Persistence of Vision*.

Mary M. Dalton is an associate professor of Communication at Wake Forest University. She is the author of *The Hollywood Curriculum: Teachers in the Movies*, co-editor of *The Sitcom Reader: America Viewed and Skewed*, and also a documentary filmmaker.

251

Mary Kate Goodwin-Kelly holds a Ph.D. in English/Film Studies from the University of Rochester. As a CWIL Fellow at Saint Mary's College in South Bend, Indiana, she taught courses in Film Studies and Women's Studies. More recently, she has taught at Western Kentucky University. Her current work examines representations of pregnant bodies in contemporary sports media and popular culture.

Mark Harper teaches at Indiana University-Purdue University in Indianapolis and is the director of the Indianapolis LGBT Film Festival. His research interests include melodrama, queer theory, and French cinema.

Kathleen Rowe Karlyn is an associate professor of English at the University of Oregon. She is the author of *The Unruly Woman* as well as articles on feminist theory, cultural studies, and film and telelvision genres. Her current project, *Unruly Girls, Unrepentant Mothers*, is a companion to her first book and examines mothers and daughters in the context of girl culture and feminism's Third Wave.

Mun-Hou Lo is an assistant professor in the University Scholars Programme at the National University of Singapore.

Tamar Jeffers McDonald is Lecturer in Film at the University of Kent, UK. Her research interests include romantic comedy, film costume, representations of sexuality, and Doris Day. Her recent monographs are *Romantic Comedy: Boy Meets Girl Meets Genre* and *Hollywood Catwalk: Costume and Transformation in American Film*.

Madonne M. Miner, Dean of the Arts & Humanities College and Professor of English at Weber State University in Ogden, Utah, has published on late nineteenth and twentieth-century American literature and popular culture. Ever since writing *Insatiable Appetites: Twentieth-Century American Women's Bestsellers*, she has been interested in representations of mothers, daughters, and mothering.

Elaine Roth is an associate professor of Film Studies and Chair of the English Department at Indiana University South Bend. Her work has appeared in *Feminist Media Studies*, *Quarterly Review of Film and Video*, and *Genders*. She is currently working on a co-authored book about the films of German director Tom Tykwer.

Gaylyn Studlar is director of the Program in Film and Media Studies at Washington University in St. Louis. She has published widely on issues of gender and sexuality in Hollywood film.

INDEX